A Book of Sikh Studies

Dr. Gobind Singh Mansukhani
M.A., LLB., Ph.D.

NATIONAL BOOK SHOP
Pleasure Garden Market, Chandni Chowk, Delhi

Copyright: Author

N. B. Shop 1989

ISBN 81-7116-074-3

Price: Rs. 120

Published by:

Rajinder Singh
National Book Shop,
32-B, Pleasure Garden Market
Chandni Chowk, Delhi 110 006.

Laserset by **data culture**, Amar colony, New Delhi 110024 and Printed
at Avon Offset Printers, Darya Gunj, New Delhi 100 006.

CONTENTS

Pages

INTRODUCTION   1

Chapter I.	Sikhism its theory & practice		7
Chapter II.	The Ten Gurus		20
	Guru Nanak	20	
	Guru Angad	53	
	Guru Amardas	57	
	Guru Ramdas	63	
	Guru Arjan	66	
	Guru Hargobind	73	
	Guru Har Rai	78	
	Guru Harkrishan	80	
	Guru Tegh Bahadur	81	
	Guru Gobind Singh	87	
Chapter III	Sikh Ethics		104
Chapter IV	Sikh Scriptrues		128
	Guru Granth Sahib		
	Dasam Granth		
	Some important sacred compositions: Japji, Asa-di-var, Sukhmani Sahib, Anand Sahib.		
Chapter V	Sikh Worship: Gurdwara, Sadh-sangat, Kirtan, Ardas, Langar, Social Responsibility, Home worship		165
Chapter VI	Sikh Rites and Ceremonies		181
Chapter VII	The Important Sikh Festivals		192
Glossary			199
Bibliography			202
Index			205

Introduction

In the modern age of reason and technology, people praise the achievements of Science. They regard it as a magic wand for finding a solution to every problem. Undoubtedly, science and technology have minimised human labour, increased comforts, and even luxuries for the rich and developed nations, yet it has not solved the problem of hunger and deprivation in most of the countries of the world.

Secondly, the stockpiling of nuclear armaments and the invention of highly destructive weapon -systems has posed a global holocaust and the very survival of the human race. The growing desire for peace, and for limitation and destruction of certain missile systems through treaties between the superpowers are indicators that science has been misused for power-politics and exploitation of communities. In spite of the bumper crops of food-grains—the mountains of wheat and butter and milk-lakes in the west—more than half the population of the world is in grip of starvation and poverty. The mal-distribution of goods made the late President J.F. Kennedy remark: "If we cannot help the many who are poor, we cannot save the few who are rich."

Religion which implies concern for equality, justice and peace is intended to correct the imbalances created by our leaders in the economic and political structures. Religion also tends to remind the scientist of his responsibility. It switches human motivation from power and exploitation, to service, aid, cooperation and harmony. In this connection, Prof. A.N. whitehead remarked: "The future of civilisation depends on the degree to which we can balance the forces of science and religion.".

The importance of religion and its serious study arises from a need of maintaining individual peace of mind and the establishment of a just society and world-order. We are torn by tensions and problems, both internal and external. It is by exploring the paths of religious teachers and studying their holy books and writings, that we may get a balanced view of life, an unpolluted environment and inner peace.

Religion, for that matter any religion, provides some norms, sets of values and a charter of human possibilities. It shows what is good and what is bad, and promotes a desire for harmonious living and a caring society. Man's progress in real terms, depends largely on efforts to follow the norms and values provided by religion. There are bound to be difficulties in following the path, only persistence and courage will enable a man to get results. It may mean subordinating one's own interests to the interests of society or the social group, but it will have its own compensations. Hence the need of the study of religion, particularly one to which one is born. It may also be added that the study of religion should begin at the school. Obviously philosophical concepts and motivations for good conduct may not be 'understood' at that age, but exposure to them will enable one to get some idea of right conduct and discipline.

Some people question the wisdom of *teaching* religion as a part of any school syllabus. Can Religion or Divinity be taught? Perhaps another way to learn about one's religion is in place of worship, as for example, the church, the mosque, the temple or the gurdwara. But religious education imparted at these places is generally traditional and inadequate. It often cannot answer the questions of children. It is therefore necessary to supplement its broader dimensions, so that any ethical and cultural heritage may be brought to the notice of its children in a rational and academic way, as for example through discussion and feedback. Religion must not be above reason or beyond analysis and class-study. Religion in its own right belongs to the field of Humanities; it provides insights and values which are of great importance to communal harmony and self improvement.

We know that it is possible to impart elementary religious education to school children, through tales from the lives of the various prophets and holy men. They can be excited by miracles and unusual events in the lives of saints and mytics. They are interested in forms and sequences of worship in church or temple. They want to understand their meanings and purposes. They enjoy religious fire-works, the splendid decorations, the special foods at particular events, the pomp and pageantry of priests and congregations. Such pageants or ceremonials arouse their curiosity, and also provide a source of dialogue and pleasure in different seasons of the year. Even routine visit to places of worship can provide worthwhile experiences. For example, a Sikh child who visits a Gurdwara observes that children look after the shoes of the congregation. The Free Kitchen (langar) attached to the Gurdwara attracts lots of children. not only for food. but also for voluntary service, in the distribution of plates and spoons to diners seated in the hall. Though children do not always understand the concept of "Free Kitchen,"or of sharing meals with others, they like to serve people and feel happy when they distribute food and water, and also some times join others in washing the dishes afterwards.

Religious ceremonies like the "Naming" and "Marriage Ceremony" are liked by all children, because they can there meet other children and make new friends. They become excited by participating in the showering of flower-petals (like confetti) at wedding ceremonies. They are thrilled by the garlands of flowers, which they or their friends may put on the bride or the bride-groom, when the actual wedding ceremony comes to an end. Sikh children who do not go to the Gurdwara often attend daily worship at home—to acknowledge their Guru Granth Sahib — and listen to any *Kirtan* (hymn-singing) which their father, mother or sister may sing in their own *Darbar-Sahib* (a room for keeping the Scripture). Perhaps, they may repeat the lines after one of them. Apart from the feelings of togetherness, they will also enjoy eating Karah-parasad (sweet pudding), which is always distributed to all present at the end of all religious services. However, the teaching of Religious studies has a wider objective. It encourages a more specific and intelligent approach to the subject by senior students. Such studies will be more meaningful to them than to younger children. At that level, they can start to understand the purpose and significance of the many stories on the lives of the Sikh Gurus. For example, the story that tells of Guru Nanak at Hardwar, throwing water in the direction completely opposite to that of the Hindus, will not only be amusing, but also meaningful, as it exposes the absurdity of ritual. It encourages them to realise that rituals which are meaningless or purposeless should be abondoned. Religion is not blind faith, but a way to find the truth, a distinction between right and wrong, the logical and the illogical. The docrinal part of religion will be clear, as they think over the stories and begin to understand the purpose and content of the Guru's teaching.

A more important objective for Sikh Studies lies in the ethical dimension, in terms of conduct and behaviour. Religion normally plays a vital role in the promotion of love for one's community. It also inculcates loyalties and inspires a person to be a good citizen. Though it cannot make a person holy or pious, it can make him appreciate an ethical person, one who distinguishes between right and wrong, and who can understand the limiting of selfishness, and the rights and dignity of other men.

When a student takes up a study of Sikh ethics, he must make an effort to discover the value-systen underlying them. For example, why

Sikhs emphasise continence and chastity, why they wear under-pants, why they do not use tobacco, drugs or intoxicants? He will be able to appreciate the Sikh Code of discipline, the four major sins—*Kurahits*—and their significance in the baptism ceremony (Amrit), since Sikh values and views on sin and atonement are based on fundamental principles, food and dress also have a purpose beyond that of culture.

Perhaps I should now explain the Guru's attitude on the use of force and why Sikhs wear a *Kirpan* (a small sword), this being specially emphasised by the Tenth Master, Guru Gobind Singh. He justified the use of force only after all other means have failed and then only to prevent injustice and oppression. If silent and peaceful protests fail, Sikhs may then fight. They cannot be indifferent spectators to injustice, murder or rape. They may resort to the use of the sword only as a last resort. The Gurus believed that war was justifiable to protect freedom, to fight against injustice or the right to practise one's own religion. The use of force is also permissible in support of basic ethical values and human rights.

The word 'Ethics' in its Sikh context needs elucidation. It is not acting in accordance with traditional morality, but work or behaviour acceptable to God. Any work or practice which brings one near to God is *ethical*. Good social conduct and character are a foundation for God-realisation. Both the *aim* and the *means* have to be noble. Honest means, make the goal worth-while. Virtue does not lie in personal excellence or glory, but in the recognition and respect of the rights of others, and the giving of humble service to them as God's children. All work and activity should be inspired by good motives and intentions.

The Sikh concept of virtue is related to the conquest of the ego through humility and selfless service. Indian religious tradition regards hunger, poverty, pilgrimage, self-mortification as virtuous. Sikhism does not. Physical well-being and the acceptance of normal comforts and amenities, are a part of one's spiritual welfare and advancement. Wealth, good living, hobbies, entertainment and social interaction, can make a contribution to man's spiritual progress. It is through the transformation of character, through the building up of moral muscle and conscience, that the ultimate mystic experience of God realisation is made possible.

The Utility and Scope of Sikh Studies

The usefulness of Sikh Studies, like any other progressive subject cannot be over-emphsised. Gradually, the reader will discover the basic principles underlying the Sikh faith and the essence of the message of the

Sikh Gurus and gain an understanding of man's spiritual dimension. Progress in the exploitation of our economic resources and the acquisition of wealth tend to make us more materialistic in outlook and selfish in behaviour; so often we incline towards trampling on the rights of others, and so become mean and cruel. Perhaps in due course, we may become automatons or robots, an insensitive and inhuman people. It is the comprehension of the Guru's teachings that can reveal to us our own deficiencies, also the need to improve our communities as a whole. The Gurus and their disciples faced similar challenges, with courage and fearlessness. They loved God and His creation. They regarded the service of mankind as an act of worship. They affirmed that religious worship without commitment, dedication; and sacrifice, was meaningless. They affirmed that political power without charity and compassion was corrupting and dangerous. They exposed the cruelty and injustice of their rulers and their armies with great boldness, and were prepared to face the consequences. Some of them sacrificed their lives for their beliefs, so setting examples for the Sikhs to follow. The study of such lives is inspiring. It can strengthen the forces of peace justice and progress.

The basic aim of Sikh Studies is to widen the readers' outlook and so promote their integrated development, to help become progressive members of the human family. All societies consist of a diversity of individuals. Without their progress, the uplift of societies is impossible. The Gurus' yard-stick for progress was: "Does a particular action or project help the development of the individual or promote social good?" They laid stress on the development of physical and mental health, honest and hard work, the sharing of one's income with others, while at the same time, rejecting any inflation of the ego through ostentatious giving in fake charity.

SIKH STUDIES

Historical	Theological	Institutional	Practical
i. The Ten Gurus (1469-1708)	The Scriptures: Covering	Gurdwara, Amrit,	Sikh way of life, the
ii. Banda Singh & later persecution (1709-1764)	concepts of God, Hukam,	Takhat Gurumatta.	family, the Community,
iii. The Growth of the Missals (1765-1800)	Guru, The Name, Salvation etc.		Worship, Sikh identity, Sikh character.

iv. Ranjit Singh & his
empire (1801-1849).
v. Panjab under British rule
(1849-1947).
vi. Sikhs after India's Independence

The above sections should not be regarded as water-tight compartments. Like inter-secting circles, they cut across mutual borders, and relate to one another. The studying of lives of the Gurus leads to formulation of their views and concepts. Understanding the concepts leads to the needs of institutions to demonstrate practicality and benefit. From this was developed the Sikh way of life, with its religious identity and worship, which is focussed on 'Plain living and high thinking.'

The Sikh way of life was demonstrated by all the Sikh Gurus. They supervised the theoretical and practical aspects of Sikhism, and guided their followers. Guru Ramdas prescribed the daily routine of the Sikh; Guru Gobind Singh completed the form of Sikhism by the creation of the *Khalsa Panth*. He gave his Sikhs an outer uniform—the *Five K's*—and an inner uniform of courage, meditation and sacrifice.

Finally, Sikh Studies will include the appreciation of the insights and perceptions of the Gurus, the significance of their poetry and music, the social and cultural value of their religious ceremonies, and the role played by Sikh institutions in their history, when the Sikhs had to pass through terrible ordeals in order to survive. In recent history, the Sikhs have had again to face terrible challenges, to secure the democratisation of their places of worship, and for the freedom to maintain their religious symbols, and be the masters of their own destiny. Apart from playing a vital role in the cause of securing freedom from British rule, the Sikhs are now making tremendous sacrifices for preserving the Sikh identity. The seed sown by the Sikh Gurus, has over the years flourished, in spite of torture and bloodshed.

Sikh Studies have a great relevance today. They offer solutions to many problems of the modern world. They encourage self-reliance, hard work and spirit of sacrifice. Its insistence on leading 'a good and purposeful life' in the secular and spiritual fields, attracts many people from east and west. The Gurus' wisdom may bring light to many way-farers. Let me recall the words of Guru Nanak; "As darkness is dispelled when a lamp is lit, so by studying books of wisdom, evil inclinations may be destroyed."

I

Sikhism: Its Theory and Practice

Its Theory

The tenets of Sikhism are based on the teachings of the Ten Sikh Gurus. Sikhism has been described as a religion propagated through its Guru's hymns. The message of its Founder—Guru Nanak—was simple and universal, with its significance and dimension being increased by the contribution of his succeeding Gurus, each one adding something definitive, or dynamic, to enable it to meet the needs of changing times and new problems.

The word 'Sikh' is derived from Sanskrit 'Shishya,' which means a student, learner or disciple. As more and more seekers of truth and virtue sought out Sikh Gurus, so their teachings were extended in scope and volume to be recorded in their hymns, poems and commandments *(Hukam-namas)*. Their rules of conduct called *Rahat-namas* were compiled by their devotees and then projected in the poetic compositions of intimate disciples like Bhai Daya Singh and Bhai Nanadlal. So that eventually the bulk of their doctrine and discipline became included in their scriptures and approved *Banis* which constitute the written basis of Sikhism.

The definition of a Sikh given by the Shromani Gurdwara Parbandhak Committee, Amritsar is as under:

"A Sikh is any person who believes in one God and The Ten Sikh Gurus, the Guru Granth Sahib and other Scriptures of the Sikh religion. Additionally, they must believe in the need and importance of Amrit (the Sikh Confirmational ceremony)." Sikhism is the religious path laid down by the Ten Sikh Gurus and includes a Code of Discipline as prescribed for the Khalsa (baptised Sikh). Khalsa is a Sikh, but not every Sikh a Khalsa. Sikhs however for all practical purposes are those who declare themselves as 'Sikhs' and included as such, under the heading of 'Sikhs' in census figures.

The principles of Sikhism were developed during the 239-year period from the first to the tenth Guru. Guru Nanak laid down its fundamentals—the Fatherhood of God and Brotherhood of man, universal love and peace—also the steps to be taken in day-to-day life to reach a goal of God-realisation, man's individual progress depending on the development of the three elements of his personality—physical, mental and moral. Life is to be lived in harmony and one's society. The body must be kept healthy and fit through good food and physical exercise. The needs of the mind for education, culture and wisdom need to be satisfied. Knowledge solely obtained through school-teaching and professional training is not enough. The mind has to be further developed by reflection and introspection in the company of holy men or those who have wide perception and intuition. Ethical progress in any human being is attained through the practice of virtue, altruism, meditation, communal worship and those other activities which bring inner satisfaction and spiritual uplift.

Side by side with normal life, Sikhs are expected to discipline their body, mind and character for higher goals. Self-discipline requires self limitation in wanting and the elimination of any undue attachment to material things, with miserliness and possessiveness being eliminated by learning to share with others. Projects of charity and social welfare, promoted and financed by individual donations and voluntary services by members of the community are recommended.

In pursuing the Sikh way of life, the disciple is expected to follow ethical code of the Sikh gurus. Its compliance is demanded not by a catalogue of *do's* and *don'ts*, or of commands and prohibitions, but an understanding of the love of God and His creation and respecting the rights of others. People are responsible for their own actions and they must understand the consequences of the chain of reactions they set in motion by all their actions. From this, vigilance over thought and action become a part of their practice of self-discpline and way of life. Charity and compassion both reflect a love of God and a sense of caring for the community as a whole.

Guru Nanak acknowledged commitment to society and rejected any system of escape from the responsibilities of life—as followed by most yogis and mystics—as irrelevant and unnecessary. He also emphasised *Nirgun Bkakti*—devotion to the Absolute and Transcendent Reality. This does not exclude the acceptance of God's attributes *(Sargun)*—like

8

mercy, generosity, goodness, fearlessness etc. God is regarded as being beyond time and space, birth and death, revenge or jealousy. According to Guru Nanak, God is Supreme Reality, that which is Absolute and Attributive, Transcendental and Immanent, Formless and yet Beauty itself. He is present within and without His own creation.

One of the most distinctive feature of Sikhism is its reconciliation of sets of opposites—peace and war, charity and dignity, humility and honour, selflessness and self-reliance, discipleship and sovereignty, *Degh²* and *Tegh.³* One of Guru Gobind Singh's important sayings was: *Degh, Tegh jag mai dou chale* (may both the cooking pot (charity) and the sword (strength for the protection of the weak) co-exist in the world:). Elsewhere, he wrote: "Blessed is that person in the world who recites the Holy Name with his mouth and at the same time, thinks of fighting against evil and tyranny." This epitomises a Khalsa Sikh, one who is strong and fearless outside, while being compassionate and generous within. The Sikhs have an inherent belief in a moral order in the universe which will ensure the ultimate victory of good over evil. The greeting of the Sikhs— *Waheguru Ji Ka Khalsa, Waheguru Ji Ki fateh*—the Khalsa is of God and the victory is of God—is inspiring, it affirms this positive and firm belief in the bright side of life—*Chardi Kala*.

One important aspect of Sikhism is its group-consciousness, its belief in *Sangat* (congregation) and the presence of the Guru in the *Sangat* . Guru Arjan respected the wishes of the *Sangat* in all matters, even personal ones. It is reported that Chandu Lal—a State official who had earlier offered him his daughter in marriage to the Guru's son—Hargobind—used words derogatory to the Guru. The *Sangat* of Lahore felt unhappy about this and told the Guru of their feelings about it and indicated to him that the offer of such an arrogant and conceited man should not be accepted. Guru Arjan respected the wishes of the *Sangat* and rejected the offer.

Guru Gobind Singh called his baptised Sikhs *Guru-Khalsa*, which means that the Guru is present in the Khalsa. He obeyed the command of his Panj-Piarye⁴ at Chamkaur and left the fortress much against his will. Thereafter a *Gurmatta⁵* became institutionalised for deciding all the important affairs of the Sikh Community in those crucial times when the Muslim rulers had ordered the genocide of all Sikhs. Even after the establishment of Sikh rule in the Punjab,early in the nineteenth century, Maharaja Ranjit Singh was not immune form obeying *Gurmatta* of the *Khalsa Panth*. He was called to *Akal Takht*. Amritsar, to receive his punishment for certain misdemeanours. In the same way, orders or proclamations issued by the *Akal Takht*, for the whole community, in the form of *Hukam-namas* which are respected and complied with, by all Sikh communities. As decided by Guru Gobind Singh, the Guru-Khalsa/ Guru-Panth is the supreme authority for the direction of all secular matters concerning the world Sikh Community.

Sikhism encourages the exercise of the intellect and gives weight to it, because man is a rational animal. In this connection, Guru Nanak says:

"One must serve the Lord intelligently.
Honour is acquired through wisdom.
Nanak says, these are matters of creative thinking;
All other ways are of ignorance." (AG, 124)[6]

The use of reason or reflection, however does not exclude any belief in certain fundamental things. Some sort of basic belief is found at the root of most human activity. We acquire professional skill in the belief that apart from enabling us to earn our living, it will provide us with some kind of social standing or status. Most human institutions and political organisations are based on the presumption of a general good conduct and law-abiding spirit in human beings. There have to be certain provisions for resolving deadlocks and crisies; by and large, people are reasonable and will solve most of their problems in a fair manner without trampling on others, in the process.

We presume that people will not be selfish beyond a certain point, since if they are, they tend to lose credibility and respect. Similarly, in matters of religion, we consider certain things as acceptable, for example the existence of God, even though we cannot prove His existence, in a class-room or a laboratory. The testimony of those spiritual leaders and saints who are accepted as experts in this field are enough to us to accept their ideas and experiences. We accept the opinions of such experts without demanding further verification. We recognise that reason and intellect do have a role to play in religion. Faith and logic too, are complimentary in leading a harmonious and integrated life. Religious practices too have common bases; they can be explained at least most simply in terms of fellowship and brotherliness.

Frequently it may not be possible to find a cogent rationale for every activity, because emotion too, has its part to play in human life. Religion in its highest sense can lead to mystical experience: the experience of God's vision and presence, but that cannot be demonstrated to another person. Our frontiers of knowledge, especially in the spiritual domain, can be extended by the perceptions and intuitions of prophets and saints. For example, stories of the Gurus impart to us a wisdom which could not be learnt form books or lectures. It is here that "associating with holy persons or evolved beings" reinforce our belief in religion, as healthy and inspiring.

Its Distinctiveness

Unfortunately, Sikhism is often considered only as an offshoot or break-away sect of Hinduism.[7] Some people regard it as being closer to Islam than to Hinduism by its rejection of caste and idol-worship; also Sikhism does not recommend the rituals of fasting and pilgrimage as stressed in both. Guru Nanak was himself born to a Hindu family, but he still rejected its ritual and orthodoxy; he refused to wear the Sacred Thread or worship its statues. Another reason for wrongly labelling Sikhism as a Hindu sect is because the Sikh Gurus referred to current Hindu concepts like *Maya, Karma, Gian, Moksha, Dharama*, even though in many cases the Gurus gave them new interpretations or modified their nuances in order to relate them to the Sikh Path. This equally applied to their concept of God and ideas of vice, virtue and sin.

Another point in the distinctness of Sikhism is its objective of salvation for all people. Man is considered as crown of creation. His soul comes form God and so must ultimately return to God. God is ingrained in man. He speaks to us through one voice of moral conscience—that divine spark—which is within all of us. We must rise above selfishness and prejudice, this requiring great effort and a keen desire to live up to the Guru's instructions. By following the Guru's teachings, one may near or goal of God-realisation. But personal salvation is not the only goal of a Sikh's life. He also hopes for the salvation of all humanity and so works for it. He also tries to inspire his fellow-men with the same spiritual goals and leads them on that path of service and meditation which could let them come to salvation, for themselves. This is a unique aspect of Sikhism.

The requirements necessary for the acceptance and viability of any religion and in its own right are satisfied by Sikhism. It has a founder and a line of successors. It has established institutions for the practice and furtherance of its faith: the *Sangat, Pangat, Gurdwara, Takhat, Amrit* and *Gurmatta*. It had missionary terminology like *Manji, Massand, Dhuan*, and *Bakhshish*, even though these orders were so misused that the tenth Guru abolished all missionary organisations. As such missionary work

11

today is done on a voluntary basis, as a Sewa,[1] because the Guru expected every Sikh to propagate the message of Sikhism. As in most other religions, Sikhs have a central place of worship the—*Harmandar Sahib* (the Golden Temple) at Amritsar, it also has its own script, called *Gurumukhi*. Its Scripture is called "The Guru Granth Sahib" a secondary scripture is called "The Dasam Granth," the latter containing the compositions of the Tenth Sikh Master. Sikhism has its own ceremonies for births, baptisms, marriages and deaths. It also has its own code of discipline—The *Rahat-Maryada*--infringements of which call for punishment by the *sangat*. It has its own festivals, fairs and celebrations. It has its own way of life, its own dress and customs. As such, Sikhism qualifies for recognition as an individual religion in its own right.

The approval of Sikhism, as one of the six major religions of the world, for school and college studies in great Britain and some other countries, only confirms the fact that it is a universal religion. It has an appeal for all the people and is there for any one to study or follow who is interested in the teachings of the Sikh Gurus. In Sikhism "The Guru is regarded as a ship which carries people across the world-ocean:

"The Guru is a boat wherein we may cross the sea of existence."
(AG, 864)

Guru Amardas clearly stated that Sikhism is a religion for all mankind, because like rainfall, it is capable of irrigating large areas and then covering them with corn and fruit. The teachings of the Gurus can bring enlightment to any person who follows their Path, through service (Sewa), holy company (Sadh-sangat), character-bulilding (Sadachar) and meditation (Simaran). All the Gurus acknowledged the state of ordinary people—that they have to live in this world—the needs of a married life and social commitment. They rejected asceticism and renunciation as unsuited to ordinary people and encouraged their active participation in community welfare work. They also examined the problems of sin and suffering, dictatorship and tyranny, they established the Khalsa Brotherhood to fight against injustice, fanaticism and oppression. These teachings and the mission of the *Khalsa Panth* are as relevant today as they were then. Sewa means selfless and voluntary service for the benefit of the community.

Sikhism also accepts the validity and co-existence of other faiths. God sends His messengers and prophets throughout the world to guide humanity in its times of difficulty and distress. Guru Ramdas says:

12

"God sends His Saints, in every age and gives them His support."
(AG, 451)

The Gurus preached to both Hindus and Muslims. They never told them to renounce their own faiths. On the contrary, they exhorted them to learn correctly, the teachings of their religious preceptors and prophets, to cut out all the dead wood which had obscured the original message. The Gurus stood for the freedom of conscience, the right of the individual to practise his own religion, and defend his belief and way of life. Even today, Sikhism does not proselytise or evangelize. It believes in persuasion and does not seek converts. Those who wish to join the fold of Sikhism are expected to undergo a period of preparation and apprenticeship before being baptised. It is totally against conversion by coercion or unfair means. The Gurus in their own day tested their followers frequently in order to assess their sincerity and devotion.

Another aspect of Sikhism is its concern for the good and the welfare of all people. The whole world is the creation of the Lord., and all its people, of different colours, features and ethnic origins have the same right to freedom, peace and progress. Sikhs in their daily general prayer—The Ardas—pray always for universal peace and the welfare of all people.

The universality of Sikhism is further supported by its Scripture—Guru Granth Sahib—which contains not only compositions of its own Gurus, but also of many Hindu and Muslim mystics of different castes and sects. No other Scripture has this catholicity of contents and outlook. It bears testimony to the unity of all revelation and demands freedom of worship. It is a unique treasure, a great heritage for all mankind.

Its Practice

The doctrines and beliefs enunciated by the Gurus were tested and evaluated by their practice in daily life. The twin objectives of moral living and spiritual evolution were demonstrated through *Sadhana* (spiritual discipline), *Sewa* (selfless service) and *Simaran* (meditation). Guru Nanak set up the first institute for the practice of his teachings, it was called a *Dharam-sal,* a place for the practice of righteousness. Here people gathered for prayers and the sharing of meals together. Later on, Dharamsal was changed to *Gurdwara*—the Guru's door or the Guru's home. Here, apart form hymn-singing and exposition of the Guru's

13

teachings, the disciples volunteer their acts of charity and projects for public welfare. One of the earlier and important projects was that of the construction of wells and tanks, to provide water for people.

Guru Nanak simplified worship and rejected all primitive austerities, rituals and omens. His practices were based on egalitarianism, common sense, public cooperation and social welfare. The ritual of fasting, pilgrimage, bodily mortification and physical exhaustion were forbidden. Idol-worship was rejected. Prayer and hymn singing only formed the daily worship of local *Sangats* (Congregations).

The ethical code laid down by the Gurus for their followers, was motivated by the needs of righteous conduct and social benefit. It was in furtherance of the Fatherhood of God and the brotherhood of man that the Gurus advocated gentle speech,chivalry and humility. They always exhorted their disciples to be ready to sacrifice themselves to noble causes. The Guru themselves led exemplary lives for their followers to emulate. Guru Arjan, Guru Tegh Bahadur and Guru Gobind Singh all sacrificed their lives for their principles and so set a tradition of martyrdom for their beliefs.

The Five K's

The original Sikh initiation ceremony, started by Guru Nanak, was called *charan-amrit*. It consisted of pouring water over the Guru's toe and then drinking it by the disciple. The drinking of this the 'foot-nectar,' was considered as proof of dicipleship. It was accompanied by Guru's blessing and initiation into the Sikh way of life. Bhai Gurdas confirms this practice in the following words: "Guru Nanak initiated his disciples with *charan-amrit* and prescribed his new code of conduct as a path-way to the truth." The initiation included instructions regarding a daily bath, meditation, the sharing of food with others, and the need to keeping the hair uncut and the wearing of the turban. Successor-Gurus added further instructions regarding the learning of Punjabi in the *Gurumukhi* script, in order to enable the Sikhs to read the hymns and hopefully be able to understand and then expound their meaning and significance to others. Subsequently, the Sikhs started the celebration of *Gurpurabs*—the birth land death anniversaries of the Gurus. Sikhs would greet their co-religionists with the words *Pairi Pauna,* which means I touch your feet, and simultaneously bow and touch each other's feet or knees in order to express love and humility. Some time later, the ceremonies suitable for birth, marriage and death were formulated with the object of seeking the blessings of God and Guru.

Guru Gobind Singh however changed the mode of baptism by replacing *Charan-amrit* by *Khanday-di-pahul* in 1699. This was necessary in order to test the disciple's total commitment to the Guru and his readiness to sacrifice himself to uphold the values of Sikhism. The demand for 'heads,' was made by the Tenth Guru to sift nominal Sikhs form dedicated ones. His new form of initiation was the nectar—*Amrit*—prepared by stirring water and sugar-crystals with a double-edged sword. It was accompanied by the maintenance of the Five K's and obedience to a code of discipline. The Guru gave Amrit to the five disciples who responded to his call for readiness for sacrifice and thereafter he himself took the *Amrit* from their hands. This implied that the Guru and the Khalsa are equal. The Tenth Guru declared: "The Khalsa is my image and I am present in the Khalsa."

Some people question the value and significance of the Five K's. Many explanations have been given by different writers, emphasising particularly their utilitarian. organisational, ethical and spiritual values. The first 'K' stands for the *Keshas* (unshorn hair), which symbolise living in harmony with the will of God. Hair is an integral and living part of the body and as such has to be maintained intact. It is kept as mark of dedication to engender group-loyalty. The Tenth Guru emphasised this and regarded the removal, shaving or trimming of hair of any part of the body as a sin *(Kurahit)*. Many Sikhs gave up their lives, but not their Keshas. Bhai Mani Singh was tortured to death and his body was cut joint by joint. Bhai Taru Singh's scalp was removed because he would not allow any one to cut his hair.

The second 'K' stands for the *Kanga* or the comb which implies cleanliness and tidiness. The Guru asked the Sikhs to comb their hair daily, and tie it in a knot and wear a turban smartly over it. The turban is necessary for the protection of hair and is a symbol of the identity of the Sikh and as such a part of his uniform. Its weaving was adopted because Guru Gobind Singh told his Sikhs to "adopt my form;" he wore a turban.

The third 'K' stands for *Kara* or the steel wrist-band. Steel holds an important place in Guru Gobind Singh's thought. God is called 'All-Steel *(Sarabloh)*. Amrit is prepared in a steel/iron pot and stirred with a steel sword. Steel is a symbol of strength and heroism. The Kara worn on the right wrist protects it form injury. The *Kara* also reminds the Khalsa that he is a servant of the Guru and must shun doing any thing evil with his hands. According to some, the Kara's round shape symbolises eternity and the wearer's link with God. The *Kara* is the only symbol which speaks

15

to its wearer each time it strikes any object, it reminds him of God (Waheguru).

The fourth 'K' represents 'Kachh' or underwear. It symbolises continence and self-restraint. It serves as a reminder against adultery or sex-perversion. It permit the complete range of physical movement without any embarrassment to its wearer and is used by both sexes.

The fifth 'K' stands for *Kirpan* or sword. The sword represents the power of God, because it destroys the wicked and the arrogant. The sword is the protector of the weak and the helpless. It may be used only in defence. Goodness must be able to defend itself and survive. The Khalsa must have means to defend others—the needy, oppressed and forsaken. Guru Gobind Singh deified the sword:

"You (sword) are the conqueror of countries,
The destroyer of armies of the wicked.
In the battle-field, you fittingly adorn the brave.
Your strength is infrangible, your brightness effulgent,
Your radiance and lustre dazzle, like the sun." (DG. 59)[9]
The sword is in an emblem of courage, dignity and self-reliance.
It is meant for the protection of the right and just.

The reader's attention is drawn to a new interpretation of the Five 'K' by J.P. Singh Uberoi[10] in terms of inversion. While in the Indian tradition, the yogis either shaved their hair or matted it together, to indicate social renunciation, the Khalsa maintains his hair (Keshas) and uses the comb(Kanga) to keep it clean and combed. Similarly, the *Kara* and *Kirpan* go together; *Kara* symbolises control over one's actions including any use of the sword. Both symbolise dignity, courage and warriorhood, as opposed to the escapism of the ascetic or recluse. The fifth symbol—*Kachh*—a garment to cover the loin and thighs is also a symbol of constraint like the comb and the wrist-band, it covers also control over sex. These symbol reflect a positive and dynamic attitude to life which includes cleanliness of the body, tidiness in appearance and conduct as demanded in the Sikh code of discipline. These put together, represent that form of Nam-Yoga/Sahaj-Yoga envisaged by the Tenth Guru in which *Kesh* and *Kanga* symbolise Sanyasa-Yoga (the virtue of detachment) *Kara* and *Kirpan* stand for Raj-Yoga (Kingly virtues), while *Kachh* represents Gristh-Yoga (family-life). This sociological and cultural interpretation of Sikh symbols needs further scrutiny.

The Five K's, supplemented by the turban form the Khalsa

16

uniform. This is an identity which remains distinct even amongst thousands of people. It preserves the unity of the community and promotes feeling of brotherhood and love. This uniform and code of discipline, have enabled Sikhs to work together in times of peace and war. Guru Gobind Singh emphasised both the outer uniform and the inner discipline (meditation) and stated that all Khalsa must stick to the discipline to maintain their progress and glory.

The maintenance of the Five K's and the observance of the four injunctions[11] called *Kurahit* (misdemeanours) form the core of the Khalsa discipline, while his outer uniform, proclaims his faith and his readiness to pay a price for it. It is not intended to foster a spirit of exclusiveness or superiority. It is a reminder of the personality and the ideals of Guru Gobind Singh.

Role of Religion

Religion is not merely something which is practised in church or temple on certain days of the week. Its role is important in day-to-day life. Each one of us is born in a family so that one's religion is something inherited. It is the duty of parents and relatives to explain the purpose and significance of religion to their children. Unfortunately, most parents fail to perform this duty with the result that their behaviour-patterns resemble those we see currently. This is particularly true in the case of Sikh families settled in foreign countries. In India also, parents are careless in this matter. In the Indian tradition, the unit is the family, not the individual. The Head of the family is responsible for the education and the religious upbringing of the children. He is the custodian of family tradition and honour. If any of his children or grand-children misbehave, the Head has to accept responsibility for neglecting his duty. It is equally important that Sikh families settled abroad, also maintain this tradition and take on the religious upbringing of their children, otherwise the children may become lost to the Sikh community.

A Sikh family is a close-knit unit. Religion is its guiding principle for conduct and activity. The basic belief in human fellowship, and the need to be selfless, humble and good, encourage Sikh children to do voluntary service both in the home and outside. Sikhs accept the natural calamities and disasters as a part of life and there is no protest or lamentation against destiny, They look forward, because a night is followed by day, so they should accept both, in the same spirit.

Many Sikhs maintain a private room or other place in the home, where they install their Guru Granth Sahib, where all members of their family may join in prayers or hymn-singing in morning and evening. On important days, like the birthdays of family-members or *Gurprabhs*, they will have special celebration in their prayer room to invoke God's blessing. They will prepare *Karah-prasad* and invite their relatives and friends to their home. Those who have no *Darbar-Sahib* (prayer-room where Guru Granth Sahib is kept) will often go to the local Gurdwara for celebrations. On the occasions of marriage and death in the family, Sikhs will hold ceremonies either in their homes or in the Gurdwara. Generally, when a Sikh starts a new business or project, he will visit the Gurdwara with his family and friends, to offer special prayers to seek God's blessing on their work, for they know that without Divine Grace, their efforts may not bear fruit.

Religion also plays an important role in the community. Social and economic activity has to have a moral base, otherwise the interests of the general public will suffer. It is necessary that the community's prosperity and affluence are shared in order to raise the standard of living for its members. The love of materialism and the lure of power are likely to make people selfish and mean. If they have these ethical values provided by understanding of their faith, they will be able to think of the welfare of the community rather than of personal gain.

Similarly, religion has a role to play for the State or nation in promoting welfare schemes and caring for its citizens. Politics without morality or principle are counter-productive and can be the bane of a nation. Theocratic States run the risk of bigotry and tyranny, because they cannot hold a balance for the scales of justice, between the interests of the followers of a State religion and of those who profess other faiths. Most of the secular States exclude any teaching of religion from their education-system, in order to prove this impartiality which in equally harmful, for they fail to provide a knowledge of fundamental moral values, which are found in all the world religions. A study of religion—of whatever choice—is an important part of education, it is also a State duty to provide its citizen with a value-system which enables them to judge right and wrong, what is moral and what is immoral. In a world which is getting smaller day by day through its technological development, it becomes increasingly important for youth today, to realise that their own prosperity and survival will depend on the peace and progress of all mankind as one entity.

Notes

1. For details, please see Darshan Singh's Indian Bhakti Tradition and Sikh Gurus
2. Degh means sharing of food.
3. Tegh means defence of the weak.
4. The Five Beloved Baptised Disciples.
5. A resolution passed by the Five Beloved Disciples and the congregation.
6. 'AG' stands for the Adi Granth, the figure indicate the page number.
7. For details, see the author's book - "Aspects of Sikhism," pp. 17-23.
8. 'Sewa' means selfless and voluntary service for the benefit of the community.
9. DG stands for Dasam Granth and the figure indicates the page number.
10. Harbans Singh, 'Perspectives on Guru Nanak', p. 502.
11. For details, see the author's book - "Aspects of Sikhism," p. 180

II

Brief History of the Ten Gurus and Their Important Messages

1. *Guru Nanak: The Founder of Sikhism*

Background of Guru Nanak's Times

1. Political Scene

India in the fifteenth century was passing through a period of political turmoil and social decadence. The Lodi emperor in Delhi had a very feeble hold on the country and the general laxity of morals and corruption affected both Hindus and Muslims. An earlier invasion of Taimur Lang in 1398 had turned northern India into a land of desolation and povery. While the Lodis (the ruling family) and their companions enjoyed a semblance of power at Delhi, the general administration of the country was a shambles. Bahlol Lodi (1451-89) was the nominal King of Hindustan and, had assigned the control of Punjab and other regions, to Governors and the Chiefs for payment of tribute or the supply of troops; this meant that the Lodi King could not directly ensure either a good administration or stability in his empire. Moreland affirms that the "great bulk of the kingdom was administered through assignees rather than salaried officers."[1] The local Chiefs killed their opponents and robbed the traders and peasant by force or fraud. Guru Nanak condemned the administration in the following lines:

> "Greed is the king, sin the minister, falsehood the mint-master. Lust, the Deputy calls men and pronounces judgement. The people are blind and without sense. They pay homage like dead men."
>
> (AG, 468)

Sikandar Lodi succeeded to the throne of Delhi in 1489, but nothing improved. Daulat Khan Lodi was appointed Governor of Lahore, by the Delhi Emperor, (It was he, who employed Guru Nanak as a store-keeper in his Sultanpur stores for a few years) The law and order situation worsened as the years passed. Latif, a Muslim historian, sums up the political situation at this time prior to the invasion of Babar as under:

> "Corruption, degradation, and treachery stalked openly throughout the land. Confusion and disorder of every kind ran riot over the length and breadth of the Empire. Murders of the most horrible type, robberies of the most outrageous and shocking character were the order of the day. Justice and position were bought and sold. The rulers of the land were sunk in sensual pleasures, and wallowed in an abyss of enfeebling debauchery."[2]

For about nineteen years Guru Nanak remained away from home, preaching his way of love and brotherhood in different countries, keeping himself away from the political uncertainties of the age. So that on his return from his missionary tours in 1521, he was very hurt by the tragedy that overtook the Punjab when king Babar attacked it. The looting and killing by Babar's soldiers at Eminabad were witnessed by the Guru. He later wrote four hymns on this subject which are called *Babar-vani*.[3] He lamented the loss of property and wilful genocide as follows:

> "Where are those sports, those stables, and those horses?
> Where are those bugles and clarions?
> Where are those who buckled on their swords and were mighty in battle?
> Where are those scarlet uniforms?" (AG, 417)

According to the *Janam-sakhies*, Guru Nanak was taken captive and produced before the Emperor. The Guru told him frankly what he thought about his atrocities and the killing of innocent men, women and children. He rebuked the emperor for the bloodshed, the looting and lustfulness of his soldiery and warned him of the nemesis of fate for him, which could be similar to that of those chiefs whom he had defeated. The Lodis who were yesterday the masters of land, were now rolling in the dust. He declared to Babar: "Do not sow the seed of cruelty. He who is cruel, himself suffers cruelty. Temper justice with mercy and forgive others, as you would wish to be forgiven. Do not covet that which is meant

21

for others, for God is just."

In turn, Guru Nanak also criticised the Lodi rulers, for inefficiency, corruption and neglect in protecting their subjects from the depredation of the Moghuls. He declared:

"This jewel (of Hindustan) has been thrown away by those dogs (Lodis),
when they are dead and gone, no one will remember them." (AG, 360)

The Battle of Panipat sealed the fate of the Lodi rulers. Sultan Ibrahim Khan Lodi died fighting on 20th April, 1526. Babar then became Emperor of India. During his remaining four years of life, he was unable to organize the administration of his Empire due to the terrible hostility and opposition of Afghan Chiefs and Rajput princes.

Guru Nanak himself did not subscribe to the theory of the divine right of kings. Any King must have kingly virtues, else he is not good. "Only one who is fit to sit on a Throne, should rule people," said Guru Nanak. A King did not have special rights and was as much subject to natural law as the common man. He must dispense an impartial justice. In this connection, one is reminded of the order that Maharaja Ranjit Singh issued to his Chief Minister Fakir Nurud Din, that the latter "should withhold and then inform him, of any order from himself, a Minister or any other functionary, that was inappropriate or oppressive."[4] Guru Nanak approved the right of the masses to resist political coercion and arbitrary use of force by the state, at the same time reminding the rulers of the transitory nature of royal power and the many examples of the downfall of kings which resulted from their misdeeds.

2. Social Scene

Braodly speaking, Indian society of those days, fell into three categories: (i) Kings, Chieftains and landlords, (ii) Priestly classes, (iii) Peasants and workers. The first category enjoyed power, privilege and wealth; the second category had prestige and status (so often misused for personal gain); the third category, the bulk of the population were poor, illiterate and miserable.

Hindu society, based on the caste and *varna-ashram* system followed its own traditions. The *Brahmins* were literate and privileged people. They ruled over the bodies and minds of other Hindus. The

22

Kshatriyas, next in the social rank, were important because they were fighters and warriors needed to defend the country, even by its conquerors, who brought large numbers of their country-men with them in their own armies. Then the *Vaishas*, the traders and agriculturists also had no rights and were taken for granted by the rulers, the *Brahmins,* and the *Kshatriyas.* Finally, fourth category called *Shudra*, included all low caste workers like sweepers, cobblers, washer-men and those menials whose duty was to serve the other classes and live on whatever was doled out to them. They suffered from several disabilities. They had no right to draw water from village-wells or to worship in temples. To see them was pollution itself. Mutual distrust and disunity so divided the four sections of Hindu society that they were unable to protect themselves.

From the twelfth century, Islam posed a powerful challenge to Hinduism. Being politically strong, the Muslims dictated to and oppressed their Hindu subjects. Islam's social equality however appealed to the lower caste Hindus. For them the advantages of conversion were many: money, status, employment to improve their own lot. The caste-system's main opposition came from the Muslims, the Sufis, Hindu saints and mystics. Guru Nanak openly preached against caste and broke its rigidity in many ways. He declared:

"Castes are folly, their names are folly;
All creatures have one shelter—that of God." (AG, 83)

"Remember it is actions that determine caste; people exalt or degrade themselves by their deeds." (AG, 496)

It may be noted that the impact of Islam on Hinduism produced unhealthy and unhappy results. Prof. A. Toynbee, the well-known historian wrote in this connection: "On the whole, the story of the relations between these two great religions (Islam and Hinduism) in India has been an unhappy tale of mutual misunderstanding and hostility."[5]

Guru Nanak was very critical of the Brahmins and so-called holy men (Sadhus), who exploited the credulity of the other sections of society and cheated them by performing costly rites and unnecessary ceremonials. He exposed their tricks. Their sole aim was to fill their own bellies and pockets. He wrote:

"The foolish Pandits love arguments and accumulation of wealth;
There are many pseudo-pious men, who do good deeds in the hope

of salvation as reward. There are ascetics who are ignorant of right living and renounce their house-holds." (AG, 468)

The *Kshatriyas*—the warrior class—was equally guilty of exploitation. They sought employment with the foreign invaders and acted as their agents in the harassment and persecution of their own people. Guru Nanak declared in this connection:

"The Kshatriyas have turned away from their proper vocation- to protect people. They now lisp the tongue of their foreign masters." (AG, 668)

The *Vaishas* (traders and tillers) and the Shudras (menial workers) had no status and lived only on sufferance, under the rulers and the upperclass Hindus.

There were the ascetics and wandering mendicants, who renounced their families, then moved off to search for Truth and Spiritualism, but still begged for food and clothes. The Yogis also were a great burden on ordinary people because they had to provide them with food, clothing and basic necessities of life. Guru Nanak called these yogis 'misguided spiritualists' and wrote:

"For his food and clothes, he (Yogi) runs from door to door;
He suffers pathetically from the pangs of hunger;
Divine wisdom he has not acquired." (AG, 879)

Yet these hungry Yogis called themselves superior to the givers of food; they boasted of their holiness and their vows of continence. Guru Nanak rebuked them:

"You (Yogi) do not restrain your lustful thoughts and call yourself continent, for while calling an alms-giving woman, "Mother," you beg and flirt with her."

The Muslim community was broadly divided into two categories: the rulers and the ruled. The Muslim rulers did not regard their co-religionist-subjects, as equals. The latter were also exploited, though not as much as the Hindus. They were the 'local' and so not as privileged as 'foreign' Muslims. However new muslims—the converts—enjoyed a measure of comfort and were gainfully employed.[6]

The position of woman in general in those times was almost untenable, it was pathetic. Guru Nanak referred to their sufferings and their massacre during Babar's invasions. Hindu women were held under perpetual tukelage and depended always on a protector—be he a father, brother, husband or son. They had no economic status and were generally used as household drudges. Poor women and widows were seduced in to prostitution. *Pardah* (the veil) was used by Hindu and Muslim women. Female infanticide was popular and Sati was common among Hindu woman. Foreign invaders carried off Hindu girls for their Harems and also sold them as slaves.

3. Economic Scene

Punjab is mainly an agricultural region. In those days, there were hardly any irrigation facilities. Food production depended mainly on rain-fall. Very little land was cultivated with wellwater being drawn up by Persian-wheels. Land-revenues and other levies were exorbitant. Besides this, the looting and destruction of standing crops by foreign armies and the depradations of robbers and money-lenders, left very little to farmers for their own maintenance.

Village industries hardly counted in the economy of the Punjab. Village craftsmen produced only basic consumer-goods for the local market. The main home industry was spinning and weaving which provided cloth for the people. There were few skilled craftsmen to produced silks and woollen-fabrics for the rich. Stone-work and metal-fittings were also produced in small quantities. Regional trade only gathered momentum during fairs and festivals. There was some trade between Punjab and Central Asia. Punjab exported shawls, carpets and textiles, and imported dry fruits and horses from Afghanistan and the north-west regions. Barter was the basis of trade, though in certain cases, silver and gold were also used to pay for merchandise.

The level of wages and expenses were low. Apart from ordinary people, the nobility, priests, military officers and professional people like physicians, money lenders etc. made good money. But ordinary people had to wallow in poverty and deprivation. Moreland wrote:

"Weavers, naked themselves, toiled to clothe others; peasants, though hungry, toiled to feed the towns and cities . . . Men and women living from season to season on the verge of hunger, could only exist as long as the supply of food held out; when it failed, their only hope was the slave-trader. The alternatives were cannibalism, suicide or starvation."[7]

4. Religious Scene

Superstition, illiteracy and credulity hall-marked the age of Guru Nanak. The Hindus believed in innumerable gods and goddesses, spirits, trees and even snakes. The priestly class neglected to guide or teach the people. They were hypocritical and corrupt. Guru Nanak rejected the externalisation of religion through the wearing symbols and other paraphernalia and emphasised always the expression for the spirit of love and service." He criticised the Brahmin thus:

"He, who has all three symbols of a pious Hindu—*Dhoti* (Sheet for covering the waist and downwards), *Tika* (sandal-wood mark on the fore-head), and *Mala* (rosary) feeds on the crumbs from the tables of foreign rulers. Inwardly he is a believer in Hindu worship, but outwardly he reads the Muslim Scriptures." (AG, 469).

Guru Nanak also protested against the arrogance and the fanaticism of the *Ullema*, the Mulla and the Qazi for patronising the ruling class. He censured the priestly classes for their corruption and exploitation:

"Without knowing God, they sing His praises;
A starving Mulla turns his home into a mosque,
Another has his ears split, to earn a living,
Another becomes a begging preacher and loses his self-respect.
Do not fall at the feet of any man who claims to be a religious teacher or Pir, but lives on begging." (AG, 1245).

In the same manner, the Guru exposed the cursing and miracle mongering of Yogis. He exhorted them to give up their shams and tricks. He declared:

"Yoga does not consist of wearing a patched coat or of carrying a staff or in smearing ashes over body: Yoga does not consist in wearing ear rings or shaving the head or blowing horns. Remain pure, amidst the impurities of the world; thus may you find the way of Yoga." (AG, 730).

Finally, even Guru Nanak was fed up, by the jealousies and distrust prevailing among the leaders and followers of both Hinduism and Islam. He exposed their fanaticism, narrowness, hypocrisy, corruption and meanness. He pointed out the 'Truths' of their respective religions, but few followed his advice. He had his own devoted followers to whom he preached a new gospel—the religion of man. His followers were called 'Sikhs' and learnt this new faith direct from him. He emphasised "righteous living," which included, love of the Truth, the service of mankind, the dignity of labour, the sharing of one's food with others and devotion to God. He declared to the world:

"The Truth," is the remedy for all the ailments of mankind; it can wash away all sins, it can bring man to perfection." (AG, 468)

II. His Life

A narration of the life-events of any religious leader is a difficult task due to the passing of time and the traditional addition of legend to hagiological biographies, also very true about the life of Guru Nanak. We have no contemporary records. The *Janam-Sakhis* (life-stories) are our primary source of information. There are four *Janam-Sakhis* written in Punjabi: *Puratan Janam-Sakhi* (also called Vilayat-vali) published in 1815, Bhai Bala *Janam-Sakhi*, *Meherban Janam-sakhi* (written in 1630 and published in 1964), and Bhai Mani Singh's account written in 1706. Additionally, we have *Vars* of Bhai Gurdas written about the year 1604, in which we find 23 verses covering Guru Nanak's times, travels and teachings. There are also the *Gurbilas Patshahi Chhevi* (1718), Koer Singh's *Gurbilas Patshahi Dasvin* (1751) and *Bansavali-nama Dasvi Patshahi Ka* (1769), finally the *Gurpratab Suraj Granth* in 13 volumes of Bhai Santokh Singh (1834). Bhai Vir Singh published his *Guru Nanak Chamatkar* in 1928. Earlier, the English writer Macauliffe had published his first volume of The Sikh Religion concerning the period of Guru Nanak, in English in 1909. Joginder singh and Daljit Singh publishing their *Guru Nanak, the great Humanist* some years later.

Recent studies on Guru Nanak's life which deserve attention are those of Kartar Singh, Trilochan Singh, Harbans Singh, Gopal Singh, S.S. Kohli, J.S. Grewal, S.S. Bal and Mc Leod. A volume of scholarly papers has been edited on the various aspects of Guru Nanak under the title *Perspectives on Guru Nanak* (1975). Dr. G.S. Mansukhani's two books:

Guru Nanak, Apostle of Love (1969) and *Life of Guru Nanak* (1974) also deal with this very subject. Some Indian universities and the Guru Nanak Foundation, Delhi, have also brought out a number of books as a part of Guru Nanak's Quincentenary celebrations, in 1969.

A good biographer ought to use discretion to select those events in Guru Nanak's life which tally with *gurbani*. Lots of miracles are narrated in the *Janam sakhis*. He ought to avoid quoting these stories, because all Sikh Gurus were against the performance of miracles to demonstrate their power and greatness. Sikhism does not reject the working of miracles, but discourages their use, because they defy natural law or God's Will. Guru Ramdas declares:

"The desire to perform miracles is a worldly attachment,
It is an obstacle to percolating the Holy Name in our hearts."

The two Sikh Gurus who suffered martyrdom, did not exercise the powers they had to prevent their own personal torture and suffering. The real miracle is not to perform a miracle, in spite of having a capacity to do so. Emerson says: "Self-sacrifice is the real miracle out of which all the reported miracles flow."

It is easy to divide Guru Nanak's life into three parts. The period of 38 yeas (1469-1506) covers his childhood, marriage, employment and family-life. The second period of 14 years (1507-20)* commences with God's Revelation to him, then his missionary tours to important centres in India and abroad. During this period, he wrote many of those hymns which contain his message to the various persons or groups he met with. He sang most of his compositions to the accompaniment of *rabab* (rebec), which was played by his companion, Mardana. The third period of 18 years (1521-39) he spent in establishing Dharamsal, a place for the practice of righteousness, at Kartarpur. Here he established a *Sangat* (Congregation) where all did their daily rota of duties. After establishing the institution of *Sangat* and *Pangat* (Free Kitchen), he then appointed his successor, to carry on his mission. Such were the beginnings of Sikhism as a religious Path.

The First Phase (1469-1506)

Guru Nanak was born to middle-class Hindu family on 15th April, 1469,* at Talwandi (50 kms. north-west of Lahore) now called Nankana Sahib. His father Mehta Kalyandas was the village accountant and his

28

mother was named Tripat. The upbringing of the child Nanak was left to the mother and eldest daughter Nanaki. They loved him and looked after him very well.

Throughout his childhood, Nanak proved to be a precocious and gifted boy. He was very friendly and charitable. He would join his friends and neighbours for play, and distributing sweets among them that his mother had prepared. His special gift was singing. He enjoyed composing and singing songs in praise of God and Nature. His friends would repeat lines after him. He had the gift of sublime poetry, words and tunes, came to him naturally. People called him *shair,* which means poet, he liked this title. He was very gentle, affectionate and compassionate. His sister Nanki was very fond of him, appreciated his unusual wisdom and his devotion to God.

Nanak went to school at the age of seven. His teacher was Pandit Gopal. Nanak learned every thing thoroughly and quickly. Being a poet, he wrote an acrostic on his letters of a Gurumukhi alphabet, called a *Patti* (AG, 432), much to the amazement of his teacher. Gopal realised that the gifted child had greater wisdom than himself and that his self-manifested spiritual knowledge was deep and profound. Nanak told his teacher that all worldly knowledge was nothing as compared to the adoration of God. He declared:

"Write the praises of the Holy Name; write that God is limit-less and supreme.
O Brother! If you learn these things, they will support you on your day of reckoning." (AG, 16).

Nanak was sent to learn Persian and Arabic from another teacher, Ruknuddin. In those days, the knowledge of these languages was necessary if one wanted to obtain a job in the State Service. Nanak learnt these languages quickly. Then he met a Muslim mystic, named Qutubuddin who told him about Sufi philosophy and mysticism. After this meeting, Nanak began to think more deeply about God and His mysteries; he visited the local jungles to study birds, bees, insects, among the trees. He began to wonder about rustling leaves and birds' songs. It seemed to him that the woods themselves were singing songs of God's praise in their own way. The residents of his village loved Nanak and often came to listen to his words of wisdom; they respected him. Rai Bular, the local Chief, discovered the genius of Nanak and told Nanak's father, to be good and generous to him, as he was an extra-ordinary boy.

When Nanak was nine years old, his father made pre-parations for investing him with the Sacred Thread—the Hindu *Janeau*. This was customary and signified spiritual birth or baptism. Pandit Hardayal, the family priest, came to perform the ritual. Family relations and friends gathering to witness the ceremony and join the feast that followed. After the priest had read the sacred verses, he asked Nanak to come forward to receive the Sacred Thread. Nanak demurred, he wanted to know the purpose and significance of wearing of the sacred thread. He questioned the priest: "Will this Sacred Thread make me a better man? What will happen if the thread gets broken or is lost?" The Pandit could give no satisfactory answers to these queries. He could only say that the Sacred Thread was a traditional ceremony, and it would confirm him in the Hindu religion. Nanak replied that he would prefer wearing a different kind of thread, one which could make him truthful and virtuous. He told the priest to prepare another Sacred Thread, according to the following prescription:

"Out of the cotton of compassion, spin a thread of contentment;
Tie in it a knot of continence then twist it with the strength of Truth;
O Pandit! If you can make such a Thread for my soul, then give it to me." (AG, 471).

The priest was baffled; he admitted that he could not make such a Thread. Nanak assured him that such a Sacred Thread was possible:

"By adoring and praising the Name, honour and a true thread are obtained;
This Sacred Thread when put on, will not break and will ensure one's entrance to God's Court."

After this event, Nanak spent more time in the forest brooding on the problems of the world. He avoided company and sought solitude for his contemplation and meditation. His parents felt disturbed, for he neglected his meals and became deeply absorbed in his meditation. His parents noting his other-worldliness, called a physician (Vaid) to treat him. Nanak recorded this experience in the following words:

"A physician is called for my treatment;
Gripping my arm, he counts my pulse
But being simple-minded, he does not know,

30

That in my heart does lie cause, in my wrenching quest for God."
(AG, 1279).

Nanak told the physician of his inner malady—of the separation from God, how he felt much better when he meditated on God. The physician told his parents that he had no medicine to cure Nanak's ailment, for Nanak was contemplating a World's malaise. How sick souls could be restored to health.

Nanak's parents thought that perhaps marriage would provide a solution to his other-worldliness. Perhaps if he under-look responsibilities of a house-holder, he would settle down in normal life. Nanak was now sixteen and ready for marriage. So his parents selected a girl called Sulakhni. Nanak's marriage took place in April 1485.

Nanak and his wife lived happily at Talwandi. He liked family life and had two sons. His father thought that Nanak should now enter business and earn to maintain himself and his family. So giving him twenty rupees he asked him to try for a profitable bargain, in the neighbouring town-market. Bala a freind accompanied Nanak on this buying venture. On the way, they met a group of holy men who needed food and clothing. Nanak thought that there could not be a more profitable bargain than that of feeding the hungry and clothing the poor. So he and Bala bought food-stuffs and clothes and gave them to the holy men, who in turn blessed Nanak for his kindness and charity. When Nanak returned empty-handed, his father beat him up, for wasting money. Soon after, his sister Nanki and her husband Jairam, came to Talwandi and then took Nanak with them to Sultanpur for employment. Jairam had a good job and was influential with the local Chief. Nanak agreed to stay in Sultanpur, and found a job, as a store-keeper, in the State Ration-shop.

At Sultanpur, Nanak was happy and satisfied with his job. His daily schedule consisted of prayers, the discharge of official duties and meeting family obligations. Nanak's friends gathered for prayers at his house in the mornings and evenings. Mardana also moved to Sultanpur and took employment. He and Nanak sang their songs in praise of God every day. Nanak preached to his companions of the Three Rules of life:

i.   That one should earn one's livelihood and maintain one's family;
ii. That one should share his food and give money in charity for the poor;
iii. That one should remember God while leading an honest and moral life.

31

Nanak himself followed these rules, and shared his income with those in need. His geniality, efficiency and hard work won him many admirers. Being free from corruption, his colleagues soon became jealous and complained to the authorities that Nanak was freely distributing rations and so depleting the commodities. An official inquiry cleared him of any deficiency of stock or of money. After being clear of any dishonesty, Nanak decided to resign from his job and devote himself totally to his spiritual pursuits.

In 1507,[10] Nanak had a very strange experience. One day, while taking his bath in the river Bain, close to Sultanpur, he disappeared in the river. It was said that he had drowned. The Chief sent men to search the river-bed and its source, but to no avail. Everyone was surprised by his disappearance; some thought that he may have committed suicide. However, on the third day, Nanak reappeared in the village, but as a changed man. His eyes glittered and his face shone with a divine lustre. Later he wrote a hymn about a mystic vision and divine mission as under:

"I am a minstrel picked from the state of inertia,
And sent on the mission and was instructed by divine ordainment,
To disseminate the gospel, by day and night.
This minstrel, was called to the presence of God,
On him the mantle of god's praise was conferred.
He bestowed on me His cup of divine Nectar,
Its sustaining substance being the Ambrosia of Truth;
In accordance with the blessed instruction of the Master,
I consumed the Nectar in full, it was truly blissful.
Now this minstrel, disseminates this Revelation, through ambrosial song,
Nanak says that through praising "The Truth," the Truthful has been attained." (AG, 150).

Soon, a crowd gathered to hear Nanak's Revelation. His first words were: "There is no Hindu; there is no Mussulman." This meant that all people are equal. All divisions of man based on creed, caste, colour and culture are futile. A man's worth depends not on his religion or birth, but on his character and actions. God judges people not by their labels but by their deeds. Then he recited the Mool-Mantra[11] which defines God and His qualities—His Uniqueness, Truth, Creativity, Fearlessness, Rancourlessness, Immunity from birth and death, Self-enlightenment and Gracefulness. Guru Nanak was now under Divine commission, to spread this message, of Truth, Equality and Peace. So ending his commitments in Sultanpur, Guru Nanak set about fulfilling his Divine Mission.

The Second Phase (1507-20)

Guru Nanak explained the purpose of his journeying in his Sidh-gosht:

"In search of saintly men, I became a wandering recluse;
In the hope of getting a vision of the Divine,
I donned a hermit's garb;
'Truth' is the only merchandise I have in my store." (AG, 939)

Guru Nanak then set off, to eastern India on his first missionary tour. As he entered Eminabad, he met a carpenter named Lalo. Guru Nanak admired his skill, as he made the wooden pegs used for fixing tents. The Guru asked him: "Lalo, will you be making wooden pegs all your life ?" Lalo was astonished by this question and could make no reply. He fell down at the feet of the Guru and wanted enlightenment with regard to the way he might lead the remainder of his life. The Guru told him that to merge with God was the goal of this life, for which there were three simple rules, namely *Kirt-karna* (doing honest work), *Wand-chhakna* (share your food with others), *Nam-Japna* (meditate on God's Name). Lalo became the Guru's first disciple and vowed to follow his instructions.

Guru Nanak went on to Kurukshetra, where thousands of Hindus, gathered on the day of Solar eclipse, for bathing, fasting and prayer. There a Zamindar who had just returned from a hunting expedition, offered Guru Nanak a dead deer as an offering. The Guru told Mardana to cook it. Soon a crowd led by Nanu pandit approached the Guru and protested about the cooking of meat during a period of eclipse. The Guru referred to those meat-sacrifices mentioned in the *Vedas* for Hindus, and declared:

"Rhinoceros sacrifice was performed to appease a goddess,
Those who give up eating meat and disdainfully,
Pinch their nostrils with their fingers, still
Eat men, under the cover of night's darkness." (AG, 1289)

The Guru rejected their protest as hypocritical, and told them that vegetarianism was not a passport, to heaven or salvation:

> Only the foolish quarrel over the desirability of eating flesh,
> They are ignorant of true knowledge and meditation.
> What is really flesh? What is really vegetarian food?
> Which one of them is sin-infested?
> They cannot differentiate between good and sinful food!" (AG, 1289)

The Guru told them that only food which produces pain or disease in the body produces evil thoughts in the mind, is forbidden and sinful. The people were impressed by the Guru's arguments and sought his blessings.

Then Guru Nanak went to Bindraban (near Mathura), where there were many, temples dedicated to Lord Krishna. When the Guru saw Krishan-lila,[12] he criticised the performers on their antics and greed:

> "The audience see, laugh and go home.
> It is for money, that actors beat out their rhythms,
> And dash themselves to the ground!" (AG, 465)

During his second missionary tour, Guru Nanak went to south of India. At Ujjain, a pilgrim-centre he found many people lighting lamps, floating them in the river, in the belief that these lamps would illuminate the dark road of the next world. The Guru pointed out to them the futility of this practice, as their lamps sank in the river's water. He declared that only the illumination of the mind was valuable. He declared:

> "Make your body the float; light in it the lamp of true realisation;
> Transform the flames of desire into devotion;
> Kindle with them an every-lasting flame;
> Merge your consciousness with the divine consciousness;
> Float such a lamp on the stream of your life;
> Such a light will illuminate the darkness of your mind and awaken understanding."

At Kanchi, the Guru saw pilgrims standing in a queue to offer flowers to an idol of Shiva. He asked them:

> "Why worship gods and goddesses?
> What can you ask of them?

34

What can they give?
The idols that you bathe and worship,
O Brother, sink in water.
How can they help any one to cross the ocean of life?" (AG, 637)

After visiting Rameshwaram, Guru Nanak crossed to Ceylon by boat. Raja Shivnabh of Ceylon, had heard of Guru Nanak from Manshukh, a local Sikh businessman. He decided to t;ry and test the Guru. So he sent a few dancing girls to charm the Guru. The girls tried their best to attract the Guru's attention, but as he was in meditative trance, they failed. So Raja Shivnabh became convinced of the Guru's holiness and sought his blessing.

During his third missionary journey, Guru Nanak proceeded to North India. Near Sialkot, lived a so-called holy man, who was called *Shah-Suhagin* (which meant 'Bride of the Lord'). His disciples did not allow any one to enter his house. The Guru told the people to gate-crash his house and see for themselves what the holy man was doing inside. They did so and to their surprise that their great man was making love to a woman in the inner room. The Guru rebuked him for his hypocrisy and explained to him that only through True Devotion could a person become the Lord's devotee or His Bride.

Guru Nanak climbed the Himalayan ranges, and there met a group of yogis at Sumer Parbat. He held long discussions with them. He exposed their asceticism and so-called penances. He advocated family-life and social commitment, declaring:

"As a lotus growing in muddy water maintains its bloom,
As a duck floating on the water does not soil its feathers,
So when meditating on the Lord's Name and being in His Presence,
The soul remains unaffected by the world's environment." (AG, 938)

Returning to the Punjab, Guru Nanak stopped on the banks of the river Ravi. He liked the spot and so sought to establish a small town-ship there for his followers. He brought the land from Karoria, the local *Zamindar* and built himself a small cottage. The Guru asked some of his devotees to build their huts there. The place became Kartarpur— "city of God."

During his fourth and last journey, Guru Nanak went west of the Punjab. He passed through the Sind province and stayed at a place called

Hinglaj. Here, in the temple of goddess Kali, he explained to her disciples what true worship was:

"They who imbibe "the Truth" as their fast, make contentment their pilgrimage,
Meditation their ablution, contentment their deity and
Forgiveness their rosary, are the most sublime persons." (AG, 1245)

Guru Nanak then went to Mecca where he gave counseil to local priests. On the outskirts of Baghdad, the Guru stayed with Bahlol Dana and gave him spiritual enlightenment. Swami Anand Acharya wrote a poem on this, entitled "On reading an Arabic Inscription in a shrine outside the town of Baghdad, dated 912 Hijra," in his book entitled *Snowbirds*:

"Here spoke the Hindu guru Nanak, to Fakir Bahlol,
For all those sixty winters, since the Guru left Iraq,
The soul of Bahlol has rested on he Master's Word—
Like a bee poised on a dawn-lit honey rose!"[13]

As Guru Nanak returned to the Punjab, he heard news of Babar's invasion and witnessed scenes of carnage and destruction.[14] His compassion flowed for the refugees and prisoners of war. Guru Nanak finally returned to Kartarpur in 1521, to spend the remaining years of his life in the company of his devotees.

The Third and Last Phase (1521-39)

Guru Nanak having again donned the garments of family life devoted his time to farming and teaching "the Sikh way of life" to his followers. He looked after his family who liked this new surrounding and the rural setting. Here both Hindus and Muslims gathered in his house for prayers. The daily routine was conducive to simple and holy living. They shared meals in the Free Kitchen after prayers and hymn-singing. This became a model colony—"the Brotherhood of God-fearing republicans," as Pincott calls them. Here the Guru gave his sermons and advised those who came with personal problems.

Kartarpur attracted people from all the Punjab. The peasant liked the simple message and healthy food. Guru Nanak told them to get up early in the morning and recite *Japji* or meditate on the Holy Name. The numbers of his followers increased day by day. They were called "Sikhs" or students, they engaged in being competitive in spiritual matters.

One day, a resident of Khadur called Lehna came to see Guru Nanak. He stayed there and served the Guru with great devotion. He did all kinds of difficult jobs. Guru Nanak was then getting old and felt it was time for him to appoint a successor. His sons thought that one of them would get the succession as the next Guru. However, the Guru made it clear to them that he would test his devotees and his sons to find the best man to succeed him, to carry on his mission. One day, the Guru's brass jug fell into the gutter. He asked his sons to pick it up, but they refused. Lehna then quickly picked it up, cleaned it and returned it to the Guru. Then the Guru held other tests. In all of them, only Lehna was successful. The Guru then announced that he would hold a special function for the installation of Lehna, as his successor. On 22nd. September, 1539, Guru Nanak embraced Lehna and gave him a new name: Angad, which meant 'my limb,' passed his light on to him and bowed to him, as Second Guru of the Sikhs.

Guru Nanak then, lay down, covered himself with a white sheet and passed away. His Hindu and Muslim devotees cut the sheet into two parts. The Hindu burnt theirs, while the Muslims buried theirs. So Guru Nanak's light, was passed from Guru to Guru. It is now present in the form of *gurbani* (hymns) in the Guru Granth Sahib. His hymns will continue to inspire humanity for all time to come.

> "The Word of the Guru is the inner music,
> The Word of the Guru is the highest Scripture,
> The Word of the Guru is all-pervading." (AG, 2)

Guru Nanak as a Teacher

Guru Nanak's concept of education was very liberal. Education for him implied the development and integration of body, mind and soul. The progress of man requires educating, the Hand, Head and Heart. To educate the Hand requires the acquisition of manual skills, an understanding of the value and dignity of labour, and a sense of service forward the community. The education of the Head demands a knowledge of the Arts and Science, an understanding of the problems that face us and the way to their solution, an appreciation of the wonders of Nature and an

37

inquisitive mind to search for Truth. To educate the Heart includes self-discipline, control of emotions, the pursuit of ethics and a sense of spiritual values.

Apart from this secular knowledge, the performance of one's duties with vigilance over thought and action, are also important. *Dharma* or righteousness in its broadest meaning should be the aim of our education. This includes a respect for our teachers and holy people, a love of our neighbours, service for our fellow-beings, and consideration for the whole of God's creation. However, Guru Nanak has given a wide reference to this realm of knowledge in his *Japji:*

> "There are many kinds of earth, air, water and fire,
> Many are the Krishnas and Shivas;
> Many also the forms of Brahmas in different colours and dresses.
> Numberless are the earths and mountains.
> Numerous Dhrus[15] receiving instruction.
> Numerous are the Indras, suns, moons and the many starry and earthly regions.
> Many are Sidhhas, Buddhas, Nathas, and goddesses of various sorts.
> Many are the gods, demons and sages, many the jewels in the oceans;
> Many are the forms of life and language.
> Many the great kings;
> Many too are the devotees of God,
> Many this humble servants;
> O Nanak, their numbers are beyond counting.
> In this domain, knowledge reigns supreme,
> Here are found many joyful sights and sounds. (AG, 8)

If we analyse the above lines, we find that Guru Nanak has referred to the wonders of God and his manifold creations. Our reason and science is limited to physical matter and the perceptions of our organs of senses. But total Knowledge, is vast and profound. Science has not yet touched the tip of the iceberg in this respect. There are millions of other solar systems, galaxies and other sources of energy. The five elements of air, earth, water, fire and ether (space) themselves contain vast stores of untapped energy. Taking them one by one, *Air* may be in the form of storm-energy, wind-power, and typhoon-power; all to be harnessed for human use. The *earth* has lots of minerals, gases and geo-thermal energy

38

within, also energy available from bio-matter and garbage. Similarly, *water* could help the present energy shortage through tidal power, hydro-electric power, rainfall reservoirs, inland water-ways, sea-minerals, also oceanic vegetation and animal forms, all potential sources of energy. *Fire* as solar and volcanic power when we learn how to harness it. *Space* or ether energy in the form of ozone-layers, electro-magnetic fields, power from satellites and space-laboratories. All may become available to us as man acquires ever greater knowledge of these new subjects and explores the means for utilising new sources of energy.

The super-naturl and supra-mental worlds have still to be developed, they would again extend our present horizons and prove to be vast fields for new research in the years ahead. Such knowledge is obtainable form these gifted and spiritual persons whose own intuitions and wisdom are enlarged by God's Revelation. God is beyond time and space and great is the power of His messengers and prophets, while ordinary people with their limited reason and faculties can only produce within the capability that God was pleased to give them.

Unfortunately all too often, with knowledge, comes pride, arrogance and selfishness. The Guru calls this use of knowledge 'ignorance' and illusion. The Guru did not approve of bookish knowledge and argument for its own sake. He says:

"A learned man is a 'fool,' if he is full of avarice, greed and pride."

The Guru criticised Brahmins for parading their learning in stead of teaching it to ordinary people. Knowledge only derived from books does not produce wisdom.

"One may read as long as he lives; one may study as long as he breathes;
Nanak says, only one thing, The Truth will be of value in the end;
The rest, is all futility and vexation to the spirit." (AG, 467)

Guru Nanak laid stress on character-building, fellowship and social service. He declared: "The essence of education lies in promoting the service of man-kind." (AG, 356) For him all humanity was the family of God, as such, education should be oriented towards learning to love our fellow-men:

"He indeed is learned who does good to others;

The acquisition of true learning is an action that proceeds from it." This form of love is best seen in acts of charity and altruism. It is the duty of a teacher to set an example to his students. The young have to face many challenges and temptations, and unless they get the right guidance, or build up sufficient potential and courage, they are likely to fall prey to their materialistic environment and other unhealthy influences.

Every individual has his own moral conscience within, which can tell him what is right or wrong. This moral sense, also called "the conscience" is present even in atheists. It has to be developed and Guru Nanak tells us that this is most easily done in the company of good or virtuous people. When a man is in doubt—whether he should do a particular thing or not—he can take it to his conscience for a decision, provided he has developed it. People have to learn to recognise, then obey, their small voice of conscience.

His Technique of Teaching

Though Guru Nanak was not a professional teacher, he was very serious about his mission. He chose to call himself a *poet* and in that capacity explained to people the laws of morality and social behaviour. Guru Nanak did not condemn any sect or cult for being different, often he showed its followers a better path, because in ignorance, they had mistaken "the chaff for the grain." He believed that every person had a divine spark in him and that it was due to ignorance or indifference that a person misbehaved. It is the duty of any teacher to try to remove this ignorance. Guru Nanak says:

"I say to you, 'When the sun rises, the moon is not seen,'
When divine knowledge appears, ignorance is dispelled."

He appealed to the common sense and intelligence of people. He told them that this human life provides a grand opportunity for the pursuit of perfection. An egoistic person throws away his human life for trivial amusements. Like a frog, he lives on slime and weeds, while a sensible person, like a honey-bee obtains his nectar from the lotus flower growing in the same pond. He declared:

"In the clear water of the pond, lives the pure lotus flower;
In the pond also grow slime and weed; the honey-laden lotus
Remains unsullied by the dirt and slime of the pond.

Forg (evil person) can you not realise that you are next to the lotus?
You eat only slime and weeds, while sitting in the pond's clear
water
While the honey-bee, that does live not in the pond, comes to it,
And sucks honey from the lotus." (AG, 990)

Elsewhere the Guru compares an ignorant person to a peasant who sows
poison and expects nectar:

"He who sows bitter seed and desires a sweet crop,
Where is his common sense? (AG, 474)

Similarly, the Guru rejected ritual and ceremony because they were
fruitless:

"If you churn curd, butter comes from of it, but
If you only churn water, you will only get water." (AG, 635)

Guru Nanak communicated with all people using the simplest language,
so reaching their hearts. He used home-spun images and colloquial
phrases, to drive his lessons home:

" A cow without milk is as useless as a bird without wings;
As vegetation withers without water, so a king without subjects, is
a nonety.
Those in whom the eyes of spirituality are closed, are equally
useless without "The Name." (AG, 354)

According to him, devotion to God destroys all sin, as a fire can burn up
a pile of garbage:

"The lamp of life is filled with oil of suffering"
Light it with the flame of God's Holy Name;
Such a flame will consume all suffering, and
Lord himself will be seen." (AG, 358)

Guru Nanak diagnosed each of his disciple's malady and prescribed a
specific cure. Like a physician, he examined their outer and inner
condition, then gave them the medicine with a list of the precautions to
take. He did not frighten the disciple with threats of hell or a curse. He

reminded them of their duty to themselves, to the family and community. He emphaised the fact that this golden opportunity of a human life, should be put to the best use, by sowing the seed of the "Holy Name" and in the service of mankind, these would win ample rewards both in this world and the next. He showed his path to the disciples in a genial and friendly way. Daud, a Muslim weaver brought a small carpet for the Guru which he had woven as a labour of love. The Guru received his gift and thanked him for it. As he was about to leave the Guru opened the door. Outside, was a bitch with her puppies, shivering in the cold. Guru Nanak told Daud to cover them with his carpet and give some milk to the animals. Daud was touched with the Guru's sense of compassion. He was happy that his gift had been given to the needy animals. Such lessons in the milk of human kindness were given to the disciples by the Guru, from time to time.

Guru Nanak imparted his teachings through poetry and song. Music can touch the heart of most people even to their inner core. The gentle strains of spiritually inspired music seep into the inner consciousness, like the drops of rain which percolate through the soil. The soul drinks such nectar to its fill, and becomes imbued with the Holy Name. Guru Nanak advised hymn-singing at dawn, because the environment of silence and calm at that hour makes the mind more receptive to the soft strains of sacred music, and the absorption of the healing power of "The Name". Music most easily links the individual soul to the Universal soul. According to the Guru, Kirtan is "food for the human soul". Those who perform or listen to it, loses their fear of death. Their tensions and sorrows vanish, and their minds become full of peace and joy: Guru Nanak says:

"The persons who perform kirtan are free from the fear of death. ... They are awakened to a love of the "Holy Name." Their souls become linked to God." (AG, 867)

Guru Nanak was an expert in the matching of his poetic compositions to the right *ragas* and *talas* (rhythms). It is this harmony that imparts both beauty and vitality to his hymns and creates the appropriate *rasa* (aesthetic feeling)in the listeners. This coordination is further reflected in the diction, imagery, prosody and theme of the hymn coupled to the choice of raga. Here is an example of such harmony between subject-matter and symbols. In Basant raga—suited to the season of spring, as its name suggests—Guru Nanak uses the image of a tree (the devotee) which in spring blooms to fruition. If the disciple leads a life of holiness and meditation, his bliss (bloom) will never end:

"When virtuous deeds are the tree and God's Name its branches,
Faith is its flowering and divine knowledge its fruit, then the
Attainment to God are its leaves, and humility provides its dense
shade. . . .
Eternal spring will be for those who perform altruistic actions.
Nanak says, Such holy persons will remain always in bloom and
merge in Divine Essence!" (AG, 1168)

His Personality

Guru Nanak was a versatile personality; he had charisma, which no
one could resist. He was a singer, a poet, a preacher, a house-holder and
a farmer. He identified himself with the lowest classes. For him, social
status, asceticism or power had no meaning or charm. While he met his
obligations to his own family, he was more inclined to see the needs and
difficulties of the greater family of mankind. He visited the huts of the
poor and neglected, and shared with them, his sympathy and wisdom. His
sweet reasonableness appealed to all. Even the arrogant emperor Babar
came to him for his advice and blessing.

Guru Nanak was a man of the people. He gave them basic moral
and religious values for life. He emphasised the unity of all religions and
the futility of ceremonial worship. Only devotion and prayers from the
individual heart could reach the God in man. His humanism found
expression when he set up Dharamsals—places of prayer, shelter and care,
for the poor. The provision of Free food, was one of their functions as in
a Sikh temple. Babar's atrocities so moved him that he took upon himself,
the task of healing the sick and caring for the maimed and helpless. Sewa
(selfless service) was introduced as a proof of true devotion. He declared:

"In this world, service to its people, is supreme; It will secure for
you, a seat of honour in the Lord's Court." (AG, 25)

Guru Nanak was a champion of equality and freedom. He stood for
the fair treatment of women. In his time women were looked on as the
embodiment of temptation and pollution. She was deemed unfit to be
literate or to read the scriptures, sold in child-marriage or forced to
concremation, if her husband died. The Guru gave great attention to the
improvement of the lot of the women of his time. Her uplift was essential
for the progress of Indian society. How could mankind progress, if

women, about half of it, are backward, despised and treated as outcastes? He pioneered the liberation of woman in the fifteenth century. He opened the doors of his *Dharamsal* to women; There, they were treated as equal to men. Later on, succeeding Gurus appointed women as missionaries and teachers.

Guru Nanak was a world-teacher and peace-maker. He brought reconciliation to many Hindu and Muslim groups. His love for mankind was limitless. Any one was welcome to his home. He loved to reclaim a lost sheep, a strayed soul. He was fair and just to every one. He rejected the claims of his sons. The office of 'Guru' had to be earned, it was not an hereditary office. He was respected and acclaimed by both Hindus and Muslims. He was recognised as:

"Baba Nanak, the best man of God! The Guru of Hindus, and Pir of Mussulmans!"

3. Guru Nanak's Message

(a) Message of peace

Guru Nanak was a man of peace and conciliation. When he and his companion Mardana sang divine music on the cutskirts of Baghdad, where music was banned, he faced an explosive situation. The local Muslims led by Pir Dastagir came with sticks and stones to teach him a lesson. The Guru asked them to calm down and listen to his point of view first. He made them understand that music in itself, was not bad or evil. It all depended on the content and wording of the verses. If it dealt with erotic theme:,it could rouse the lower passions of man and that was the type of music which was banned. But if the words only contained the praises of God, it was good and blessed, for sacred music, nourishes the soul of man. He declared:

"Devotional music is like a priceless jewel, it gives spiritual bliss and many other blessings! (AG, 893)
"Whoever recites or listens to sacred music, will have Their evil inclinations and sorrow ended." (AG, 1300)

Then Guru Nanak sang a divine hymn. The hearts of the Muslims were at once filled with peace and joy. Those who had come to chastise the

Guru, sought his blessings before dispersing.

According to Guru Nanak, another source of peace is in the service to God's creation. In selfless service, one illustrates the "presence of God', within the individual. There is the story of a Sikh of Guru Gobind Singh, called Bhai Kanahiya who served water to friend and foe alike on the battle-field. When questioned as to why he served water to enemy soldiers, he replied: "Sir, I see God in all men. How can I refuse to serve water to the Lord!" Guru Gobind Singh was pleased with his answer and blessed him.

(b) Universal Brotherhood.

Guru Nanak rejected the caste system and the division of any people on bases of religion, birth, power or wealth. He realised the Divine presence in all people and so valued every human being. No person need be lost for ever. Even the worst sinner, if he repented and turned to God, would be forgiven. As all mankind was of the one family, all forms of discrimination—social, political, ethnic, racial and religious should be ended. Today however, inspite of the charter of Fundamental Rights of UNO, discrimination still persists in many countries. A truly religious man should be recognisable through the practice of equality and impartiality in all relations with others. Guru Nanak says:

"Religion consists not only in words,
He who looks on all men his equal, is religious."

The idea of brotherhood implies giving to those in need and helping the helpless. Altruism is a basic human duty, but it must be organised to do the maximum good for the greatest number. That is why the Gurus introduced the system of *Daswand*—the 1/10th (tithes) for charitable and religious projects, Such organised charity can bridge the gulf between rich and poor. Similarly, *langar* (Free Kitchen) was started to ensure that no one coming to the Guru's house left hungry. Such Kitchens are also started in places of famine, flood or other calamity to relieve distress and suffering. In modern states most of these functions have been taken over by Governments.

The idea of a universal brotherhood was carried to its logical conclusion by Guru Nanak in collecting the hymns of Hindu and Muslim saints for incorporation in his *Pothi* (hymn-book). This volume in its manuscript-form was given by Guru Nanak to his successor, and by his

45

successor, to his successor Guru. Guru Amárdas compiled another volume called *Mohan-Pothi*, which contained all the hymns of the first three Gurus and of some Indian saints. This formed the basis of the Sikh Scripture compiled by Guru Arjan.

(c) His Moral Values

Guru Nanak did not write any Code of Rules or Discipline, as such his teachings and discussions with various persons in his life crystalised into the norms of human behaviour which he expected of his Sikhs. Such norms are not based on commandments, but on advice, their violation does not constitute a religious offence with specific penalty or penance. He believed in the general goodness of men and women and thought they should exercise discretion and behave like rational human beings. Some of these norms or *guide-lines* of conduct are mentioned below.

(i) "None is a stranger, no one is an enemy"[16]

Guru Nanak gave his advice to any one who wanted guidance. Sometimes, his own behaviour illustrated this way of thinking. He did not mind if a wicked man came to him for help. Some times he himself, would volunteer to guide him. On his way to Kamrup (Assam), the Guru came across a group of sorceresses had who kidnapped Mardana and kept him as a captive. The Guru approached the leader of the group named Nurshah. She tried her black magic on Guru Nanak and it failed. Then it dawned upon her that the visitor could only be a holy man. She begged his forgiveness for detaining Mardana. The Guru told her to give up her magic and be of service to all the people in her neighourhood. He said to her: "Be a queen of mercy and not of magic; fulfil your divine mission by sowing in the hearts of all boys and girls, the seeds of virtue and then teach them by your own example that courage and truth are rooted in every being." There are many other stories which illustrate the above saying.

(ii) We reap as we sow

In terms of human action, the above dictum is known as the law of *Karma*. What we are today is the outcome of past actions; our present actions will determine our future. Guru Nanak asked his followers to be vigilant about their words and deeds, because they all produce results;

46

their futures depend on what they do in the present. All their actions are recorded by God's agents, and there is no escape from their consequences. Initially they did have a choice of action: of sowing whatever seed they liked, but once done, they would not be able to change the results of that action. For this, the world is referred to as *Karam-Bhoomi*—the realm of action. Whatever we do, we should first think of its probable consequences. Hence a need for good and noble action. Guru Nanak says:

"Men do not become saints or sinners merely by calling themselves so;
They carry the record of their own acts within themselves."
"Those who practise Truth and perform service, will obtain their reward;
When their hair grows white, they will still shine without using any cosmetics."

It may be noted that all actions of frequent repetition leave their impression on one's character. A man doing evil deeds continuously will become of bad character. His evil actions will deprive him of peace of mind, for he will carry a burden of fear and guilt-complex, even if he escapes punishment in a court of law. However, according to Sikh credo, any punishment for bad words or deeds may be mitigated through prayer and the grace of God.

(iii) The proud must fall

Ego or self-conceit is the root of pride. Some worthless people have an extra-ordinary sense of self importance; they ill-treat and insult others. Such conduct, not only alienates them from their own fellow-men, but also merits divine disapproval. Egoistic acts are chains round the neck of a conceited person. Sooner or later, such a person is always found out; then his company is shunned and complained about. Guru Nanak preached humility, particularly to the rich, the mighty and the violent. He told Rulers to remember that their reign is only temporary, that they should not brag of their power or wealth, for God could turn a king into a pauper instantly. When Babar came to visit Guru Nanak and Mardana in prison at Eminabad, the Guru questioned the invader about his atrocities. Why were the innocent villagers rounded up and compelled to grind wheat on hand-powered grinding stones? At this time Mardana was actually grinding corn, his right hand turning the handle of the grinding mill and his left hand dropping grain into mill-hole. Flies were constantly settling on Mardana's face, with the result that he had frequently to free his right hand from the handle, to wave the flies off. The Guru told Babar[17] that as a king he should order the flies to keep away from Mardana's face. Babar was non-plussed. How could he order the flies to keep away form Mardana? The Guru told him, "If you cannot control flies, how can you rule over men". Babar's pride vanished as he thought over the Guru's words. The Guru reminded him of the former Lodi ruler and his present plight. Babar then set all his prisoners free and sought the Guru's pardon for his high-handedness and cruelty.

Another story tells how Guru Nanak cured a land-lord of his pride. As mentioned earlier, the Guru wanted to buy some land to establish a new village for his followers. The land that he selected belonged to Karoria— a proud and arrogant *Zamindar* (land-lord), who decided in his own mind that he would not sell the land to the Guru, for he might lose popularity and status, as a big land-lord. When he went to visit the Guru about this transaction, he met with an accident on the way. Karoiria saw this as a punishment from God for his intended refusal to sell the land to the Guru; so he changed his mind and gave the land to the Guru. There the city of Kartarpur was built. Readers may find many other stories from Guru Nanak's life.[18]

(iv) "Truth is higher than every thing, but higher still is truthful living." (AG, 62)

Knowledge of "The Truth" is not enough on its own. We talk big, but our actions are small and selfish. Guru Nanak declared:

"We are good in talk, but evil in deed." (AG, 85)

He wanted his followers to be Truthful in thought, word and deed. He knew the difficulties that lay in the way of The Truth and salvation; he said:

"Truth is the remedy for all ills. . . .
Nanak seeks the blessing of the Truthful." (AG, 467)

Examples of truthful living are set by saints and holy men. From their lives, the disciple can draw inspiration. Without a virtuous life, no one can reach their spiritual goal. The highest of all virtues is "devotion to God and a love for His creation."

It is essential that in pursuing of a life of truth, the means employed should be equally good. Many people have the right goal, but they try to reach it by the wrong means. According to Guru Nanak, the right means alone, make the attainment of a goal worth-while. That is why he laid so much emphasis on inner purity and refinement of character; these can bring joy and bliss to the heart.

(v) Earn your living

All of us try to earn our living, one way or the other. Guru Nanak, emphasised "honest labour" or the use of fair and right means for earning one's living. Some people live on crime, some on the exploitation of others, and others by begging and parasitism. Some who devoted themselves to so-called holy or spiritual pursuits, like ascetics, mendicants, sanyasis, and yogis were criticised by the Guru for neglecting this duty of earning their own living.

Guru Nanak set his example by working as a store-keeper and later as a farmer. Whatever he earned was partly spent on his family and partly, on supplying the needs of the poor and helpless. He established a colony of workers at Kartarpur where work and worship were combined to promote simple living and high thinking. Apart from working, the Guru exhorted his disciples to set aside some part of the earnings for charitable and welfare project, to show a concern for the community.

(vi) He who conquers his mind, may conquer the world. (AG, 6)

The mind controls the motivation and functioning of the body. The mind's powers are manifold-comprehension, analysis, synthesis, memory etc. The mind is the originator of good and bad actions. Guru Nanak says:

"What the mind says, the will performs.
The mind is our director of good and evil."

Generally, the mind is dominated by selfish aims. The Guru says:

"Duality and evil thoughts dominate the mind;
It is only through the Guru's instruction, and
By meditating on the Guru's Word, that these are overcome."

49

If the mind becomes the slave of passion and wealth, it will end up condoning evil action. If the mind is disciplined, it can remain in a state of equilibrium and peace. Controlling the mind is a difficult task. With great effort, the mind can be brought in contact with the Guru's Word for its illumination. The Guru's Word gives right direction and guidance to the mind and so enables it to gain stability and exaltation. In this way only can the mind become free of illusion and desire.

The conquest of the mind also eliminates the ego. Then one can accept 'God's Will' as being the guiding force in life. Like a child, a devotee surrenders himself to his heavenly Father and is prepared to follow him, in every way. He has a feeling that he is in the right hands and cannot go wrong. 'The conquest of the world' does not mean the domination or exploitation of other people, it indicates a successful and progressive life. Self-realisation is possible only through self-discipline and control over one's own mind.

(vii) True prayer is devotion to God

There are different ways of coming to salvation (Moksha), as for example, the Way of Action (Karma Marg), the Way of Knowledge (Gian Marg), the Way of Mind-control and Self-search (Raja-Yoga Marg) and the Way of Devotion (Bhakti Marg). Guru Nanak recommended the last, but with a difference. While the Hindu Bhagats practised the worship of idols, as symbols of god, Guru Nanak emphasised the worship of a Formless God *(Nirgun Bhakti)*. This is also called *Sahj Marg* or *Nam Marg*. In the Sikh credo, the recognition of *Nam* takes the form of *Kirtan* (hymn-singing) and *Simaran* (meditation).

Many people question the need for worship and prayer. The purpose of prayer is to offer thanks to God for all His Blessings. It is also a way to ask for His blessing and for obtaining inner peace. *Simaran* is the practice of realising God's presence, by keeping HIm ever in mind, with love and devotion, by remembering and reciting His excellences. It must not be lip-repetition only or a display of piety by rosary or other symbol. The Guru says:

> "Everybody says 'Ram, Ram!,' but by only saying 'Ram,' one doest not become holy,
> Only when the Holy Name is imbued in the mind, can one come to real bliss."

To remember God's qualities is the purpose of meditation. By frequent or constant reflection on HIs qualities, man may acquire these qualities in himself. As one thinks, so one becomes. The Guru says: "Man ultimately becomes like the one he is devoted to"—*Jaisa seway taisa hoi*. Guru Nanak clarifies meditation as under:

"First the Guru teaches the disciple to repeat God's Name;
This practice eliminates his ego.
Then he practises meditation on the Divine attributes and intones God's Name;
This intonation with love, brings about an association with the super-self;
In this state, a Gurmukh needs no yogic exercise for inspiration;
Only vivid perception of God's proximity can procure this fulfilment;
Nanak says, that this is the way for a Gurmukh to become omniscient!" (AG, 946)

(viii) God is everywhere

To Guru Nanak, God was no concept or a hypothesis, but reality. He realised the presence of God in every thing and in every place. He says:

"Wherever I look, Thou art there;
Thy worth cannot be estimated or described;
Those who can describe Thee are already absorbed in Thee;
No one knows the extent of Thy Being!"

Guru Nanak explained that there is a divine spark or light, in man; if man can discover it, he will do nothing which may be displeasing or unacceptable to God. He says:

"In all things is His Light, it is from His light, that all things find light.
He is always present and watchful; nowhere is He absent."

God pervades all places and yet is Transcendental. God when "Absolute", is called *Nirgun;* when we think only of His qualities, He is *Sargun* (Attribute-ful). God is both in and above the universe. We can only know of Him, as much as He allows us to know.

51

Saintly persons realise the existence of God through His creation. Some one must be responsible for this creation. He is the Creator and His presence is embedded within His own manifestations. The Guru says that He cannot be seen by 'physical eyes.' The eyes which can find His presence, are only those of devotion and enlightenment. People worship God in temples, caves and forests, but His Abode is also within man's body itself. God is in every human being; it is one's ego which forms a curtain between God and man. As soon as the wall of the Ego is demolished, God can be seen face to face. Guru Nanak says:

"He fills all spaces, O Nanak, I carry Him in my heart;
His Light fills all the worlds.
In every being the Endless One and the True One is present;
You can join Him by subduing your own self."

If man were to realise that God is present everywhere and is watching him, he would not do any evil. His faithful devotees hold their communion with Him in the inmost recesses of their hearts.

(ix) Respect for woman

One of Guru Nanak's main teachings was that men and women are equal before one another and before God. Society respects man; it must give equal respect to woman. Guru Nanak rejected the traditional domination of males and pleaded for female justice. The latter look after the family, specially children; they are the pivot of the family and their education must have the same priority as that of men. For this reason, the Guru opened the doors of his *Dharmasal* and the *Path-shala* to women. He complained of Hindu cruelties to widows; why compel her into concremation (Sati) when her husband died? Why not test her courage to live without her husband?

Another way in which Guru Nanak raised the status of woman was the idealising married life. The Guru idealised the love of a wife for her husband and regarded it as the model for a devotee's love for God. He wrote of the chaste wife's love and obedience to her husband in terms of divine love as under:

"Do whatever your Lord bids you;
Apply any perfumes, surrender yourself, body and soul, to him.

art is there?
Thus speak the happy wives, O Sister, by such means the Lord's love is won!"
"We are the Lord's brides,
We bedeck ourselves for His pleasure.
But if we are overtly proud of our beauty,
Our bridal robes will be of no avail." (AG, 62)

Guru Nanak's message was directed to all women.[19] His teachings of virtue and truth were as well received by women, as by men. Congregations in those days, as today, were mixed. Women attended the *Dharamsal* and joined in hymn-singing. Guru Nanak addressed them as sisters. Here are a couple of quotations:

"Hear, O far-sighted woman! words of deep and sublime importance:
Examine the commodity first, and then trade in it." (AG, 1410)
"Come, O sisters, let us embrace as bosom-friends!
Let us recall our stories of the Omnipotent Bridegroom!" (AG, 17)

In short, Guru Nanak affirmed the dignity and worth of woman and treated her as the equal of man in every way.

2. Guru Angad

Guru Angad became the Second Guru of the Sikhs in 1539 at the age of 35. It is valuable to consider his early life and study his background. Born in a trader's family in 1504, Lehna—who was only called Angad when he became Guru—was a man of simple habits and pious character. He went every year to the Durga Temple at Jwalamukhi. One early morning while he was resting in his bed at Khadur, he heard a hymn sung by his neighbour and was so moved by it that he wanted to meet the writer of the hymn. His neighbour told him that the composer was a saint-poet who lived in Kartarpur. So Lehna want to Kartarpur, met Guru Nanak and was charmed by his personality. He decided to settle permanently in Kartarpur. The Guru however told him to go back to his village, inform his parents and relatives and only then settle at Kartarpur. Lehna followed the Guru's advice and some time later moved with his family, to Kartarpur.

53

Here he learnt the Sikh way of life from Guru Nanak. He memorised *Gurbani* and took part in hymn-singing. He served the congregation with great humility and sincerity. During the day, he worked on Guru's farm and in the evening served in the Free Kitchen. Off and on, he visited his old village to supervise the congregation he had previously established there.

Eventually Guru Nanak felt that he was getting old, so he decided to appoint a successor to carry on his mission. The Guru tested all his devotees and his own sons. His choice ultimately fell on Lehna, as the worthiest of all. So he invested him with the responsibility of Gurudom in 1539. Guru Nanak, before his passing away, advised Guru Angad to move his residence from Kartarpur to Khadur. He gave his personal property to his descendents, but gave the volume of his hymns to Guru Angad. Guru Angad thus moved to Khadur, where the whole congregation welcomed him on his arrival.

Guru Angad felt the loss of his mentor—Guru Nanak very much. This sense of separation he expressed in song. Here are a few of his verses:

"Surrender yourself totally to The One you are devoted to;
To live without Him in this world, is futile and contemptible."
(AG, 82).
"Every one has some one very close; I have no one but you (Guru Nanak);
Why should I not die in lamentation, if I neglect to remember you?" (AG, 82)

Guru Angad realised that the mission of Guru Nanak had to be strengthened and let into new channels. He knew that people were illiterate, and that the first and fore-most task for him was to make them literate. The Brahmins—the custodians of scholarship and learned in the Vedas—regarded it as below their dignity to teach Sanskrit—the sacred language—to ordinary people. While the Guru felt that the existing Punjabi script ought to be modified and made easier for people to learn quickly, so he simplified the script and called it *Gurmukhi*.[20] He also wrote Primers and had small wooden boards made, for teaching the Alphabet. There was no building with class word. So the *Dharamsal*—the place of worship—was used as a class-rooms *(Path-shala)*. The enthusiasm for learning was great; children and adults came in large numbers to learn the the phonetical alphabet Gurmukhi from the Guru. Soon, the people began to read and write the Guru's hymns. Small hymn-books were hand-written by devotees as a labour of love and then presented to the Guru who in turn passed them on. In this way a literacy campaign was started by the Guru at Khadur.

Education and sport go together. The brain and the brawn, should be developed together. The Guru asked for play-grounds; the village-common and other open spaces became wrestling-arenas and play-areas. Soon, inter-group competitions and tournaments were organised. Sports, physical culture, learning Gurumukhi and hymn-singing became important functions of the Sikh Temple at Khadur.

The Guru's commitment to social welfare and the educational uplift of all people brought him in conflict with vested interests. The high castes and the ascetics protested against the Guru's nation-building activities. One ascetic—Tappa—was very hostile and revengeful. When the village crops were threatened by bad weathers, the farmers feared a drought. Tappa announced that the Guru's presence in Khadur was the cause of the drought. If the Guru left the village, then his Tappa, would read some *mantras* and appeal to the rain-god. He felt certain that it would then rain and so the village would have enough grain for the people. The villagers, in their desperation, asked Guru Angad to leave the village and so save them from starvation. The Guru agreed to this and moved in to a hut in the country-side. Tappa did his best to invoke the god of rain, but to no purpose. After waiting for a few days, the villagers got tired of Tappa's tricks; they realised that their sending the Guru out of the village was a mistake. So they went to him and brought him back to Khadur and then requested him to save them from the effects of the drought. Guru Angad told them to pray to God for rain, which they did, in sincerity. Shortly after, the rain fell and the standing crops were saved. The villagers apologised to the Guru for their mistake and served him even more zealously than before.

At this same period, Hamayun, the Moghul emperor of India was defeated by Sher Shah Suri and had to flee from Panipat. While going through the Punjab with his retainers, he happened to pass near village of Khadur. One of his friends suggested to him that in his hour of distress, he should seek the blessing of the Sikh Guru Angad, who lived close by. Hamuyun welcomed the idea and came to visit Guru . When he arrived the Guru was teaching Gurmukhi to the children. So the Guru's attendant told him to wait for a few minutes until the Guru had finished his teaching work. Hamayun, though defeated, was very arrogant and would not wait for the Guru to finish his lesson. He thought that he would teach the Guru a lesson by his manliness. In his anger, he drew his sword from its

55

scabbard and entered the Guru's room. The Guru told him to calm down; a little later, the Guru said to him: "How come, you want to use your sword against an innocent person like me. Did you not have opportunity enough to show your mettle against Sher Shah on the battle field?" Hamuyun felt ashamed of his indiscretion and asked the Guru's pardon.

All the Gurus had the idea of establishing a village or colony to serve as a centre for the propagation of Sikhism. Guru Angad bought a large area of land from Gond Marwaha on which he wanted to establish his new village. Fortunately at this time, he had a very faithful disciple—named Amardas—who at that time was in his sixties but very active and fond of facing challenges. Guru Angad asked Amardas[21] to move from his own village of Basarkay—and undertake the development of the new site, which was to be called Goindwal. Amardas took up tis work in all earnestness and persuaded many of his friends and relatives to move with him, to the new village. Even so every morning he walked from Goindwal to Khadur to serve Guru Angad. At dawn, he would go to the bank of the river Beas at Goindwal to fill a pitcher of water for the Guru's bath, then he would walk with it to Kahdur. He would then join in the prayers and serve the congregation. Then off to the jungle to cut trees and bring fuel for the Free Kitchen. He would also help in cooking food and scrubbing the floor after meals. In spite of his age, he did all these difficult jobs with great devotion. The service of people, was dear to his heart. At night, he would return to Goindwal to rest. He followed this schedule for many years. Guru Angad was pleased with his service and gave him an annual turban as a token of his appreciation. Amardas was so much devoted to his Guru that he would not throw away his old turban—a gift from the Guru—when he got his new one. He would wash it and tie his new turban over the old washed one.

One wintry night, Amardas was carrying water for the Guru's bath from Goindwal to Khadur. It began to rain and the road became very slippery. As he passed near a weaver's hut, his foot slipped and he fell down; some how he saved the water pitcher from spilling over. The weaver's wife, awakened by the sound, used disrespectful words against Amardas. When he reached Guru Angad's home, the latter blessed him, calling Amardas 'shelter of the shelterless and helper of the helpless.' Guru Angad decided to pass on the succession to Amardas in 1552. Before passing away, he delivered his collection of hymns to Guru Amardas, thus preserving the authenticity and integrity of *Gurbani* and maintaining its purity and richness. He never thought that age was any disqualification for Gurudom and nominated Amardas—then 73 year old as his successor—

again, in preference to his own sons.

A few words now about the work and personality of Guru Angad. He carried on Guru Nanak's mission, obeying his instructions to the letter and spirit. He lived to the qualifications he laid down for a true devotee:

"Obedience produces devotion and discipline;
All other things are futile;
O Nanak, those who are imbued with God's Name are honoured;
This truth is known only through the Grace of the Guru." (AG, 954)

Guru Angad was both philosopher and a practical man. He passed on the spiritual succession to Guru Amardas, but left his personal property to his sons. He told Guru Amardas to move to Goindwal, because he did not want any bitterness between the Guru and his own descendents who lived in Khadur. It is true that Bhai Datu, the son of Guru Angad set up a spiritual establishment at Khadur for a while, but the main body of Sikhs followed Guru Amardas to Goindwal. During the thirteen years of his pontificate, Guru Angad did yeoman's service to Sikh faith by spreading literacy and popularising physical culture among his followers. He also made sure that the compositions of Guru Nanak and his own, were made available to all Sikhs.

3. Guru Amardas

Born in 1479 at Basarkay, Amardas was known as a very kind boy. As a student, he learnt thoroughly and quickly. He became a person of simple habits and charitable disposition. In his twenties, he became interested in his Hindu religion and practised both fasting and pilgrimage. Annually he went to Hardwar for his ritual bathing. It was on retuning from one of that visits to Hardwar, there he met a monk who asked him who his religious preceptor was. He replied that he didn't have one, for upto that time, and—he was then 61,—he had not felt the need to have a spiritual guide or Guru. This answer horrified the monk who then ran away from him. This odd incident proved to be the turning point of his life. He started search for a spiritual guide.

One morning at home, he heard a soul-stirring hymn being sung by his nephew's wife; he listened and realised that its words reflected his inner condition. It effects on him was such that he immediately wanted to know about the writer of the hymn. He was told that it was a song of the Sikh Guru, Nanak, who had recently passed away and that her father—Guru Angad—was his successor. On his insistence, the lady then took him to her father at Khadur. It was love at first sight. Amardas became an instantly true devotee of Guru Angad. Eventually, on account of his devotion and service, he was appointed by Guru Angad to be his successor.

Guru Amardas consolidated the works of his predecessors and made a considerable contribution to the recognition of Sikhism as a distinct religion. First of all he set up a missionary organisation throughout northern India. He established 22 manjis or diocese. Devoted Sikhs were appointed as the Guru's agents and missionaries in the respective regions. These were in the nature of life-long, personal posts, and not hereditary positions. The incumbents of the *manjis* could initiate people into Sikhism and collect offerings for the Guru. They wore expected to visit Goindwal twice a year to meet their Guru, where views on matters of common interest and problems of Sikhs in their regions were discussed.

Secondly, Guru Amardas also established the Free Kitchen as part of a Sikh Temple, so that in all Sikh temples, there would be an arrangement for the supply of cooked food to the disciples and visitors who attended prayers. *Thirdly,* he collected all the compositions of the first two Gurus and his own, to compile an anthology, which came to be known as the Mohan Pothi. This was necessary because many fake poems were circulating as hymns of the Gurus. This method then protected the sacred hymns and preserved them from interpolations. *Finally,* Guru Amardas detailed simple ceremonies for the events of birth, marriage and death. His idea in devising these ceremonies was to do away with the performance of the Brahminical ceremonies which were conducted in Sanskrt and were not understood by ordinary people and were very costly. In his Sikh ceremonies, only hymns in praise of God are sung, or *Gurbani* is recited, both as acts of devotion and for seeking Divine Grace.

Guru Amardas also undertook the excavation and construetion of an open well-cum-deep reservoir, with 84 steps leading from the ground-level to the surface of the water below. This was completed in 1559 as a humanitarian project, by voluntary labour. It was to supply water to the growing population of Goindwal. The well was called Baoli Sahib, and daily congregation was/is still held by its site both morning and evening. One day, as Guru Amardas was passing through the streets of Goindwal. which had many old houses, some having been damaged by heavy rain, were in a very poor condition. Suddenly the Guru crossed the street at a

58

run and told his disciples to do the same, as there was a great likelihood of some of structures collapsing while they were passing. His Sikhs were surprised by this sudden hurry and began to feel that the Guru,—being a very old man in his seventies—was afraid of death. The Guru anticipating their question then told them:

> "I am not afraid of death. Human life is a precious gift of God and one must not take unnecessary risks with it. The more one looks after the care and health of the body, the greater is God's Blessing. The Sikhs considered the Guru's point of view and realised that the human body should be preserved and cared for. In opposition to this Sikh view, there are other sects in India which regard the mortification and torture of the body as being virtuous and praise-wothy. Sikhism regards self-injury or putting the body to unnecessary pain or risk as deeds of no spiritual merit."

Guru Amardas was a great social reformer. He ordered all Sikh women to discard the veil. This was contrary to the customs prevalent among the Hindus and Muslims of his time. When the Raja of Haripur came to visit the Guru, his queen as usual, veiled her face. The Guru admonished her for covering her face. He also rejected the idea of female pollution and female infanticide. He forbade the use of wine and intoxicating drinks. He also prohibited Sikh women from following the practice of *Sati* (widow burning). Sati was a horrible practice, even though traditional sanction was behind it. The death of a husband itself was a great blow to the wife; she should be encouraged to accept the Will of God and to lead the remainder of her life, with virtue and patience. The Guru also prohibited his Sikhs from consulting astrologers and palmists, saying that the belief in good or bad omens is due to superstition and ignorance. In these ways, he made Sikhism different from Hinduism. As one writer put it: "He constructed a fence, to protect Sikhism from ancient Hindu practices."

Guru Amardas had a number of staunch devotees. One of them was Prema who owned a farm near Goindwal. He brought a pail of milk everyday for the Free Kitchen. He was slightly lame and used a crutch for walking. One day it rained heavily, but Prema, as usual, wanted to take the milk to the Guru's Kitchen. On the way, people teased him, saying: "Why don't you ask the Guru to rid you of you limp? When the Guru came to know of this taunt, he told Prema to go to a Muslim saint in the neighbouring village and request him to cure him of his lameness. When

Prema went there, he told the saint his story. The latter was astonished by Prema's naivety and told him to go away. As Prema did not go, the saint took up a stick to scare him away. To avoid being beaten up, Prema ran as fast as he could and forgot his crutches at the saint's house. Then he realised that he was no longer lame as he had already run some distance without a crutch. He returned to thank the saint, who then told him that he had not performed any miracle; in fact Prema's leg was normal when he had come to him on his crutch. The Guru had given him (the Saint) credit for working a miracle when in fact he had no such power.

There were also devotees however who failed the Guru's tests and had to learn their lesson the hard way. We have the outstanding example of Gangu, the Lahore trader. He suffered losses in business, his friends left him in the lurch. He was advised to go to Guru Amardas for help in his hour of distress. So Gangu came to Goindwal and started doing voluntary service in the Free Kitchen. One day, he told the Guru about his problems in business and sought his advice. The Guru told him to go to Delhi and start new business there. When he became successful, he must help the poor and needy, and also pray to God regularly. Gangu proceeded to Delhi and started a business. After a few months he not only became wealthy but vain. One day, a poor Brahmin came to Guru Amardas at Goindwal and sought financial assistance for his daughter's marriage. The Guru gave him a letter to Gangu, asking him to help the bearer of the letter. By this time affluence had turned Gangu's head the needy and he had become very arrogant. He had forgotten the instruction of the Guru to help. So when he received the Guru's letter, he became worried lest the Guru might send him more people to help in the coming months. Better for him to turn away this first needy person. He told the Brahmin that he could not offer him any help in cash or kind. The Brahmin then returned to Goindwal and reported Gangu's indifference. The Guru asked his congregation to donate money and added a sum from his own pocket and sent the Brahmin off, satisfied.

A few months later, Gangu's business at Delhi began to fail. He then realised his mistake and came to Goindwal to seek the Guru's pardon. Feeling ashamed of facing the Guru, he started serving in the Free Kitchen. After a few days, the Guru called him and asked him what he wanted. He sought the Guru's forgiveness for his mistake. He assured the Guru that he would follow the Guru's instructions strictly in the future. The Guru blessed him; his business throve once more and he became known as Gangu Shah (Gangu, the king).

Another devote of Guru Amardas was Bhai Paro Jhulka, also called Param Hans. He used to visit Goindwal daily by crossing the river Beas. The Guru was pleased with his devotion and humility and expressed a desire to nominate him as his successor Bhai Paro declined the honour, saying: "I am content with being the Guru's disciple, through him I have received the treasure of the Holy Name." Abdullah, the Nawab of Jalandhar was so impressed by the holy living Paro, that he too became an ardent follower of the Guru.

Guru Amardas's best devotee was Jetha.[22] The Guru took great interest in this young man who made a living by selling boiled gram. Jetha served the Guru with patience and devotion. The Guru was trying to find a suitable match for his daughter Bhani. His choice fell on Jetha, who was overwhelmed by such good news and declared: "A worm like me has been blessed by Guru!" After the marriage had taken place, Jetha accompanied the Guru—now his father-in-law -to Kurukshetra and to Hardwar on a missionary tour.

One, day, a rich Sikh banker offered a pearl necklace to Guru Amardas. The Guru told that he would not wear it, but that he would give it to his best disciple. The banker, not knowing who was the best devotee, therefore requested the Guru to give it to his favoured one with his own hands. The Sikhs who were present, then began to guess the name of the person who would be lucky enough to be given the necklace from the Guru's hands. Many thought that the Guru would give it to one of his sons, but the Guru called, Jetha, and put the necklace round his neck. This indicated to all that Jetha was the Guru's best devotee.

In 1570, Guru Amardas decided to set up a new township to serve as a Sikh centre. He entrusted the task to Jetha, who then purchased land from the Zamindars of Tung and started on the construction of a big tank, knowns as the *Ramdas Sarovar*. Many Sikhs came to provide voluntary labour and a Free Kitchen was set up on the site. Residential buildings and a few shops were also constructed. Jetha travelled to Goindwal from time to time, to consult Guru Amardas about the details of the new development, which came to be known as Ramdaspur. Later, the township was called Amritsar.

Undoubtedly, Jetha had won the Guru's confidence through total obedience and holiness, even so the Guru decided to test all the disciples and his sons to find the worthiest of his Sikhs, to be his successor. His sons did not want to compete; there were only two candidates for the tests—his two sons-in-law, Rama and Jetha. Guru Amardas asked both of them to each build a masonry platform of certain specifications from which he would address the congregation, near the site of *Baoli Sahib*. Both Rama and Jetha built platforms, but the Guru rejected both as unsuitable. Then both started building again, after demolishing the first platforms. For the second time, the new platforms were disapproved. When the platforms were ready for the third time, the Guru rejected them again. At this stage, Rama felt disgusted and quit the test. Jetha then built the platform for the fourth time and again it was rejected. Similarly the fifth and the sixth platforms were found unacceptable. Only when the seventh platform was completed, did the Guru approve of it and also declared Jetha as his successor. At the installation ceremony, Guru Amardas gave a new name to Jetha—'Guru Ramdas.' He also asked him to move his house from Goindwal to Amritsar and to complete the construction of the new township.

Summing the character and achievements of Guru Amardas, he was essentially a man of peace and humility. When the Sikhs complained to him of the harassment caused them by the Muslim residents of Goindwal, he advised them to remain patient. Then the Muslims broke the water-pots of the Sikh women who went to the village well for water. Again the Guru advised restraint and said: "It is not good to take revenge." He also avoided conflict with Datu, the son of his predecessor, who kicked him and insulted him. He declared to his followers: "If one ill treats you, bear it three times, God Himself will fight for you for the fourth time and punish your enemy." He taught forbearance, self-control and compassion to his disciples by personal example. His simplicity is evident from the fact that he kept only one spare set of clothes for himself and gave away all his other clothing in charity to the needy. His enemies, in spite of their frequent mischief and nuisance, could not disturb his peace of mind.

During his 22 years of Pontificate, he gave new direction to the Sikh faith by making it an established original religion. He set up a missionary organisation and prepared a hymn-book. He improved the status of women by removing more of their disabilities. Above all, his foresight enabled him to initiate as a permanent project the provision of a centre of worship for Sikhism and a place of trade and commerce, later called Amritsar. His selfless service to the Sangat, both before and after he became the Guru, until the age of 95 should serve to inspire all seekers of 'The Truth.'

4. Guru Ramdas

Jetha, who became Guru Ramdas, was born at Lahore in 1534 to the family of a small trader named Haridas. Unfortunately, he lost his parents at the age of seven and was therefore taken away from Lahore by his grand-mother to Basarkay, for her care and rearing. At the age of eight, Jetha began to support himself and his grand-mother by selling gram. Fortunately, at this time, he came to know Bhai Amardas, a devoted disciple of Guru Angad. The old man took him often to Khadur to meet Guru Angad. In his company, Jetha learnt Gurmukhi and a lot about India's religious heritage and the tenets of Sikhism. At the request of Bhai Amardas, who treated him like a grand son, he moved to the new village of Goindwal and started serving in its Free Kitchen. When Bhai Amardas became the Third Guru in 1552, Jetha was only eighteen. Guru Amardas loved him and was very pleased by his service and devotion. When the matter of finding a match of his young daughter came up, he approved Jetha becoming his son-in-law. The marriage was solemnised at Goindwal, and the new couple first lived in the Guru's house.

The period from 1552 to 1574 (22 years) was a period of apprenticeship and training for Jetha at the hands of Guru Amardas. His daily routine consisted of serving the Guru and the congregation in the morning, and working in the Free Kitchen for the remaining period. In addition, he also performed the various other tasks assigned to him by the Guru.

The first test for Jetha came when Guru Amardas deputed him to defend the charges made against the Guru by high caste Hindus at the Moghul Court. The charge related to the Guru's egalitarian practices, like the Free Kitchen, which the Hindus alleged were against the doctrines of Hinduism and the caste-system. Jetha went to Lahore and explained to the Emperor Akbar, who then ruled, the principles of Sikhism and its practice of equality and universal brotherhood. Guru Amardas had not done any thing against Hinduism as such; he had only given practical shape to the idea of equality and fraternity, by serving food free to every person who came to meet him or join the congregation. The Emperor appreciated Jetha's clarifications and dismissed the petition of the Hindu leaders.

The visits of Guru Amardas, to places of pilgrimage like Kurukshetra and others with his followers, was not to placate the Hindus, but to explain the Sikh attitude to the subject of pilgrimage. Guru Ramdas, in one of his hymns (AG, 116) clarified the purpose of Guru Amardas's mission during his visit to Kurukshetra on the occasion of the 'Abhaijit' festival. The true purpose of pilgrimage is not to bathe in a so-called holy river or water, but to meet any saintly persons who visit these places and to remember the nobel deeds of those who founded or worked there. It is the environment of such sites that is conducive to mental peace and which serves as a source of inspiration and spiritual endeavour.

Jetha was a man of charity and compassion. One day, Guru Amardas felt pleased with him and gave him a pearl necklace as a gift. There was a Muslim mendicant (fakir) in the neighbourhood, who was always asking for charity from the Guru, but when the Guru gave him nothing, he began to use disrespectful and offensive language. Next day, Jetha gave him his pearl necklace. Thereafter, he began to sing the praises of the Guru. In the meantime, the Guru came to know of Jetha's gift to the mendicant. The Guru asked Jetha why he had given the necklace to such an unworthy beggar. He replied: "Sir, I have already got the real necklace, that of the 'Holy Name.' So I gave away the pearl necklace to one who needed it." The Guru was pleased with his reply.

Now let us examine the contribution of Guru Ramdas to the establishment Sikhism. *Firstly,* the new township of Ramdaspur, later known as Amritsar, attracted lots of Khatris who wanted to start their business in the new township. The town was built on the main trade-route from Lahore to Delhi, so that it had great importance as a centre of import and export. The message of the Gurus also appealed to the Jats, because they understood the teachings of the Guru in terms of the needs of the people. The excavation of the reservoir also attracted a number of sangats from neighbouring villages, to provide the voluntary labour for this project of public benefit. The dual role of the township—provide employment and spiritual uplift—and a Free Kitchen, attracted many new followers to the Sikh faith.

Secondly, the new missionary organisaton of *massands,*[23] which Guru Ramdas set up, was very helpful in carrying the Guru's message to many new areas, and attracted financial assistance for his various welfare projects and charitable activities. The *massands,* apart from the *manjidars* collected the Sikhs' offerings from their areas and deposited them in the Guru's treasury. The development of Ramdaspur was thus ensured as money began to flow in for the supplies of cereals, vegetables and pulses needed for feeding the large number of labourers and skilled workers, employed in the construction of the new town-ship.

Thirdly, Guru Ramdas's contribution to the Sikh way of life is both great and significant. The Guru laid down the daily routine of his Sikhs and also the prayers they should offer when starting any new venture or business. He also composed the *Lavan*—the Wedding Song—for the Sikh marriage ceremony. These verses tell a couple, how to integrate secular duties with spiritual practices. He also composed *Ghorian*—the songs to be sung as prelude to marriage. Similarly, he wrote some special compositions like *Pahray, Vanjara,* and *Karhalay*. He also set the *Dhunis* (tunes) for three *Vars* (ballads). In addition to the clarifying the basic concepts of Sikhism, he composed songs of adoration for his Guru (Amardas), the significance of the human body in man's spiritual effort, the value of family life and references, to contemporary events. His hymns carry conviction and inspire a disciple, a devotion to and longing for God.

Fourthly, his contribution to poetry and music (Kirtan) is remarkable. His poetry falls into three categories: *Realistic, Disciple* and *Nature* poems. All are set to music in appropriate ragas (musical patterns). They deal with secular and spiritual themes. Guru Ramdas throws light on the problems of the age—the corrupt bureaucracy, the hypocritical clergy, the social stratification, the rituals, poverty and helplessness of the people. He tells us about man's inner condition, his ego, his involvement in maya and worldly pelf and power, the need to develop the character and cultivate virtue, efforts that are necessary for raising one's spiritual stature. As a poet, he calls himself a bard of God's Court—a minstrel commissioned to propagate the Divine Message:

> "I am a minstrel of the Lord, my Master. I have come to His Gate;
> God listened to my cries from inside then called me into His Presence;
> Once inside, He asked me the object of my visit;
> I said: 'O my Merciful Lord! Grant me the gift of meditation on Thy Name for ever!
> God, the Benevolent, asked me remember His Holy Name,
> And clothed me with this robe of honour." (AG, 91)

Guru Ramdas had many devotees. He tested them from time to time to find out if they had rightly understood his teachings and also checked to see if there was any improvement in their character and style of living. Bhai Soma was one of his disciples who used to sell boiled gram near the tank which was being dug at Ramdaspur. One day, the Guru asked him to donate his day's earnings to charity. Soma obeyed the Guru's command and gave all the money he had earned to the Guru for use in charity. Next day, the Guru asked him to do the same again which Soma did faithfully. For six days on the Guru's bidding, he gave his income in charity. On the seventh day, the Guru called Soma and told him that 'this' day, it was his turn to give and Soma's to receive. The Guru blessed him and predicted that he would be a great businessman. After some time, Soma started a new business and quickly became a very rich man. He was called 'Soma Shah' (Soma, the king). Charity yields big dividends.

Hindal was another disciple who was fond of working in the Free Kitchen. He was so busy there, that he found no time to attend morning and evening congregations. He saw to it that the Free Kitchen was open all the time, that food was served to one and all. One day, Guru Ramdas went to the Free Kitchen to see Hindal. At that time, the latter was kneading flour. When he saw the Guru approaching, he got up in reverence and kept his hands at his back because they were covered in dough. As he bowed to the Guru, the Guru looked at his hands and smiled. The Guru blessed him for his service and after a time put him in charge of all missionary work, at Jandiala, his home-town.

Guru Ramdas was a self-made man. From an early age, he had to earn his own living. He learnt the Sikh way of life and virtues, from his association with Guru Amardas. The spiritual link was not based only on close personal relationship—he was the son-in-law of Guru Amardas—but on the love and devotion of a child for his father or of an innocent bride for her husband. The Guru expresses this sentiment thus:

"I am your slave-girl, you are the Infinite Lord of the Universe,
I am under your command. What can I do on my own?
Could any one else save a sinner like me?
The True Guru, has both saved and liberated me:" (AG,167)

Summing up, Guru Ramdas had a charismatic personality. He won hearts, not only of his disciples, but also of his detractors and opponents by his grace, sweetness and generosity. His life is a beacon to any ordinary Sikh who wants to rise to a state of spirituality through self-discipline, humility, and devoted, unselfish service.

5. Guru Arjan

As mentioned earlier, each Guru laid a particular stress on one quality or virtue; for example, Guru Nanak personified universal brotherhood, Guru

Angad obedience and discipline, Guru Amardas selfless service, Guru Ramdas humility and Guru Arjan selfsacrifice. The life of Guru Arjan is outstanding example of humility and a readiness to suffer in support of one's principles and ideals.

Born in 1563, Arjan was a grandson of Guru Amardas. In infancy, he learnt his first lesson form the Third Guru. As a child, he would crawl on his grand father's lap and sit with him. He was blessed by his grand father as a "Ship of the Holy Name". As a boy, he took a keen interest in the development of the town of Ramdaspur which had been founded by his father. His two elder brothers—Prithichand and Mahadev—were jealous of him, because he enjoyed their father's confidence. It has been stated that his visit to Lahore on the instruction of his father was as a form of apprenticeship in his training as a devotee, eventually earning for him, the succession to Gurudom, at the age of eighteen.

The first important work of Guru Arjan was the completion of the tank (Ramdas Sarovar) which had been started by his father. He finished this task in 1588 and renamed it Amritsar (tank of nectar). His next task was to complete the building of the new temple, the foundation-stone of which was laid by a Sufi Saint, Mian Mir, in 1588. It took another two years for him to complete this House of God, the *Harmandar Sahib*. Guru Arjan built another tank called *Santokhsar,* for the supply of water to the township's outskirts.

Guru Arjan did a lot to consolidate Sikhism and put it on a solid footing. He undertook preaching tours to Manjha, Doaba, Gurdaspur and the Shivalik Hills. He set up new congregations *(sangats)* and strengthened the old ones. He improved the missionary organisation and gave *massands* new instructions for looking after the secular and economic interests of all Sikhs in their regions. He taught them to give guidance in all matters of agriculture, trade and industry. He appointed new *massands,* so that the offerings to the Harmandar Sahib and the Free Kitchen, increased. He also set up the new township of Tarn-Taran, Kartarpur and Hargobindpur. He established *Sangats* in Delhi and Kabul.

During his missionary tours over a ten year period, Guru Arjan placed great emphasis on the excavation of wells, tanks and reservoirs, to supply water for drinking and farming. This was done to reinforce the principles of self help and community service. During his visit to Lahore in 1598, the Guru built a deep well (baoli) in the heart of the town This was the period of drought, famine and infectious disease. The Guru served the needy and attended the sick for the eight months period. Daily many corpses were collected and burnt, by him and his disciples. It is said that it was on the insistence of Guru Arjun, that Emperor Akbar, remitted his land revenue from the region on account of the effects of drought.

Many of Guru Arjan's missionary difficulties were due to the hostility of his eldest brother—Prithichand who had been found unfit for the Gurudom and therefore he left no stone unturned, to take revenge on his younger brother. For some time he occupied the Guru's quarters and collected offerings, directly form the congregations which resulted in the contributions to the Free Kitchen dwindling for a while. Bhai Buddha and Bhai Gurdas then exposed the tricks of Prithichand to all the new Sikh groups coming in from other towns and themselves collected the offerings for the Free Kitchen.

In order to avoid conflict with Prithichand, Guru Arjun moved form Amritsar to another village six miles away, called Wadali, where, a son was born to him in 1595. Prithichand become desperate for he knew that he had lost his chance of ever getting the Gurudom in future. Three times, he tried to destroy the child, called Hargobind. First he sent a wet-nurse with poisoned nipples to breast-feed the child, but the child would not suckle. Then he sent a snake-charmer to the Guru' house to place a poisonous snake before the crawling child, but this trick also failed. Finally, he sent poisoned milk for the child through a trusted servant, but the infant did not touch the milk. Prithichand wanted to punish the Guru and his family, at any cost. He sought the aid of bureaucrats and political leaders to crush the Guru. He persuaded Sulhi Khan, a local commander of troops to attack the Guru, but the former died on the way to Amritsar. He incited Birbal, a high official of the Moghul Court, to take punitive action against the Guru. However, Birbal was very busy in State matters, and died before he could do any thing against Guru Arjan.

The most important work of Guru Arjan, was the compilation of the Sikh Scripture—the *Adi Granth*. He collected the *Mohan-Pothis* and all the hymns of his father and of his own, he obtained those compositions of Indian saints and minstrels which agreed and supported Sikh philosophy. He rejected the hymns of those contemporary mystics which were not in accord with Sikh tenets. Then taking Bhai Gurdas with him, he found a quiet spot near *Ramsar* and dictated to him, the compositions in a proper order and set according to Indian classical *ragas* and folk tunes. It took more than a year to prepare the Master Copy of the Adi Granth. The total number of hymns included were Guru Nanak: 974 hymns; Guru Angad 62 verses (Salokas); Guru Amardas: 907 hymns; Guru Ramdas: 635 hymns; Guru Arjan: 2218 hymns; Bhagat-vani: 938 hymns; Bhattvani and miscellaneous verses find a place at the end. The total number of *Vars* (ballads) is 22. The hymns are in 30 ragas. However one more raga (Jaijawanti) was added by Guru Tegh Bahadur later. The number of pages in the edition published by the Shromani Gurdwara Parbhandhak Committee, Amritsar is 1430.

The only original Copy of the Adi Granth is preserved at Kartapur and is displayed to the public on important festivals. Another copy was made by Bhai Banno. This was an unauthorised copy and contained two additional hymns. This copy can be seen in the village called Mangat, now in Pakistan. The contents of the Scripture are prayers in praise of God and hymns pointing the need for cultivating morality and virtue. A few of the hymns throw light on the political and social conditions of the times. Most of the poems are in Punjabi, and very few in Sanskrit and Persian. The prologue contains the Basic Creed (Mool-mantra), and the epilogue is a thanks-giving for the completion of the volume by Divine Grace. At the end, Guru Arjan declares:

"O Lord: I cannot measure Your grace; You alone have made me worthy of it;
I am full of imperfection; I have no merit; You have been kind to me.
You have shown Your Grace, to me; I have met the True Guru, the Lord!
Nanak says, 'I survive only on the Holy Name. It keeps my body and mind in Bliss." (AG, 1429)

Guru Arjan installed the Scripture in the *Harmandar Sahib* in 1604. He bowed to it, because it represents the Word of God. The Guru while living, showed the utmost respect to the Adi Granth. He appointed Bhai Gurdas as first ever *Granthi* (Reader of the Granth Sahib). In the morning it was ceremoniously opened and covered with a *Rumala* (an ornate covering of stitched cloth). Bhai Gurdas waved a *chauri* (a tuft of yak-hair extended form a handle) over it, as a mark of veneration. Musicians sang the hymns in its presence for most of the time. At night it was laid to rest. Those visiting the Harmandar Sahib were expected to cover their heads and take off their shoes. Thus traditions set up by the Guru are still followed today.

If readers are able to have a look at the contents of the Adi Granth, they will notice that it contains more hymns of Guru Arjan than any other Guru plus the hymns of the Indian saints which it incorporates. The Guru's most popular composition is The *Sukhmani Sahib*—the Psalm of peace.

The main theme is of salvation through meditation, through service and the winning of God's grace. God assists his devotees in every way. The Guru says:

"O man! Why worry, when God Himself is concerned about you;
He who has created living things inside stones provides them with food;
He who abides in the company of holy men is liberated;
With God's grace, he may attain the highest state." (AG, 495)

The hymns of Guru Arjan are full of sensitivity, refinement and sublimity. They bring joy and inspiration to those who read them understandingly. They lay stress on holy living in a family-environment. They tell us about the Sikh way of life. Guru Arjan's poetry reaches a high water-mark of religious fervour and piety.

Guru Arjan was not only a great singer but also, an eminent musicologist. He used to sing hymns while playing a new musical instrument called *sarinda* with a bow of his own design. He sang hymns in seventeen rhythms *(Ghars)*. He started an amateur class of musicians, because the professional musicians of his court called *rababis* had become arrogant and greedy. He personally trained his new musicians who were called *ragis*. He taught them how to sing hymns in the appropriate tune and rhythm. He also started a tradition of music-sessions *(chowkis)* in the *Harmandar Sahib,* after the installation of the *Adi Granth.* According to *Kirtan* tradition, in the Harmandar only the appropriate hymns in their right ragas may be sung, according to the time, of day or night.

Guru Arjan's devotees undertook any type of difficult job. Bhai Manjh collected fuel from the jungle and carried it to the Free Kitchen every day. Bhai Bahlo collected garbage for the brick-kilns needed for quality bricks for the construction of the buildings in Amritsar. One day, a Sikh named Gurmukh came to the Guru with a request that he show him, an ideal Sikh whom he could emulate. The Guru sent Gurmukh to a saintly disciple called Bhai Bikhari. When Gurmukh went to Bikhari's house, he saw that preparations were being made for the wedding of Bikhari's son. After a while, he met Bikhari and found him stitching a white sheet of cloth and singing:"O Lord: Thy Will is pleasing to me." Gurmukh felt surprised that Bikhari was not taking any part in the preparations for his son's wedding. Next day, the wedding took place with the customary fun and joy. After the wedding, the bride-groom came home and died suddenly on account of a heart-attack. Bikhari was not the least disturbed. He covered his son's body with the white sheet which he had stitched the previous day. Gurmukh was amazed at the calmness and spirit of resignation shown by Bikhari; he neither wept nor lamented; instead he sang hymns of the Gurus. When questioned by Gurmukh as to why he did not prevent the marriage of his son, when he knew of his death in advance, Bikhari replied :"How can I interfere in God's will: It is the duty of a Sikh to be resigned to the Divine Will."

Another devotee of Guru Arjan was Bhai Langah. He carried a pot of curd and butter from his village to the Guru's house in Tarn-Taran every day. The Guru wanted to test Langah. One early morning, Guru Arjan left for Amritsar. When Langah arrived at the Guru's house at Tarn-Taran, he was told that the Guru had gone to Amritsar. So Langah proceeded to Amritsar. When he reached there, the Guru had again left for Tarn-Taran. So Langah hurried to Tarn-Taran, because it was then very late for the Guru's break-fast. It was noon when he reached Tarn-Taran. When he entered the Guru's house, he apologised for his delay. He said to the Guru: "Sir, I am sorry for being late. I entreat you to forgive me for bringing this pot so late to you, for your break-fast," The Guru replied: "Bhai Langah. I was putting you to the test; I am so glad that you have come out successful. I bless you for your patience and devoted service."

Guru Arjan successfully carried on with his preaching mission during the regime of emperor Akbar. As the number of Sikhs increased, both Hindus and Muslims visited Amritsar to hear the Guru's sermons. By this time, Sikhism had attained the status of an original and independent religion. This point was affirmed by Guru Arjan in one of his hymns:

"I do not keep Hindu fast or that observed by the Muslims in Ramazan;
I serve only that Lord who is my refuge.
I believe in the same Gosaeen who is also known as Allah.
I have broken away form Hindus and Muslims." (AG, 1136)

Earlier, Guru Amardas had made it clear that the Sikh Faith was not a branch or sect of any existing religions. The *Revelation* of the Guru was original and meant for the whole world, for all people.

Emperor Akbar was succeeded by the bigoted Jehangir, who was a man of contradictions and caprices. He prohibited the sale and use of wine, but was himself a drunkard. The Fundamentalist-Muslims of his court, insisted on the rigourous application of Muslim law against non-believers. So Jehangir took on the role of "Defender of Islam." He reversed the tolerant policy of his father and became hostile to Guru Arjan, the more so because the latter was a very popular preacher of Sikhism. In his autobiography Jehangir wrote about Guru Arjan as under:

"A Hindu named Arjan lived at Goindwal on the bank of the river Beas, in the garb of a saint and in ostentation. As a result, many of the simple-minded Hindus as well as ignorant and foolish Muslims were persuaded to adopt his way of living as he raised aloft a standard of sainthood and holiness. He was called *Guru*. This business had flourished for three or four generations. For a long time, it had been in my mind to put a stop to this vain affair and to bring him into the fold of Islam."

Thus Jehangir had decided in his mind that since a number of Hindus and Muslims had accepted Guru Arjan as their religious guide, the mission of Guru Arjan should be ended and he should be converted to Islam.

Jehangir waited for his chance to take action against Guru Arjan. The opportunity came when it was alleged that the Adi Granth compiled by Guru Arjan, contained some derogatory words against the prophets. Jehangir without calling for any evidence immediately imposed a two lakh rupee fine on the Guru. The Guru made the following defence:

"Whatever money I have is for the poor, the friendless and the stranger. If you ask for money, you may take what I have, but if you ask for it as fine, I shall not give you even a *Kauri* (shell), for a fine is imposed on wicked and wordly persons, and not on priests and preachers. And as to what you have said about my erasing any of hymns in the Granth Sahib, I cannot erase or alter anything. The hymns which find a place in it are not disrespectful to any Hindu deity or Muslim prophet. My main object is to spread the truth and destroy falsehood. If, in the pursuance of this object, this perishable body must depart this life, I shall account it a great good fortune."

Jehangir then found another excuse, with the news that his rebel—son Khusro, had sought the blessing of Guru Arjan for his claim to kingship. This was not true. Khusro had gone to Guru Arjan, but the Guru had not supported his claim to the throne, because that was political. The Guru had aided him, as he would have done to any person in distress. But the prejudiced Jehangir believed his own version of the news without asking for any proof; it suited him to get the Guru out of the way. In his anger against the Guru, he decided to order the execution of the Guru. He wrote in his auto-biography: "I knew of this Guru's heresies and ordered that he should be brought into my presence,. His house and children are to be made over to Murtaza Khan and his property to be confiscated, and he will be put to death by torture."

Guru Arjan was convinced that he would have to sacrifice himself for his faith. History contains many examples of the sufferings of religious leaders who resisted injustice, tyranny and fanaticism at the hands of their rulers or other powers of their time. Ultimately Truth triumphs over falsehood and tyranny, but in the struggle against evil, the good have to bear the brunt and sacrifice their lives. Victory belongs to those who give up their lives, but not their principles and ideals.

The basic principle of Sikhism—sacrifice—is mentioned by Guru Arjan in one of his hymns as under:

"First be prepared for death; forget the desire to living;
Become like the dust under the feet of men, then come to me:"
(AG, 1102)

Guru Arjan was summoned to Lahore on the order of the Emperor. Before leaving Amritsar, he nominated his son—Hargobind—as his successor. When the Guru reached Lahore, he was put in charge of Chandulal, one of the important officials of the
Moghul Court. Chandulal inflicted great torture on the Guru to break his spirit. For five days he was tormented with burning sand, boiling water and seated frequently on a hot iron plate. The Guru 's body was partly burnt. He offered prayers and thanked God for being able to stand up to His test. Then he was thrown into the Ravi river.

Guru Arjan was the first Sikh martyr. Note that martyrs never die. They proclaim their Truth in the sacrifice of their lives. They affirm eternal life. They are the conquerers of death and hence immortal. Martyrs live in the memory and songs of the people and continue to inspire succeeding generations with a willingness for sacrifice, in a good cause.

6. Guru Hargobind

Guru Hargobind was born on 16th June, 1595. He received his education and training at Amritsar. His father died as a martyr in 1606 at Lahore, and he became the Guru at the tender age of eleven. His father's last message to him was that he should prepare himself for the struggle against tyranny and injustice, keeping himself armed and equipped for battle. This meant the entry of militancy into Sikh polity, with emphasis on self-reliance and self-defence.

One should try to understand the concepts of *Piri* (holiness) and *Miri* (royalty). These concepts are connected with the life of Guru Hargobind. The word *Piri* is derived form the Persian word *Pir* which means a holy person or a religious leader. The word *Mir* is derived form *Amir* (which means Ruler) hence, secular power or sovereignty. So the combination of these two words was that a Sikh Guru would now possess both secular and spiritual power, which he could then exercise to establish an egalitarian and just society. At the time of his formal installation as the Sixth Guru of the Sikhs, he donned two swords one of *Piri* (spiritual power) and the other of *Miri* (temporal power). He was called *Sacha Padshah* (True King). He adopted regal paraphernalia—a throne, a royal court, and golden umbrella and a retinue of trained soldiers. Bhai Gurdas wrote about Guru Hargobind that he was "an heroic scourge of evil-doers and at the same time, a great philanthropist." Thus the foundation of a saint-soldier Sikh was made by the Sixth Guru.

Guru Hargobind's main mission was to make the Sikh community strong and brave. It had to develop the strength to face critical times. His change in strategy was not understood by some Sikhs; they said that it departed form the earlier previous one which had stressed saintliness and pacificism. Bhai Gurdas explained the need for modification in the following lines:

"Just as a fence is necessary to keep stray cattle away from the farm;
Just as the thorny Kikar tree guards the orchard,
Just as the snake protects the sandal-tree,
Just as a dog guards the house against strangers,
In the same way, a man of God must learn to protect himself with the sword."

Guru Hargobind combined prayers with parades. Free Kitchen and sports, horse-racing and hunting, shooting and shikar were alternated with hymn-singing sessions. The musicians sang heroic ballads called *Vars* in congregations to inspire the Sikhs by the heroic deeds of old warriors.

Wrestling matches and athletics were organised to keep recruits fit and healthy. Mock-battles were often arranged among different groups to test their mettle. The Guru asked his Sikhs to bring horses and swords. He engaged fifty training officers to train over 500 Sikhs, Hindus and Muslims. This was the beginning of the formation of the Guru's own army. They had contingents of 100 soldiers, each under a leader.

Sikh character was being moulded to purposes of self-defence and opposition to tyranny and injustice. The Guru lived in a kingly style. In 1609 he started the building of the *Akal-Takhat* (the Throne of the Timeless) opposite the Harmandar Sahib. Here he dealt with secular and political matters. He also built a fort and named it *Lohgarh* (Iron fort). The Guru was preparing the community for the difficult times ahead.

Emperor Jehangir liked Guru Hargobind, and many times they went hunting together. On one occasion, the Guru saved Jehangir form the claws of a tiger. The friendship between the two lasted for some time. Jehangir once went to Amritsar to meet the Guru in 1620. Jehangir however, was a man of moods. Once he sent the Guru to the Gwalior Prison. Later, he realised his mistake and ordered his release. The Guru insisted that all the other prisoners of royal blood who were languishing in jail should also be released with him. Jehangir accepted this condition and 52 princes were set at liberty. The Guru became popular as a liberator of the bonded.

The martial exercises and hunting did not interfere with the missionary work of Guru Hargobind. Baba Srichand—son of Guru Nanak—met the Guru during one of his tours at the village of Ramdas. Srichand formally abolished the sect of *Udasis* of which he was the Founder and requested the Guru to take charge of four of his preachers— Almust, Gonda, Phool Shah and Balu Hasna. The Guru agreed to this arrangement and sent these missionaries to different regions for the propagation of Sikhism. The Guru went on preaching tours to Srinagar (Kashmir), Gurdaspur, Kartarpur, Goindwal and neighbouring villages. He inspired people with courage and fearlessness. He exhorted them to remain in a state of preparedness, for the rulers did not want Sikhism to flourish. The death of Jehangir in 1627 was a signal for hostile forces to challenge the Guru.

The first attack by the forces of the Governor of Lahore under the command of Mukhlis Khan was made in June 1628. Amritsar was plundered. The Guru's soldiers fought back bravely and later routed the Moghul forces which fled back to Lahore. This conflict is known as the battle of Lohgarh. The second skirmish between the Moghul forces and the Sikhs occurred in the village of Rahela near Hargobind-pur in 1630. Again the Sikhs were victorious. The third time, the Governor of Lahore sent troops under Lal Beg in 1632 this time the Moghul forces were defeated at a place called Gurusar.

The fourth battle was forced upon the Guru in 1634 by one of his own deserters named Painde Khan—who the Guru loved and trained, but who later, joined the Moghul army. He told the military commander of Jalandhar that the Guru's power could be crushed. He also assured him that the Guru had no regular army and that his soldiers consisted only of disciples, who did not know the strategy of war. Kale Khan, leading a Moghul army surrounded Kartarpur. Painde Khan, then arrogantly, challenged Guru Hargobind to a duel. He struck the first blow, which the Guru parried with his shield. Then the Guru dealt him a fatal blow. During his last minutes, the Guru showed Painde Khan the measure of his compassion. Kale Khan died on the same battle-field, his soldiers fled away.

Like the other Gurus, Guru Hargobind established a new township and named it Kiratpur. It was situated in the Sarhind region, near the foot of the Shivalik hills. This centre was established particularly for the welfare and training of Hindu hill-men, who were very backward and superstitious. The Guru managed this township for about ten years. He also lived with old admirer named Budhu Shah, who the Guru blessed and later attended his funeral in Kiratpur. Here the Guru also kept a small contingent of cavalry and artillery always ready for action as an emergency measure. Kiratpur—in course of time—became a centre of trade and for the service to the poor and needy.

Guru Hargobind had many devotees. Some of them participated in his wars against tyrant rulers and leaders. Bidhichand, once a dacoit, became a holy man in the Guru's company. He retrieved the Guru's two horses from the stables of the Governor of Lahore. He was also an excellent soldier and performed many deeds of valour on the battle-field. In the last battle between the Moghul forces and the Guru's soldiers, Bidhichand, though wounded, struck Shamas Beg and killed him on the spot.

Among the pacifist disciples, devotion of Sadhu and Rupa (father and son) proved to be exemplary. One day in summer, they were working on their farm. It was very hot and so they hung a water jar on a tree to cool. After a while, they felt thirsty and took the jar down. The water felt very cool, so they decided to offer the water to the Guru first and afterwards take their own drink. But the Guru lived ten miles away and there was no chance of his coming there in such scorching weather. They prayed to the Guru to come and drink the cool water. If he did not, they would rather die than drink it before the Guru had some. They were sure that the Guru would listen to their prayer, and he did. The—Guru rode from his house to their farm, braving the heat. In the meantime Sadhu and Rupa were exhausted; their lips and throats were dry. They were expecting the Guru to come there in time to save their lives. They were delighted when they saw Guru Hargobind galloping towards them. He said to them: "My beloved Sikhs! I am very thirsty, give me first some cold water to drink. "He blessed them for their love and devotion.

There was an old woman named Bhagbhari who lived in Srinagar. She had stitched a silk dress with great love for the Guru. She prayed to the Guru day and night that he would visit her and wear the dress before her death. After a few days, Guru Hargobind went to Kashmir and visited the lady and asked for his dress. She was very happy when the Guru wore the dress she had specially made for him.

Guru Hargobind was against the performances of miracles. When his son. Baba Atal performed a miracle by restoring a dead boy to life, he told him to pay for it with his own life. So also Baba Gurditta, another son, suffered the same fate for resuscitating a poor man's cow by occult power. Miracle-mongering was regarded by the Guru as an interference with Divine Will. One must distinguish between the Guru's answering the prayers of his disciples and miracle-perfomances. Reading of the heart or mind through telepathy or clairvoyance, is not a miracle.

Guru Hargobind had a charismatic personality. Tall and handsome, he attracted many young men to his fighting ranks. He loved good soldiers and rewarded them handsomely. His great contribution was the change that he brought about in the Sikh way of life. Before him, Sikhs were peaceful and pious; he transformed them into good warriors, without the loss of holiness. When non-violence failed, violence had to be used as the last resort. Moreover, tyranny and injustice had to be uprooted for the sake of survival. Guru Hargobind was compelled to wage wars with tyrant rulers, but in spite of his victories, he never acquired any treasure or occupied any territory. By his bravery and love, he won the hearts of many Hindus and Muslims. He showed that the right is the might and that good will ultimately triumph over evil. He infused new life and blood into his disciples. He groomed his grand-son Har Rai for Gurudom. In 1644, he nominated Har Rai as his successor and soon passed away.

7. Guru Har Rai

Guru Har Rai became the seventh Guru at the age of fourteen. The times were very difficult for Sikhs in the reign of Shah Jehan. He ordered that restrictions be placed on the building of any new Hindu temples. Fortunately, by this time, it was generally recognised that the Sikhs were a separate community and practised a different faith. So the royal order did not apply to Gurdwaras, and their numbers grew. However, for three years (1646-49) there was drought in the Punjab, so great scarcity of food. During this long famine, the Guru's Free Kitchen was a great help to all people, specially to the poor and other vulnerable sections of the public.

Dara Shikoh—the son of Shah Jehan—was the Governer of Punjab in that period. He realised the value and importance of the Guru's humanitarian work. Apart from feeding and clothing the poor and needy, Guru Har Rai established a big health clinic at Kiratpur, where lots of people received free medicine and every day care. The Guru collected and stocked many rare medicinal herbs at this clinic. It so happened that once Dara himself, became seriously ill. The royal physician prescribed a rare herb, which was not available at Agra or Delhi. He knew that the Guru had a stock of valuable herbs, so a request was made by the Emperor to the Guru for a supply of prescribed herb for the treatment of Dara. The Guru was only too willing to give him the required herb. This kind act left a great impression in the mind of Shah Jehan, whose troops had forced four wars on Guru Hargobind, the grand-father of Guru Har Rai. The emperor also came to know of the Guru's feeding of a large number of people during the period of famine. He also learnt that the Guru had many Muslim disciples and admirers, so he made no difficulties for the Guru's work.

Guru Har Rai undertook a missionary tour of the Punjab for about four years. He visited Kartarpur, Amritsar, Goindwal and many other places. He preached holiness and the need for service to the sick and the aged. He also maintained a small army and went out hunting. By and large, he devoted himself to welfare projects, like manning clinics for the treatment of the sick and handicapped.

The illness of emperor Shah Jehan in 1657 was a signal to start new war of succession. Shah Jehan had shown a preference for his eldest son— Dara Shikoh as his successor. The other claimants were his three brothers—Shujah, Aurangzeb and Murad. Aurangzeb, the strongest and the cleverest of them, imprisoned his father and waged war against his brothers. Dara fled to Punjab and sought Guru Har Rai's advice. The Guru did not want to take sides in the royal family's quarrels. He met Dara with cordiality as usual. Dara had his own army and a lot of treasure and ammunition. He thought he could settle his claim with Aurangzeb by force of arms. He retreated to Sind, where pursued by Aurangzeb's troops he was later captured and executed.

Aurangzeb was not happy to seeing the Sikh religion gathering momentum. He also received complaints about the alleged aid of Guru Har Rai to his brother Dara. He summoned the Guru to his court to speak of this, but Guru's Sikhs were not in favour of him meeting the emperor. The Guru therefore deputed his son Ram Rai, to Delhi to meet the emperor and sort things out. He also told his son to maintain the sanctity of The Adi Granth and not to perform any miracles. Ram Rai explained his father's stand to the Emperor and stated that he had done nothing against the emperor. Then the emperor asked about the contents of the Adi Granth—the Sikh Scripture. One of the courtiers quoted a line from the Scripture which seemed to offend the emperor. Har Rai made an unauthorised correction in the line on the spur of the moment, to please the emperor. Aurangzeb was satisfied with the explanation furnished by Ram Rai. He also liked his conduct and granted him a Jagir (estate). Guru Har Rai was very displeased with Ram Rai's doings at the royal court, particularly his change of a word in the Adi Granth. No one has the authority to make any change in the Scripture which is regarded as the Revelation of God to the Gurus. He felt that Ram Rai was not fit to be his successor.

One of his Guru's devotees was Chaudry Kala. One day, he brought his nephews—Phul and Sandli—to the Guru's court. The parents of these two brothers were dead, and Kala used to maintain them. The boys bowed to the Guru and began to beat their stomachs. This indicated that they were poor and needy and they sought his blessing. The Guru was pleased with them and predicted that they would be the rulers of the region. Next day, Kala brought his own sons for the Guru's blessing. The Guru also blessed them. Phul became originator of the Phulkian rajas who later ruled over Patiala region, while others became Jagirdars (landlords) in the neighbouring areas.

Guru Har Rai had a very compassionate and generous temperament. He specially loved his poorer disciples. Once an old lady stitched a gown for him and also cooked a meal for the Guru. She came to the congregation, but on account of coyness, did not present both things to the Guru. She took the things back to her home, not knowing what to do

79

next. In the evening, Guru Har Rai went out for a walk; he inquired about the old lady's house and entered it. The old lady was surprised by this unexpected visit. The Guru then asked what she had prepared for him. She produced the gown and the cooked food which the Guru accepted with thanks. The lady was overwhelmed by the Guru's gesture of goodwill.

Finding that his end was approaching, Guru Har Rai nominated his youngest son—Harkrishan—as his successor in October 1661.

8. Guru Harkrishan

Guru at the age of five! Indeed a wonder! There are precedents, however we have examples of saints like Dhuru and Prahlad in ancient Indian history, who in their infancy devoted themselves to God. Spiritual enlightenment does not depend on age. God has the power to enlighten any person at any time, irrespective of age. We have other examples of Sikh Gurus at an early age. Guru Gobind Singh assumed the Gurudom at the age of nine, Guru Hargobind at eleven, Guru Har Rai at fourteen, and Guru Arjun at eighteen. So we have five Gurus who assumed their responsibilities in their teens. If we include Guru Nanak, then the majority of the Gurus began their missionary work before they were adult.

A Brahmin who lived at Panjokhra near Ambala was very proud of his scholarship, particularly his knowledge of the *Gita*. When Guru Harkrishan happened to visit this village, the Brahmin told a local Sikh that he wanted to meet the Guru and ask a few questions on the Gita. The Sikh took him to the Guru's house where he expressed a desire for a clarification of some passages in this Hindu Scripture. The Guru told him that any man in the street could do that. Luckily, at that moment a water-carrier who was passing by, was called. The water carrier bowed to the Guru and was blessed. Then the Brahmin recited some difficult passages of the *Gita* and asked the illiterate man to explain their meanings to him. Much to the amazement of the Brahmin, the water-carrier explained the passages to the Brahmin's satisfaction. The Brahmin felt humbled and sought the Guru's pardon for his arrogant behaviour and desired to become the Guru's disciple. The Guru told him that true learning breeds humility, a characteristic of a scholar.

Ram Rai, the Guru's brother had complained to Emperor Aurangzeb of his suppersession and the nomination of his younger brother Harkrishan, as the successor-Guru. Aurangzeb took advantage of this opportunity to foment disunity among the Sikhs. He wanted to call Guru Harkrishan to Delhi in this connection. Very cleverly, he persuaded Raja Jai Singh to invite the Guru to Delhi. Guru Harkrishan had no mind to see the emperor, but Raja Jai Singh pleaded that the Sikhs of Delhi wanted to meet their Guru and that they should not be disappointed. The Guru agreed to go to Delhi on the condition that he would not be compelled to meet the emperor. Raja Jai Singh agreed to this condition. Guru Harkrishan reached Delhi and stayed in the Raja's palace where Gurdwara Bangla Sahib now stands. Here, the emperor was not allowed to meet the Guru, so he sent his son to see him; the prince was very impressed by the Guru's wisdom and maturity and conveyed this impression to his father.

In 1664, Delhi was ravaged by a cholera epidemic. The Guru used this opportunity to serve the entire population of Delhi with whatever he and his followers could collect. He served the sick with food and medicine. The Sikhs collected corpses from different parts of the city and disposed them of with dignity. The Guru himself felt sick with small-pox and his condition worsened day by day. Before his death, he uttered the words "Baba Bakalay" to indicate that his successor would be found in the village of Bakala.

Guru Harkrishan is lovingly called 'the child Guru.' Children and students regard him as their Guru and Patron. Many schools in the Punjab and elsewhere, are named after Guru Harkrishan.

9. Guru Tegh Bahadur

Born in 1621, Tegh Bahadur spent his first few years at Amritsar. Bhai Buddha trained him in the arts of archery and horsemanship, while Bhai Gurdas taught him Gurumukhi, Hindi, Sankrit and Indian religious thought. He also learnt music and hymn-singing. From his father Guru Hargobind, he learnt swordmanship and war-strategy. Later at the age of thirteen, he took part in the battle of Kartarpur where he performed valorous feats. Soon, Guru Hargobind's family moved to the new town of Kiratpur. He married Mata Gujri in February 1633 at Kartarpur. Guru Hargobind nominated his grand son Har Rai as his successor in 1644. He then asked Tegh Bahadur and his wife to move to Bakala.

Baba Tegh Bahadur (as he came to be known) and his family, spent over twenty years at Bakala. He looked after his family responsibilities.

but devoted the major portion of his time to meditation and to the service of the people, between, which he went on preaching tour to the U.P., Bihar and Bengal. After his return to Bakala, he received news of the death of Guru Harkrishan in 1664.

Many critics question the double by-passing of Guru Tegh Bahadur by his father Guru Hargobind and by his nephew Guru Har Rai. It was the right of the current Guru to select his successor, closeness of relationship, was not a criteria. Guru Hargobind thought that his grandson Har Rai, son of the late Bhai Gurditta, was more suitable than any one else. He had advised Tegh Bahadur to devote himself to contemplation and meditation at Bakala. Guru Har Rai before his death, appointed his son Har Krishan, the reason perhaps being that Tegh Bahadur was busy preaching to far away *sangats* in Bengal. When Guru Harkrishan and died suddenly in 1664, he made a cryptic declaration—*Baba Bakalay*. No one was named specifically as his successor Guru. The result was that imposers of the Sodhi clan, claimed succession at Bakala, in the hope that the Sikhs, in their uncertainty, would accept one of them as the real Guru. There were 22 claimants waiting for recognition. Fortunately, at this time, a devout Sikh named Makhan Shah Labana came to Bakala. He was a big trader and wealthy man. His ship, carrying merchandise was caught in a storm at sea, he had prayed to the Sikh Guru for help. He vowed that if his ship and goods came safe to port, he would give 500 gold *Mohurs* to the Guru. His prayer was heard, his ship and merchandise were saved, so he went to Bakala to make his offering of the promised gold coins to the Guru. He was amazed by seeing so many persons claiming to be the Gurus. He then started to visit each of the claimants and presented each two gold coins. He knew that the true Guru would ask for the promised amount. Only finally did he come to the home of Tegh Bahadur where he placed his two gold coins and bowed to him. Tegh Bahadur said to him: "How come, that you are not keeping your promise? Your ship was saved by God's grace and you must fulfil what you vowed in you distress." Mkhan shah immediately knew that He, was the True Guru and made his offering of 500 gold coins. His joy at discovering the Guru knew no bounds. He went to the roof of the house and shouted to the people standing below: "I have found the True Guru! O Sikhs, come and seek his blessing!" The Sikhs came there in large numbers, the pretenders ran away. Guru Tegh Bahadur was formally installed as the Ninth Guru in August 1664.

Like the other Gurus, Tegh Bahadur set up a new township. He purchased land from Queen Champa of Bilaspur in June 1665. He named it after his mother *Chak Nanki*—, later to be known as Anandpur Sahib.

Soon some houses and shops were built to meet the needs of the people. The Guru then proceeded to the eastern U.P. and Bihar on a missionary tour. He took his family and close relatives with him. He consolidated all the *Sangats* of U.P. and Bihar under Bhai Dayaldas, a man of great ability and devotion. Then the Guru left his family at Patna and proceeded towards Dacca. There he received the news of the birth of a son at the end of December 1666. In Dacca lived a devoted *massand* named Bulaki Das, whose mother had stitched a cotton dress for the Guru with great devotion. The Guru asked for the dress and blessed the old lady. Here the Guru blessed many *Sangats*. He called Dacca "the home of Sikhism."

Raja Ram Singh of Amber, who had come to Dacca at the instance of the Moghul emperor to subjugate the Ahom ruler, became friendly with the Guru. Finding that the Rulers were fighting an unnecessary war, the Guru brought peace between the two armies. Both parties were happy with the Guru's intercession and were reconciled. In the meantime, emperor Aurangzeb promulgated an order in 1669, for the destruction of all schools and temples of the Hindus. He was keen that Islam should be accepted by his subjects, while the peasants only felt the rigour of the exactions of the *Jagirdars* and the military Commanders. The Guru realised the gravity of the situation and decided to return immediately to the Punjab. He wanted to console the people in their distress and to bolster their morale, so that they would find the courage to resist injustice and despotism. So in June 1670 he hurried back to Delhi. He sent a message to his family to join him at Lakhnaur; here Guru met his family and saw his son Gobind (aged nearly four) for the first time.

Guru Tegh Bahadur began a tour of Malwa and Bangar Desh in 1673. He met Saif Khan, a Muslim admirer, in Saifabad, now called Bahadurgarh, then went to Talwandi Sabo (Damdama Sahib) where he had a tank constructed which was called 'Gurusar.' His tour of this region lasted for over a year. The Guru established more *Sangats* and inspired landlords with the need for social service. Projects of public good like the construction of tanks and wells were put in hand and lots of enthusiasm for voluntary labour was generated. The Guru rewarded and honoured the leaders of those village-communities who had undertaken welfare works.

Repression and intolerance again raised its ugly head under Aurangzeb's regime. The Emperor issued an order in 1674 to Iftikhar Khan, Governor of Kashmir, to put pressure on the Hindu Pandits to make them embrace Islam. They asked for six months grace in which to consider this matter. In their desperation, they decided to seek the advice of Guru Tegh Bahadur. So a delegation of sixteen Kashmiri Pandits led by Kirpa Ram met the Guru at Anandpur on 25th May, 1675. The Guru listened patiently to their tales of woe and repression and consoled them. He thought over their problem and came to the conclusion that only the sacrifice of a holy man could stem the tide of forcible conversion. At this moment, his nine-year old son—Gobind Rai—told his father that he, as the Guru, was the fittest person to uphold "Freedom of belief and conscience."

Guru Tegh Bahadur, as a man of great courage and determination, decided that he would offer his life to protect the Hindus who had sought his support and protection. He told them to inform the Governor of Kashmir that they would follow the Guru's leadership, and if the Guru complied with the emperor's order, they would do like-wise. The Governor sent the message to Aurangzeb, who soon passed an order for the arrest of Guru Tegh Bahadur. The Guru nominated his son Gobind Rai as his successor, before leaving Anandpur on 10th July, 1875. Two days later, he and three of his followers were arrested at Malikapur and sent to Sarhind. They were put to great hardships during their stay in jail, for over three months. Then the Guru and his men were taken to Delhi under heavy police escort where they arrived on 5th November.

Guru Tegh Bahadur and his followers were then tortured in Delhi prison. When the Guru refused to change his faith and principles, in spite of all allurements and threats, he was told to perform a miracle to confirm his sainthood. The Guru refused to perform a miracle and declared: "Men of faith do not perform miracles to save themselves from suffering. Miracles are not performed for the exhibition of one's power or glory." The emperor issued an order for the Guru's execution—but prior to this, and to break the Guru's spirit, his followers were tortured to death in his presence. Bhai Matidas was sawn into two pieces. Bhai Dayaldas was thrown into a large cauldron of boiling water; Bhai Satidas was wrapped in cotton-wool and burnt to death. On 11th November 1675, Guru Tegh Bahadur was taken to a public square in Chandni Chowk for his own execution. He said his prayers; his face glowed divinely. Then the executioner dealt the fatal blow with the sword. The Guru's head flew some distance, while his body dropped to the ground. Soon there was a dust-storm. Bhai Jaita, a Sikh of the Guru picked up the head of the Guru and took it to Anandpur. Bhai Lakhi Shah Labana, a Sikh contractor, snatched up his body, put it in on his bullock cart and took it quickly to his house on the outskirts of Delhi. Fearing discovery, he set fire to his own house which then contained the body of the Guru. At this spot now stands Gurdwara Rikabganj. Guru Tegh Bahadur is thus appropriately called *Hind-di-chadar*—the Saviour of the honour of India.

Some historians like Mir Munshi Ghulam Hussain (vide his Persian work entitled *Sirarul-Mutakhiran*) have deliberately distorted the mission and martyrdom of Guru Tegh Bahadur to try and justify the actions of Aurangzeb in ordering his execution. Pleading that the Guru was a rebel and seditious leader who organised the masses against the emperor's rule, and also collected lots of money, given as offerings, that the increasing number of his followers and the influence he had, threatened Moghul rule. The Guru's views on "freedom of belief and conscience" was misrepresented, as sedition and revolt. The news-writers also submitted exaggerated reports of the Guru's preaching tours and regarded his mission as a movement of the masses for civil rights. It may be noted that the Guru never wrote or spoke against Emperor Aurangzeb or forcibly raised money. His struggle was basically the fight of good against bad.

The message of Guru Tegh Bahadur was the same as that of Guru Nanak and his successors. All the Guru preached universal brotherhood and love of their fellow-men. Guru Tegh Bahadur had both Hindu and Muslim followers and admirers. The Guru's message of freedom and fearlessness for the people were intended to give them the moral courage to stand up for their rights, and to maintain the dignity of ordinary people.

The reason for the arrest and later execution of the Guru was for the support he gave to the cause of Kashmiri Pandits in their fight for religious freedom, and for the great success of his preaching tours. His main platform was his fight against tyranny and despotism, against the intolerance and fanaticism of the rulers of the land. His tours were intended to awaken the masses and to espouse the cause of religious freedom. He backed his cause with his life. His martyrdom produced the desired result. According to I.B. Bannerjee: "the whole Punjab began to burn with indignation and revenge." His sacrifice was instrumental in banishing sloth and cowardice and awakening the people to the need for courage and determination. They realised that human dignity and tolerance, were causes worth fighting for. Later, the Guru's son and successor continued the struggle for the defence of human values and the maintenance of *Dharma* or righteousness.

Guru Tegh Bahadur was a poet of freedom and compassion. He composed 59 hymns in Hindi and set them to 15 ragas. He also wrote 57 verses. There is a large number of hymns in Sorath raga (12) and Gauri raga (7) which are meant for singing at night. This indicates that the Guru devoted a lot of time to singing at night, and slept very little, always rose early to attended dawn hymn-singing. His hymns were later included in the Adi Granth by Guru Gobind Singh in 1706. They contain a strong plea for detachment and desirelessness. All wordly relationships and possessions are temporary and impermanent. The goal of human life is its liberation from the transitory and unreal, to union with the Eternal Reality. For this purpose, a course of self-discipline and meditation on the Holy Name is necessary. The God—oriented man—the *Gurumukh* or *Jiwan-mukt* is the one who conquers egoism, passion, praise or slander, honour and dishonour:

"Renouncing egoism and attachment to the world,
Turn your hearts towards devotion to God.
Nanak says: This is the true path of liberation,
Attain to it by turning your hearts to God." (AG, 219)

Liberation is communion with God; total-compassion and kindliness for all the forms of creation. A man of God has to be ready to sacrifice himself, to uphold Moral Law, for in life and in death, he is in tune with God.

The poems of Guru Tegh Bahadur radiate feelings of peace and joy. The Guru uses simple words and images, but these are loaded with lots of meaning and significance. He says not a single word in them about his detractors, they are free from any trace of hatred or revenge. He emphasised the positive values like detachment, altruism and compassion. His compositions have both aesthetic and life-values. The use of classical tunes adds to the appeal of the hymns and produces in audiences, feelings of calm and equanimity. His devotional poetry extends the horizon of human destiny and expands cosmic vision and the realisation of divine ecstasy.

Some of his poems were in the form of answers to the queries of his followers who sought his guidance on personal and spiritual problems. One day, a grain-dealer of Kiratpur came to the Guru and told him of his condition. He had been successful in business and won the respect of the people, ;and yet had no peace of mind. The Guru diagnosed his malady and told him that he must rid himself of his attachment to worldly things. It is man's possessiveness that leads to selfish actions which in turn produce reactions and thus set in motion the chain of cause and effect. If one gives up Ego, he can feel happy in carrying out the Divine Will. He is then free of tension, worry and fear:

"One who discards all hopes and desires,

Who lives detached from the world,
And is not disturbed by lust and anger,
Is the one who radiates the light of God." (AG, 633)

Guru Tegh Bahadur had a many-sided personality—a warrior at the age of thirteen, a family-man with a social concern, a preacher of great understanding and sympathy. The Guru wore the crown of martyrdom so that others may be spared from persecution and frustration. He believed in the triumph of Divine justice and the power of God to help and support His devotees. He upheld the sovereignty of moral life, by rejecting material allurements and pleasures. He was a great poet, thinker, philosopher and peace-maker. With his exalted vision and high idealism, he shattered the dream of the dictator-emperor that he could do whatever he liked with the lives of millions. Guru Tegh Bahadur is rightly regarded as the champion and saviour of the Hindu people.

The cause of the martyr is never forgotten. It inspires whole communities and serves as a beacon to others. Emerson, wrote: "A martyr cannot be dishonoured. Every lash inflicted is a tongue of flame, every prison a more illustrious abode, every burned book or home, enlightens the world, every suppressed or expunged word reverberates through the earth from side to side. Hours of sanity and consideration are always coming to communities and to individuals when The Truth is seen, and its martyrs justified." Guru Tegh Bahadur's sacrifice broke the myth of Aurangzeb's infallibility and piety. The emperor himself realised his mistake very late in his life and wrote: "There is no hope for me in the future . . I leave this earth leading a caravan of sin."

Summing up the achievements of Guru Tegh Bahadur, it may be said that he occupies a place of eminence among the world's martyrs. Additionally, he is remembered for founding the city of Anandpur, and for his welfare projects and missionary work in the whole of northern India. His stand on the supremacy of moral life and conscience, his triumph of spirit over material possession and physical dissection ensure the ultimate sovereignty of truth and justice in the scheme of the universe.

10. Guru Gobind Singh

Guru at the age of nine and advising his father to offer himself for martyrdom, is a rare phenomenon in world history. Guru Gobind Singh was the heir to a rich heritage. His great grand-father Guru Arjan had been a martyr. His own life developed as an obstacle course in which he had to meet a continuing crisis in spite of which over a period of forty-two years, he proved to himself as a great warrior and leader of the Sikhs, also as a poet and thinker, who gave us a Scripture comparable to the Adi Granth.

Guru Gobind Singh's life may be studied under three categories: From birth until 1675 when he became Guru, his consolidation of the Sikh community and victories over the hill-chiefs, finally, his creation of the *Khalsa Panth*, his wars with the Moghul rulers and his abolition of personal Gurudom.

The first shocking experience for the Tenth Guru was receiving the severed head of his own father, at the age of nine. Fortunately, this, did not make him despondent or isolated, but rather steeled his spirit and inspired him to resist the forces of evil and tyranny. His hour had arrived, he felt that he would have to be, the Saviour of all Sikhs who assembled under his banners.

A later stay at Paonta Sahib for about four years, he used to inspire his Sikhs with courage and heroism. For the purpose, he gathered some 52 poets to his house, he also gave military training to his followers. He and his court-poets reset in Brij-bhasha, stories of those ancient Indian warriors who had faced dare-devils. These poems dealt with history and the wars between gods and demons. The Guru rewarded his poets generously for all their creative work. Often, he would place costly woollen shawls or gold coins under their pillows, to avoid embarrassing them. The Guru himself wrote *Var Sri Bhagwati Ji Ki*—popularly known as *Chandi-di-Var* in Punjabi to inspire his peple when fighting in support of righteousness. His war-peotry is like an orchestral clash of arms alternating with the galloping of horses, the zooming of arrows and the twanging of bows. The principles of *Dharam-yudha* struggle for the victory of morality and truth over evil and injustice, had already been accepted by Guru Hargobind, but it was Guru Gobind Singh—his grandson—who later came to organise the people in their fight against the mightiest empire of his time. The writers and the musicians of his court, he involved in the task of mentally preparing his followers to get ready for the coming struggle. On the practical side mock battles were waged at Paonta Sahib and at Anandpur, to give his Sikhs the taste for battle and the strategy for war.

His Sikhs brought horses, swords and gems, as offerings, when they realised that the survival of their community was at stake. Wealthy Sikhs gave precious and regal gifts. A Kabul Sikh presented a huge ornamental canopy for the Guru's Court. Another devotee, a young prince from Assam, named Ratan Rai, came with his mother and brought valuable gifts to Anandpur. These included five pedigree horses with golden saddles, an ornamental throne, a costly goblet, a multi-purpose weapon which could be used as a sword, lance, dagger, pistol and club, an intelligent performing elephant, and beautiful dresses and jewellery. The elephant was remarkable in that it could wash the Guru's feet and wipe them with a napkin; it could pick up the Guru's used arrows, he could wave a *chauri* over the Guru's head. It also performed many other unusual feats. The hill-rajas were very jealous of the Guru's unique possessions. The Guru had a war-drum made; it was called *Ranjit Nagara*—the drum of victory. It was beaten in the mornings and evenings.

The local rulers of the Shivalik hills became very unsettled by the Guru's growing power. Raja Harichand and Raja Fatehchand, sent their troops to Bhangani in 1686, to attack the Guru. A Muslim saint, Pir Buddhu Shah brought a contingent of Pathan soldiers for employment by the Guru, which he recruited, for his army. Unfortunately, they deserted the Guru before the battle began. Pir Buddhu Shah being then disgraced brought himself, his four sons and 700 followers, to the Guru's aid. The Guru wrote a vivid account of this battle in his composition, *Bachitra Natak*. Mahant Kirpal who had never handled a weapon, picked up a club and challenged a seasoned warrior of the enemy—Hayat Khan. The latter aimed a powerful blow with his sword which Kirpal first parried with his club, and then gave Hayat Khan a fatal blow to the head: an amazing feat of courage. Similarly, another Sikh of the Guru—a confectioner named Lalchand took up a sword and shield for the first time and mounted a horse. He then challenged Mir Khan, decapitating with his sword. The Guru challenged Raja Harichand to a duel; an arrow, fired by the Guru then killed Harichand. On seeing their leader fall, the hill soldiers ran away. Budhu Shah's two sons were killed in the battle. Later the Guru consoled him and presented him a sword, a comb and a turban for his services. These relics are preserved at Nabha.

Raja Bhimchand was also jealous of the power of the Guru but he expressed his hostility in a different way. When the Moghul Governor of Jammu sent Commander Alif Khan to collect his annual tribute, Raja Bhimchand asked Guru Gobind Singh for help. The Guru ignoring, Raja Bhimchand's earlier disgusting activities, took on the command of the allied forces in a battle fought at Nadaun. Here Guru's army won a resounding victory over the Moghul forces. After a period of peace, the

Governor of Kangra again sent an expedition to collect tribute from the hill-rajas. This time Bhimchand and, the other Chiefs were scared and quietly paid what the Moghuls demanded.

The Khalsa

Guru Gobind Singh decided that the time had now come when he needed to order of the Sikhs who were to be totally devoted to him. Ready to sacrifice their lives in espousing the causes of Truth and Justice. The obstacles he would have to overcome were: the Moghul rulers and the hill-chiefs, also the then Sikh missionaries, called *massands*, who had become greedy, oppressive and immoral. Though the Guru had a trained army of devoted Sikhs and many Muslims followers who agreed with his mission, he needed a large number of "committed followers." To this end he arranged for a special assembly to be held on Baisakhi day in 1699. Sikhs from all over India were invited, their response was very encouraging. So on 30th March, 1699 thousands of the Guru's followers gathered at Anandpur. As soon as their morning prayers were over, Guru Gobind Singh stood before them, holding a sword in his hand and asked: "Is any one here prepared to die at my command?" His audience was stunned. How come that the Guru is asking for the heads of his followers? When he repeated the question for the third time, a Sikh from Lahore named Daya Ram Khatri, stood up with folded hands and said: "Sir, it is my privilege to offer my life to you. Do as you please with it." The Guru took him away to his tent. After a short while, the Guru returned to his dais, his sword dripped blood. The audience thought that Daya Ram had been killed. Again the Guru asked the audience: "I want another Sikh who is prepared to die for his faith." The second Sikh who responded to the call was Dharam Das, a Jat of Delhi. the Guru took him to the tent and again came back after a while, with his sword dripping blood. Again he asked for another Sikh to sacrifice himself for the Guru's mission. This time, some people panicked and ran away, even though after a few seconds, a third Sikh came forward. His name was Mohakam Chand, and he was a washer-man from Dwarka. The Guru took him to the tent also. On a fourth call, Sahib Chand, a barber of Bider offered himself and at the fifth call, Himath Rai, a water-carrier of Jagan Nath Puri came forward. Guru Gobind Singh then returned to his tent and after an interval, reappeared, leading his five devoted disciples, now newly dressed and equipped. Referring to them as his five Beloved ones—*Panj Piyara*—he led them to the dais. A new initiation-ceremony was about to begin.

Firstly, Guru Gobind Singh poured water into an iron bowl and stirred it with a double-edged sword, while he recited the five *Banis* (holy compositions). The five disciples faced the Guru, all wore the Five K's, namely unshorn hair, a comb, under-pants, an iron wrist-band and a sword. The Guru's wife, then brought some sugar-puffs—*Patasa*—and put them in the water as the Guru stirred it. The *amrit* (nectar) was now ready. It was called *Khanday-di-pahal*. Guru Gobind Singh then announced that from that time on, this mode of initiation would be followed in place of the former *charan-amrit* (using water touched by the Guru's toe). The stirring sword introduced courage and strength, while the sugar symbolised sweetness and virtue. The Guru then administered the Amrit vows to his five disciples—that they recite their daily prayers and follow the Code of discipline, that they worship no idols, graves or mausoleums, that they never eat ritual-killed meat *(Halal* or *Kosher)*. That they never use tabacco or anything intoxicant in any form, and never commit adultery. After the five had pledged themselves to follow these orders and injunctions, he held the bowl of his new *amrit* in his hands. All five then knelt before him. One by one, he looked into their eyes, and threw palmfuls of water on their faces. At each shower he asked them to say aloud the Sikh greeting—*Waheguru ji ka khalsa, Waheguru ji ki fateh.* Then he sprinkled the *amrit* (nectar) five times onto their hair and into their eyes. Finally, he gave five palmfuls of nectar to each, to drink. The bowl was then given them to drink from and finish communally.

Originally the five disciples had belonged to different castes. Daya Ram was a *Khatri*, Dharam Das a Jat, while the remainder were untouchables, washer-man, water-carrier, a barber, but drinking the nectar from the same bowl they renounced their caste distinctions. The Guru then added "Singh" (a lion) to their names. Daya Ram became Daya Singh; Dharam Das became Dharam Singh and so on. Thus the first group of Khalsa Sikhs—Pure Ones—were initiated, personally by the Tenth Master.

The Guru then addressed his new initiates as followes:

"You have now been reborn into the house of the Guru. Being children of the same Guru, you are now related to each other. therefore, you should not quarrel among yourselves, but live as members of one family. By the acceptance of the *amrit*, you became warriors, on both physical and spiritual planes; therefore you may no longer live to die as an ordinary person. It is now your duty to sacrifice your lives for the protection of Dharma. It is essential that you now devote yourselves whole-heartedly to God, your Adi Granth's teachings and all Guru Khalsa. You speech should be sweet, truthful, firm and full of love. Your should control your sexual instincts by considering all ladies as mothers, wives or daughters. You should control your anger by considering the faults of weak people as of your own; you should control your greed by considering the property of others as the vomit of a dog; you should control your attachment by regarding all beautiful things as being fragile; you should control your ego by considering the abilities of your elders. Each one of you should be try to become expert in many branches of knowledge. You must set the example for bravery in the world; you must become expert in the use of all weapons. Consider yourselves as being always in the service of your country. The needy and the lowly are to be helped. You must rise above deceit, fraud, calumny, falsehood, undue praises etc. You are now obliged to make known the praises of the Lord, through the *Word* of the Guru. You should serve the saints and earn your own living through hard work and honest means, giving a portion of your earnings in charity, for the needy."[24]

Now was the time for the Guru himself to become Khalsa. He stood before his newly initiated 'Five Beloveds' with folded hands and requested them to give him the *amrit*. The Beloved Five were very diffident, so he explained:

"I have given you my form and my glory. You are now Khalsa. Understand that the Khalsa is the Guru and the Guru is the Khalsa!"

They then prepared amrit in the same way and administered it to their Guru, changing his name from Gobind Rai to Gobind Singh.

Then the Guru demanded of the audience that they now come forward and take amrit and live as Khalsa Sikhs, as servants of the community, as helpers of the underprivileged and down-trodden. By this one event the Guru changed his followers psychologically and gave them a distinct uniform. He warned those who took amrit, that they must behave like warriors and remain free and fearless. He told them the story of the donkey who was clothed in a tiger's skin, but who brayed and so was found out and beaten up. The Guru impressed on them the need to conduct themselves with honour and dignity, to give up caste-taboos, their old rituals and ideas and to keep intact their outer and inner uniform. So long as the Khalsa maintains its vows, they will wear the crown of glory. He declared:

> "So long as the Khalsa maintains its identity, it will retain its honour and splendour; Once it follows devious (Brahminical) ways, it will lose the blessing of the Guru."

Why did Guru Gobind Singh lay down those conditions? How do they help one to lead a pure and holy life? How are they reflected in the personality of a Khalsa? Let us examine them one by one.

(i) The Maintenance of uncut hair

The shaving or removal of hair is regarded as a challenge to the Creator and His Divine Will. The ban on hair-cutting for the Khalsa was demanded in order that God's design of man should be left as He intended. Hair is a protection for the head. Who are we to alter God's great design.

(ii) The Ban on tobacco and other intoxicants

Tobacco contains nicotine, which is a strong poison, as any inhalations of its smoke poses serious danger both to the smoker and the non-smoker who inhales its fumes. The cigarette-wrapper itself made of cellulose pulp is a cause of lung-cancer. Smoking adversely affects the throat, heart, blood-vessels, lungs and digestive organs, even fumes inhaled by passing non-smokers are hazardous to them. Narcotic drugs like opium, cocaine, morphine, barbiturates, cannabis and alcohol cause depression and are all addictive. Though their intoxicants may stimulate temporarily and give a sense of excitement, their addictive use destroys both body and mind. More importantly, as with alcohol, they destroy the mind's control.

(iii) The Ban on eating ritually killed animal-meat

In ancient times animal sacrifice was made to appease gods. Frequently these sacrifices produced guilt-feeling in the one who offers the sacrifice in causing the death of another, be it human, animal or bird. Frequently it was used as a substitute for richly deserved self-misdeeds. The Guru rejected sacrifice of life as hypocrisy. Each one has to answer for their own deeds and cannot use a 'scape-goat' in that place. Secondly ritual meat is supposed to possess magical power, though this cannot be proved, The main objection is because of its inherent cruelty. How can any one justify the incantation of prayer over any creature delibrately allowed to bleed to death—for the main purpose that its meat can be eaten white?

The Guru did not prohibit the eating of meat as such; animals can be killed, but by swift and instantaneous stroke (Jhatka). This applies to fish, fowl and chicken. What the Gurus definitely prohibited was the ritually killed *Halal* meats, or *Kosher* meat.

(iv) Ban on adultery

The Gurus emphasised the cultivation of virtue and moral behaviour. Family-life and domestic stability were regarded as necessary to the basic development of a Sikh. Guru Gobind Singh prohibited sex outside marriage, also sexual promiscuity and perversion as they produced disease guilt and emotional problems. Sex restraint requires the self discipline of being mentally healthy, brave and faithful. When the Sikhs argued with Guru Gobind Singh that because the Mogul soldiers consistently outraged female modesty , they (Sikhs) should be allowed to do the same, but that the Guru would not permit. He wanted to preserve and develop purity in the Sikh charecter.

A few words about the five symbols *Five K's* of the Khalsa. These symbols have a personal and corporate purpose to serve. They are to remind the individual that he is a member of the Khalsa Brotherhood; they are to strengthen the unity and cohesion of the *Panth.* The symbols should remind all Sikhs who wear them of the qualities which they represent. To become effective a practically moral life is essential. Keeping uncut hair *(Kes)* asserts self identity and courage. It also gives the individual a distinct appearance. It should also confirm that the person wearing it and other four symbols, is Khalsa, one who abides by the Guru's code of Disciplene. The comb *(Kanga)* represents cleanliness and is necessary for keeping the hair clean and tidy. The iron wrist-band *(Kara)* being round in shape-without a beginning and an end symbolises the infinity of God and reminds one of Waheguru's presence. The under-pants *(Kachh)* are necessary for the maintenance of personal decency and chastity. The sword *(Kirpan)* is for the protection of oppression and injustice, also which penetrates the curtain of ignorance. Other interpretations are also espoused.

The symbols of the Khalsa are as relevant today, as they were at the time of their inception. We live now in a permissive society, where immoral things like mugging, torture, debauchery, drugs, intoxicants etc. are in fashion. No true Khalsa Sikh would become involved because being instantly recongnisable, would bring public shame. Guru Gobind Singh would strongly condemn the sexual morals which exist in the world today. Lord Lane, the Lord Chief Justice of Great Britain in his Annual Darwin Lecture at Cambridge recently, regretted that this community as a whole did not declare itself against those present vices of civilised society which are taken now accepted eg. permissiveness, abortions at will. A community which approves homo-sexuality is immoral and contemptible. If any one deserves capital punishment, it should be the heroin-pusher and the durg-pedlar, they ruin not only individuals but whole families and lead them into crime to sustain the cost of their addiction. Similarly dirty films, horror videos cassettes on sex rape, robbery, murder, vulgarity and bestiality, are regarded as entertainment, even those that seek to glorify crime and lead to the erosion of human values. It is for the leaders of the community and the legislature to censure such anti-social and demoralising activity, and to restore standards, for decent behaviour, family stability and honest living.[25]

According to Guru Gobind Singh, the ideal of the Khalsa is self perfection—physical, moral and mental. A Khalsa is the ultimate model, for a saint-soldier-scholar. He is also the social worker and the reformer. According to A.C. Bannerjee: "The Guru's conception of the Khalsa Panth was a fully democratic, compact community, well armed to maintain its struggle for the promotion of what it considered to be the right path, waging an incessant battle against tyranny and injustice in all its forms." The Guru did not believe in the superiority of numbers. He wanted quality, and therefore baptised only those who came up to his standard. Think of the great names in the history of the Khalsa Panth— Bhai Mani Singh, Baba Dip Singh, Bhai Mahan Singh, Bhai Sangat Singh: Their individual demonstrations of valour, virtue and wisdom were remarkable. Some of his own Sikhs went even to the length of pointing out so-called mistakes of Guru Gobind Singh, when the latter did something purposely wrong in order to test the vigilance and the wisdom of the Khalsa. One of such examples was the salutation which the Guru made to the grave of saint Dadu. He did so deliberately to see whether his followers had remembered his instructions. One of the Khalsa objected to the Guru bowing to a grave, as it was against Sikh principles. The Khalsa Sangat imposed a fine on the Guru which he paid gladly, though he knew he was testing his Sikhs. The Guru regarded himself as a servant of the Khalsa Sangat and paid compliments to them for any deed of heroism that was brought to his notice.

The Last Phase (1699-1708)

The growing power of Guru Gobind Singh and the rapid increase in the numbers of the Khalsa aroused fear in the Moghul rulers. An army under General Sayyad Khan was sent to Anandpur. This general's sister was an admirer of the Guru. Sayyad Khan challenged the Guru to a duel, but actually faced by the Guru, he was overcome by the Guru's personality and touched his feet. The Guru blessed him. Sayyad Khan then refused to fight the Guru and left the battle-field. He spent the rest of his life in meditation. The moghul army was dismayed by General Sayyad Khan's change of heart; so another commander—Wazir Khan—immediately took charge. The Guru's army now took refuge in the Anandpur Fort. where they were besieged for many months, with all supplies and communications cut off. Eventually Sikhs became desperate and starving. Forty of them demanded to leave the fort; the Guru asked them to write a disclaimer which they did, then they left. The Guru intended to hold the fort for some time. Emperor Aurangzeb then sent a written assurance of safe conduct, if the Guru agreed to leave the fort. At the insistence of his mother, the Guru agreed to leave only on the condition that the Moghul army would allow his treasure safe conduct first. This the Moghul Commander agreed to, the Guru knowing that he (Commander) would not keep his word. Instead the Guru sent rubbish and garbage covered with pieces of cloth of gold, on the pack mules as his treasure. No sooner had the mules left fort then the Moghul army pounced on it as booty. Later when they examined it, they found nothing but filth. In this way the promise-breakers were ashamed.

Eventually by force of his circumstances, Guru Gobind Singh left Anandpur fort in wintry night in December 1705. The darkness of night and drizzle, added to the confusion of evacuation. As the Sikh army came out of the gates, the Moghul attacked them. Soon the Guru and his elder two sons got separated form the younger sons and their mother. The Guru hastened to Chamkaur where he took refuge in an old mud-fort. Soon the fort was surrounded by the Moghul army. There was a fierce fight in which the Guru's two elder sons and 35 Sikhs were killed. Under the cover of night, the Guru and three Sikhs managed to escape. The Guru got separated form his companions, as he entered the jungle of Machiwara. They were all being pursued by the Moghul army; eventually he was found by Muslim followers (Ghani Khan and Nabi Khan) who wanted to take him to a place of safety. They dressed him as a Muslim Pir and carried him on a palanquin, calling him *Uch-Ka-Pir* (Holy saint of Uch, a place near Multan). On the way, they met a detachment of Moghul soldiers. The Guru being in disguise was not recognised by the commander and so was allowed to proceed. Later the Guru rewarded his Muslim followers when they finally left him at a safe spot.

Later, Guru Gobind Singh was again pursued by the forces of Nawab Wazir Khan of Sarhind. Again he escaped and they went to Khidrana. It was here that the forty Sikhs who had deserted him at Anandpur and had returned to their villages, but they had been shamed by their women-folk for disloyal conduct, and sent back to the Guru's army. A Sikh lady, Mai Bhago joining and leading them to a place near Khidrana. At this time, they saw the Moghul army and decided to give battle. The Guru was still some distance away, but he saw the battle. The Guru quickly arrived at the spot and examined his Sikhs one by one. Bhai Mahan Singh one of the deserters was still breathing. As the Guru came to him he said: "Sir, I seek a favour; please tear up our letter of disclaimer before I die." The Guru tore up the letter before the Sikh breathed his last. The Guru then blessed the Forty Sikhs, for they died as martyrs. They are now known as the. Forty immortals. Mai Bhago, the Sikh lady still, lay unconscious on the battle-field. The Guru had her nursed to recovery. She remained in the Guru's service till his death.

Guru Gobind Singh finally reached Dina where he wrote a poetic letter in Persian entitled 'Zafarnama' to the Emperor Aurangzeb. Here he exposed the tyrannies and sins of Aurangzeb and warned him of divine punishment:

"For spilling the blood of innocent, ply not your blade;
Think of the Sword Divine, and then be afraid."

He informed the emperor, that armed revolt against injustice is a moral duty:

"When all peaceful methods fail.
It is justifiable to unsheath the sword."

The *Zafar-nama* was the testament of the Tenth Guru. It embodies the spirit of fearless struggle against misrule and fanaticism. It explains the basis of the Guru's fight against Moughul Imperialism and feudal tyranny. His argument was that if the good and the strong condoned

97

injustice and high handedness, it would lead to the end of all organised life and sane society. The armed struggle for the preservation of basic freedoms and human dignity was now unavoidable and essential.

Aurangzeb died in 1707 and was succeeded by Bahadur Shah who was friendly to Guru Gobind Singh. They travelled together towards the Deccan. When they reached Nander, the Guru decided to stay there. There he met Madho Das Bairagi whom he converted to Sikhism and gave him a new name, Banda Singh, after baptism. The Guru gave him instructions, a sword, five arrows and sent him with Sikh soldiers back to the Punjab to help the down-trodden and punish the wicked.

One day, as Guru Gobind Singh was retiring to his bed, a young Pathan said to be an agent of the Nawab Wazir Khan of Sarhind and who had earlier claimed to be the Guru's devotee entered his tent and there plunged a dagger in the Guru's abdomen. The Guru reacted by chopping off the head of the assailant. It is said the Emperor Bahadur Shah sent an English surgeon to dress the wound of the Guru. The wound however did not heal. The Guru now knowling that his end was approaching called a special congregation on 7th October, 1708. He told his Khalsa that he would now abolish the personal Guruship and the Adi Granth would become the Guru Granth Sahib and be perpetual Guru of the Sikhs. He declared:

"By divine command, I have proclaimed the Faith,
All Sikhs are now commanded to regard the Granth as Guru;
Consider the Granth as the visible body of the Guru;
Those whose mind is clean, will find the Guru in the Word."

The place where Guru Gobind Singh was cremated is now a Gurdawara and called Takht Sri Hazur Sahib, Nander.

His Personality

Like his father, Guru Gobind Singh was a man of moral ideals and equally fearless in defending them. His personal example inspired many of his devotees to consider death for a worthy cause as the noblest goal of their lives. His creation of the Khalsa Panth was an act of great daring and foresight. Sri Aurobindo Ghosh wrote in this connection: "The Khalsa was an astonishingly original and novel creation with its face turned to the future, not the past." The Guru did not aspire to personal power or glory, but for a just society and human dignity. His stand was based on moral ethics and open diplomacy. He also demonstrated the democratic spirit which made him obey the commands of the Khalsa. He established the institution of *Gurmatta* (unanimous decision of the Khalsa council) which was binding on all Sikhs including the Guru. Daulat Rai, when contrasting Guru Gobind Singh with Shivaji—both opposed to Aurangzeb,—said that Shivaji's main claim was to found a Maratha Empire, while Guru Gobind Singh had no territorial or personal ambition. His aim was for the social and moral uplift of all and free the country from oppressive rule, also Shivaji's strategy was based on political expediency and opportunism, while the Guru's methods were open and ethical. Perhaps, his great merit was that while being a family-man, he was able to remain unattached. He treated his Sikhs as his own family that is why his Sikhs were ready to die for him.

Here are the views of some non-Sikhs on the many-sided personality of Guru Gobind Singh. Sayyad Mohammed Latif wrote: "He was a law-giver in the pulpit, a champion in the field, a king on the *masnad* (throne), and a faqir in the society of the Khalsa.' Prof. I.B. Banerjee remarked: "(Guru Gobind Singh) who preached that `the temple and the mosque are the same' was not the enemy of any community or class. . . He left leadership to the collective wisdom of the community, knowing well that it would throw up its own leaders in times of need none but a person of saintly disposition, highly spiritual and with a complete resignation to the will of God, could have behaved as he did during the various crises in his life." The late Dr. Zakir Hussain, a former President of the Indian Republic, paid a tribute to Guru Gobind Singh as follows: "Men of Guru Gobind Singh's vision and wisdom, courage and faith are rarely born. There is hardly a sacrifice which this son of God did not offer his Maker. He sacrificed his own father, his sons and many beloved followers and comrades in arms. He was for ever on the move, enduring all manners of hardship, betrayal and suffering in the process. His life knew no moments of spiritual weakening or lack of will. History always honours the hero who remained steadfast to his ideals and gave battle to the forces of evil. . . . As long as the cause of unborn fear and hatred is alive in man, so long must the quiet and unmistakable voice of conscience, one that brooks no compromise under political threat or pressure be listend to within. So long as a disgust for social inequality, religious fanaticism, hollow ceremonies and rites, remain an active condition of the mind, the world can never be allowed to forget the name of Guru Nanak and his supreme successor Guru Gobind Singh."

His Message

Guru Gobind Singh was a practical philosopher. His way to God is through universal love. He wrote:

> "Listen for once and all, the supreme truth which I declare is:
> That those who love all of God's creation will merge in the Lord."

It is love that forms the basis for peace, freedom, equality, and the hope of one unified world. This is the love which won Buddhu Shah, General Sayyad Khan, Nabi Khan and Ghani Khan to the cause and the mission of Guru Gobind Singh.

Guru Gobind Singh rejected ritual and the formalism of religion. True holiness or coming nearer to God is through serving one's fellow-mem. Vigils, fasts or penances are of no avail. They inflate the Ego. True devotion is of humility and selflessness.

The Guru also outlined his pattern for the ideal man—a person who fights against evil within himself and in the world outside. Such a person cannot be an ascetic; he has to be a man of action—a *Karam-Yogi*--a person keen on reform of himself and his community. Such a person has certain values which he tries best to follow in day-to day life. The values are of truthfulness, compassion, courage, discipline and sacrifice. They can all be learnt in the company of the good and the holy. The Guru believed in *Degh* (Free Kitchen or charity) and *Tegh* (sword or courage). Many individual Sikhs of his time, ran personal free kitchens in their own houses for the benefit of the needy.

Some people think that Guru Gobind Singh's message is different form that of the first, five Gurus. They say that while Guru Nanak and his immediate successore preached love and peace, Guru Gobind Singh preached revolt and militarism. This is not correct. All the Gurus had the same message. Guru Nanak and all the other Gurus preached a doctrine of self-surrender and sacrifice. Guru Nanak wrote:

> "If you want to play the game of love,
> Come to my faith with your head on your plam;
> Once you step on to this path, have no
> Hesitations in surrendering your head." (AG, 1412)

Similarly, Guru Arjan sang:

"First accept death; give up the desire for living; become
As the dust at the feet of all, then come to me." (AG, 1102)

The Guru wanted committed Sikhs, those who would be ready to
die for the cause. Guru Arjan gave his life, but did not renounce his
principles, so did Guru Tegh Bahadur. Then the times changed. During
the reign of Aurangzeb, the problem became one of survival. Should they
die fighting or should they die quietly like sheep? Guru Gobind Singh
liked the first option. He preferred to die fighting:

"when the end of my life comes,
I would like to die fighting on the battle-field of life."

Finally, Guru Gobind Singh's message is one of optimism, of the
victory of good over evil. Victory comes to those who are truthful and
fearless. He composed the greeting of "The Khalsa is the Khalsa thus:
God Victory is God's!" Rabindra Nath Tagore sums up the message of
Guru Gobind Singh in the first person, as under:

"I will firmly control
The wild horse of blind fate;
Taking its reins in my hands,
I will overcome all danger and trouble;
I will make it run my own way
Against all odds and obstructions . . .
Fear no more and doubt no more,
Let there be no hesitation;
I have attained the Truth; I have laid the Path;
All mankind treks to follow me,
Caring not for life or death."

Notes

1. Moreland: The agrarian system of Muslim India, p. 67.
2. M. Latif: History of the Punjab.
3. Adi Granth pp. 360-417, 722.
4. Harbans Singh: Perspective on Guru Nanak, P. 426.
5. Selections from the Sacred writings of the Sikhs' Introduction, p. 107
   UNESCO.

101

6. See Sidh-gosht, Adi Granth, p. 973.
7. Moreland: The Agrarian System of Muslim India, p. 250.
8. There is a difference of opinion among biographies with regard to the years of journey of Guru Nanak. H.R. Gupta in his "History of the Sikh Guru" mentions 1499-1521, S. S. Kolhi in his "Travels of Guru Nanak" indicates 1495-1521; Trilochan Singh writes in his "Life of Guru Nanak" 1505-1522, Dr. Sahib Singh mentions in his book on "Guru Nanak" 1508-1521. I have followed Sahab Singh's version, as at appears to be more authentic. Almost all biographies agree. The long journey of Guru Nanak ended early in 1521, when he was captured by the soldiers of Babar in the Punjab, and later he settled at Kartarpur.
9. There is no unanimity among his biographers on the date of his birth. Some say, he was born on Katak Poornima day (Nov. 1469), but most of the writers agree on Baisakh Poornima given above. In view of the Katak Poornima tradition, the birth anniversary is observed on the full moon day in November in stead of in April.
10. Some writers mention 1500 and others 1507, as the year of this spiritual experience. The latter date seems to be more accceptable to many writers.
11. For the meaning and aspects of the Mool-mantra, see the author's book entitled - Aspects of Sikhism, Chapter II.
12. 'Krishan-Lila' is a dramatic performance based on the events in The Life of Lord Krishna.
13. Anand Acharya, Swami: Snow-birds, London, 1919, p. 182.
14. For details, see the previous section on Guru Nanak's Times.
15. Dhru, a child-prince, who left his home and got spiritual instruction from Narad, a holy man.
16. Many such stories are found in The works of Kartar Singh, S.S. Bal, B.S. Anand and Sahib Singh, on the Life of Guru Nanak.
17. G.S. Mansukhani, Guru Nanak, the Apostle of love, p. 29.
18. See, Joginder Singh and Daljit Singh "Guru Nanak, the Humanist."
19. The reader's attention is particularly drawn to the stories of Nurshah of Kamrup and the dancing girls of the court of Raja Shivnabh of Ceylon.
20. Gurmukhi literally means 'coming from the Guru's mouth.'
21. For the details of the early life of Amardas, please see the next section.
22. For the early life of Jetha, please see the next section (Guru Ramdas).
23. The missionary order of manjis as supplanted by the new mass and

organisation. Manjidar were the missionaries appointed by Guru Amardas.

24. G.S. Mansukhani & S.S. Kohli: Guru Gobind Singh and his personality & achievement, p. 87.

25. The Daily Telegraph, London, dated 9-11-83.

III

Sikh Ethics

Every religion provides a code of conduct for its followers, and Sikhism is no exception to this rule. There is no formal list of commandments and prohibitions in the Sikh Scriptures. But they have been tabilised in the *"Rehat Maryada."* The Gurus by their words and deeds guided their followers to a holy and purposeful life. Guru Nanak declared:" Without virtuous living , there can be no devotional worship." (AG, 4) He elaborates this idea through the homily of the love of a bride for her groom. The good wife adorns herself with patience, contentment and sweet speech in order to win the love of her husband. Then gives up anger, covetousness and pride, so that she may enjoy bliss with her lord. Hence, morality is the basis of spiritual life. Holiness and altruistic action go together. The perfect man will always try to help others.

The sources of Sikh Ethics are the Guru Granth Sahib, the Dasam Granth, compositions of Bhai Gurdas, *Janam-sakhies, Rahat-namas* and *The Sikh Rahat Maryada* as issued by the Shromani Gurdwara Parbandhak Committee, Amritsar. The Sikh principles of conduct and dynamic participation in secular matters are based on the stories and poems (hymns) contained in this literature.

Concept of Virtue

It is difficult to difine virtue or morality. Dictionary definitions cannot possibly cover its entire dimensions, but they all agree on "Righteous action and honurable conduct." In the Sikh credo, virtue in its essence is love. That universal love which finds espression in the brotherhood of man and in respecting the common man. This love is the source of selfless service and charitable work. It drives out ego, which is the root of conceit and exploitation. In its real sense, virtue means the love of God and His creation. Guru Gobind Singh declared:" Only those who love God unite with God." So basically, any action which takes one nearer to God is virtuous. Guru Nanak says: "All meditations, disciplines, happiness, repute and respect   O Musan, I will sacrifice again and again, for a moment of love." (AG, 1364) Putting it in different words, all that is pleasing to God is virtuous and holy. According to the Gurus, fasting, mortification, asceticism, poverty are not virtues, for they affect the body adversely, as do an over-regard for eating, drinking, dressing and amusement. The Guru lays down a simple rule, namely, "Shun those things which cause pain or harm to the body or produce evil thought in the mind." This rule is basic to the Sikh way of life.

Sikhism believes in divine justice and the morality of the world order. Evil will ultimately fail, though it may often seem to succeed for a while. God alone is the Perfect Judge; He cannot be deceived by hypocritical acts or any cunning of man. He reads all hearts and knows every person's innermost motivation. Goodness is to be rewarded and wickedness punished. Ultimately Truth alone will prevail.

Sikhism does not regard altruistic acts or good conduct as ends in themselves. These are a means to achieve the goal. Man's divine spark is dimmed only by his ignorance or indifference to the force and suddenness of the temptations that constantly beset him; it is this inbuilt weakness that leads to his surrender to such forces and pressures. It is only by association with good and virtuous people that he will feel encouraged to "gird up his loins" and face the challenge of life.

Another important touchstone or yard-stick for man is the quest for "The Truth." The Gurus considered Truthful living to be better than only a belief in "The Truth." Many people swear by truth, knowing very well that they are following the path of falsehood or cant. Such double-conduct is found not only in political leaders, but also in men of apparent goodness and piety. The Gurus insisted on overcoming these negative forces before one attempted purity of conduct. The Guru says:

> "Shun vice and run after virtue; those who commit sins will have to repent;
> Those who cannot distinguish between right and wrong will, sink in mud repeatedly ..
> Shun greed, give up calumny and falsehood, then you may come to "The Truth." (AG, 598)

A common human weakness is to criticise the vices of others, without trying to eradicate them in one's self. One should endeavour to correct himself, before he criticises others. Generally he finds excuses and compulsions for his own defects and lapses. This means that he is not true

105

to himself. Progress follows where one can see oneself objectively. Sikhism itself enjoins positive action and moral conduct. It must originate from good motivation and tend to further the right objective. We do many traditional things, little realising that they have no meaning or value.

Concept of Sin

The general concept of sin is that it is "action in wilful disobedience of the Will of God or the Commandments of the Scriptures." According to Dr. S. Radhakrishanan, "Sin is not the violation of a law or a convention, but of the central source of all finiteness through ignorance or an assertion of the independence of that ego, which seeks its own private gain at the expense of others." Amongst Christians there is the concept of 'Original Sin.' This refers to the disobedience of God's order by Adam and Eve in eating the fruit of Knowledge in the Garden of Eden. Sikhism has no such belief. Man is essentially of divine essence. However, on account of his self-assertion or ego, he ignores his divine source and then pretends to act in sheer ignorance. He then thinks that he is distinct from God and builds around himself, like the spider's web, a shell of the ego (haumai) which makes him forget the God in himself. Man's building up of this separate identity and his own self-conceit cause him to do things which then set in motion a chain-reaction.

Man's ego takes many forms. The most obvious is selfishness or pride due to position, power, money or knowledge. It promotes a sense of superiority within him and also a sense of a disregard for others. This alienates him from his fellow-men and leads to sin and exploitation. Egoistic actions are like chains round the neck of the individual. Egoism is the root of man's evil thought and action. The Guru says:

"The Lord has produced a play on the role of egoism.
There is one mansion and five thieves who do evil within." (AG, 1096)

The five thieves mentioned above are the five major vices in Sikhism, namely, Lust (Kam), Anger (Krodh), Greed (Lobh), Worldly attachment (Moh), and Pride (Ahankar). Some of the others sins mentioned by the Gurus and Sikh theologians are atheism, inertia, deceits, slander and ingratitude. Guru Gobind Singh further laid down four prohibitions, which are regarded as "major sins"[1] for the Khalsa. Additionally some "minor sins"[1] are mentioned in the *Rahat-namas*.

Is it possible to undo or escape the consequences of one's sins? Some methods of atonement are provided by some religions by way of confession, sacrifice, austerities or fine. Generally speaking, the minor sins are said to be forgiven by holy works, prayers and voluntary community-service. There is no particular penance provided by the Sikh Scriptures. Remembrance of the Holy Word or God's Name washes away the pollution of sin. Similarly association with saintly beings removes the stain of sin:

> "Listen, my friends, to the benefits of attending in the company of saints:
> Filth is removed millions of sorrows vanish and the mind becomes pure!" (AG, 809)

INDIVIDUAL ETHICS

DUTIFULNESS

For which the world is the field of action. The Gurus called it *Dharamsal*—a place for the performance of one's duties and righteous deeds. Duties imply obligations—to oneself, to the family, to society, to one's country and humanity at large. Some duties are mentioned in the Scriptures and some are laid down by the State. Man has to obey both, because if he infringes them, he will reap the consequences thereof.

Man's duties as an individual: Firstly, he must look after his body and his health. He must avoid that food and drink which will impair his physical or mental well-being. Moderation is the principle which should guide one's choice in this field. Secondly, man must develop his mind through education and training and be able to earn his living. He must support his family (and his near relatives). Married life is the normal state for an a individual, unless they are either physically or mentally retarded. One must earn his living by fair and honest means. The amassing of wealth by the exploitation of labour is forbidden in Sikhism. Thirdly, one must serve others as far as possible, share one's food and also support projects of public welfare. Voluntary service to the poor and sick are recommended by the Gurus. There are also certain duties required of an individual as the member of an organisation. For example Khalsa Sikh has to maintain the Five K's and follow the Khalsa discipline.

Man's duties to others: The basic principle is that one must so conduct oneself that he sets an example which others can follow. In any event they should behave to others as they expect others to behave towards them. The duties to others may also depend upon the holding of a particular office. As a member of the human family others must be treated with consideration. Neither slander others nor cause mischief nor harm to them. He should be kind not only to his neighbours, but to one and all. He should be ready and willing to help those who are less fortunate than himself and participate in projects of social concern like orphanages, widow's homes and institutions for the care of the sick and the handicapped. There is also a duty to one's superiors like parents, teachers and the Head of the community or the State. One must respect national leaders, obey one's parents and teachers. Seek the advice of the family elders in cases of need. Teachers should be respected for they give knowledge through precept and example. Similarly, one must show courtesy and consideration to the aged and the handicapped.

The duties to equals or peers include politeness and cordiality in one's dealings with them. Frankness and fairness will play a large part in oiling the smooth flow of social life. The duties to one's subordinate include trying to understand their problems, and being able to sympathise with them in their times of crisis or distress. It is one's duty to help any who seek one's help, even those who on account of shyness may no ask for aid.

PRUDENCE

Certain religions exclude social morality and the betterment of the environment from the sphere of duty. Sikhism believes in moulding one's environment for moral goals. The Gurus paid a lot of attention to social reform, particularly in abolishing cruel practices like untouchability, infanticide and suttee.[3] Prudence lies in considering what is right or wrong for society or the social group as a whole. Man has the faculty of discrimination and he also has the capacity to distinguish between good and bad. There are choices or options open to man in many cases and then he must exercise his intellect to find out what is in favour of human sociability and the public good. Sometimes the choice may be difficult, as for example, traditional practice versus moral compliance. In such a case the choice should fall on the ethical option or the one which promotes the quality of life. The Gurus protested against the tyranny of their Rulers and the corruption of bureaucracy, as well as caste prejudices and rivalries. They exposed the priestly class for their greed and hypocrisy. It is man's duty to monitor his own environment and raise his voice against inequality and injustice. He must use his power of reason for the betterment of society and the improvement of his surroundings. Prudence would even seem to recommened force, for a good purpose or a moral issue. Similarly, the social practices which promote inequality among men, the segregation of sexes, superstition and pollution, were condemned by the Gurus, They took steps to remove these promoters of inequality and myth. The begging mendicants pretending to holiness were dubbed as social parasites. The Gurus emphasised the use of reason in demolishing social ills and abuses.

Professional duties pertain to the relationship which a professional person has with his client, for example the duty of a doctor to his patient, of a lawyer to his client, of a merchant to his customer, or a landlord to his tenant. Besides there are also the duties of elected representatives or of holders of honorary position like the President of a mutual-benefit Society or the Secretary Trustee, of a temple or a charitable organisation.

The general duty of a professional is to discharge his functions efficiently, and with a sense of responsibility and sincerity. He must safeguard the interests of his client and give him the necessary truthful guidance and direction. A doctor's duty to his patient is very delicate, for he is dealing with a human being in trouble, therefore he must give him his undivided attention and greatest professional devotion. He cannot afford to be indifferent or negligent. Similarly it is the duty of a lawyer or attorney to offer sound advice, to his client. He must not prolong the case to make more money or do any thing to obstruct the course of justice. Many litigants get dissatisfied with their legal counsel, because the latter have adopted unfair means to gain advantage from them. Honesty and fair play are the tests of professional competence.

With regard to elected or fiduciary positions, the duties are even more onerous and sensitive. There is an element of morality in such appointments. The representative is duty bound to pay attention to the wishes of the electorate or the people he is supposed to serve. As a trustee, he must safe-guard the interest of the entire group which elected him. He must look after the assets and property of any Trust, as if these were his own. Though law regulates the nature and functions of office-bearers it is important that people in power perform their functions, impartially and with care and integrity. Office bearers must act consciously in the interest of their beneficiaries and man's duty to speak out against the malpractice of vested interets and parasitical institutions.

JUSTICE

Justice as a virtue implies respect for the rights of others. It also stands for fairness and impartiality. The neglect or violation of the rights of others is a moral lapse. The Guru condemned the usurpation of another's right as irreligious like the eating of pork by a Muslim or beef by a Hindu. Delay and the denial of justice, is generally due to greed and selfishness. Justice must be done with a good heart, and not by shedding crocodile tears. Justice lies in apportioning correctly, what is the due of others, even if they have not the courage to ask for it.

In a wider sense, justice means the non-exploitation of others. Unfortunately in our modern competitive society, exploitation is sometimes condoned on the grounds of the survival of the fittest. Trampling on the rights of others is justified as an ingredient of ambition and go-getting. It is generally agreed that many get rich as quickly as they can, even when this cannot be done without employing dishonest and underhand means. Making a quickbuck is an art which involves cunning and trickery. Moreover, in our present-day society, the rich or the strong often get away with it. The Gurus censured the Rulers for looting the peasants and compared it to 'Devouring men at night.' Moreover, justice in its real sense connotes equity and not legalisticism. It forbids preferential treatment to any person, religious or social group. Justice in its essence manifests selflessness or the conquest of the ego, and is one of the means for self realisation.

TOLERANCE

People belonging to different regions and faiths have different customs, habits and manners. it is therefore necessary that the individual should not be upset by them. He must accept non-conformity and diversity as an inescapable fact of life. However, this does not imply that he should change his stand because of others. He must remain firm in his own convictions and make no compromise on principles; he must control any feeling of prejudice or violence when he sees people whose manners or customs are not to his liking. Racialism is a prevalent disease among the most civilised societies today; it is in fact a form of superiority writ large. The golden principle of tolerance demands 'live and let live.' Tolerance puts a human and charitable construction on the apparently

110

peculiar conduct of others. The tolerant person does not feel angry or upset. He keeps his cool in times of excitement or anger. Even if he feels mentally disturbed he will not show his impatience or annoyance. Just as a sensible person tolerates the foolish behaviour of a child, in the same way, the tolerant person will be able to stand ignorance or lack of politeness in others. Why should one expect that others will always behave to us as one wants them to behave? Tolerance accepts dissent and even opposition. This quality is particularly needed by Rulers and religious teachers, because without it, they are likely to allow or condone many follies and atrocities against those who differ from them.

TEMPERANCE

Self-control is necessary in desires, words and actions. It is generally agreed that man's mind runs after lower things as a matter of course. The Guru says: "The mind seeks evil things, but through the Guru's Word, it can be controlled." Such control is not to be violent or mortifying like the practices of Hath-Yoga, but mental control through a process of harmony and moderation. Thus man's faculties are rightly channelised and gently guided. This method is natural—Sahaj—and not forced or punitive. Guru Amardas has advised in his "Anand"[4] how to regulate the human organs of action for high and noble tasks. The eyes, the ears, the tongue, the hands and feet are to be used for good purposes to act at the right moment. Temperance is like a fence which prevents one from straying into the wilderness. It is the golden mean between self-indulgence and rigid regimentation. Temperance is just the right way for the householder. He should enjoy the normal comforts and amenities of life, but at the same time, he must keep his passion and desire under control. This self regulation would result in a balanced and harmonious existence.

SIKH VIRTUES

The virtues recommended by the Scriptures are many, but five of them, corresponding to the Five vices are regarded as major virtues. These five are Chastity, Patience, Contentment, Detachment and Humility.

1. Chastity

Chastity or continence, is emphasised in Sikhism, because in the

111

human body lies the divine presence and as such, the body has to be kept clean and perfect. Those things which harm the body or cause sickness and disease have to be scrupulously avoided. Sex is to be limited to one's wife. Pre-marital or extra-marital sex is forbidden to a Sikh. He should consider females older to him as his mother, equal to him as a sister, and younger than him as a daughter. He should never entertain evil thoughts in the company of women. Marriage is a sacrament and the purpose thereof is companionship and help on the spiritual path, rather than sexual enjoyment. The marriage ideal is summed up in the maxim: 'one soul in two bodies.' Fidelity to one's married partner is the essence of continence. Monogamy is the rule in Sikhism.

In order to avoid evil thoughts, one should keep away from obscene books, nasty plays and films, and sexy music. Drinking of alcoholic beverages and wines or the wearing of scanty or flashy dresses and dancing of men and women together is prohibited for the Sikhs. The Guru says:

> "O Lust! You consign people to hell and to the cycle of transmigration,
> You cheat all minds, influence the three worlds and destroy all contemplation and culture;
> Your pleasure is momentary, you make one fickle and poor and punish the high and the low;
> I have overcome your fear by associating with saintly persons and taking shelter with God!" (AG, 1358)

Even in married life, sex is to be mutually regulated. Those who are spiritually inclined, consider the sublimation of sex into divine love as a great virtue.

2. Patience

Patience implies forbearance in the face of provocation. Some say that it is natural to be angry, but one should think twice before giving vent to anger. Patience gives moral courage to bear the unexpected, such as sudden hardships and sorrows. Guru Amardas says:

> "There is no greater penance than patience, no greater happiness than contentment, no greater evil than greed, no greater virtue than mercy, and no more potent weapon than forgiveness."

112

It may be noted that saints and great men are tested by God through the fire of suffering, though they have not done any thing to deserve that suffering. The challenge of life are intended to evaluate the mettle of man. Even the performance of duty may involve the facing of difficulties and personal injury, but that is no excuse for shirking one's duty. One must pray for God's help and grace to overcome the difficulties.

There are people, who are in a position to injure or even to crush their opponents with the power they possess, but they control resentment and anger, because they firmly believe that if another loses his head, they should not lose theirs. Moreover patience keeps their mental faculties in balance. Their minds are tranquil. They do not cry or rail bitterly against their enemies or at God for their misfortunes or deprivation. They maintain their peace of mind and keep calm when faced by threats or tragedy:

"Patience is the sustenance of angelic beings!" (AG, 83)

3. Contentment

Contentment is an attitude of mind which accepts victory or defeat in the same way. A contended man is active; he tries his best to go forward, but he does not despair if he cannot achieve what he wants. Contentment has no place for fear, fatalism, inertia or sloth. Guru Nanak tells us of a contented person in the following lines:

"They (the contented ones) do not tread the path of evil, but do good and practise righteousness;
They loosen worldly attachments and eat and drink in moderation." (AG, 467)

The contented man is free from envy, jealousy and greed. He is frugal and thrifty. He may have his ambitions, but he knows that every one does not get every thing. The Guru says:

"No one feels satisfied without contentment." (AG, 275)

Contentment does not mean a compromise with poverty and privation. In the modern world, the common man has opportunities for

113

self-advancement and affluence. He must develop his own potentialities and work hard to move forward; at the same time, he should not become proud through his achievement or feel frustrated in case of failure. God is the ultimate arbiter of man's destiny, and He will not leave 'an iota of a man's effort uncompensated.' Unfortunately, in this modern competitive world, one seems to keep multiplying one's needs and commitments, in order to keep up with the Jones, thus only adding to one's tensions and difficulties. The contented man knows the limits of his own needs and so does not feel frustrated if he is unable to get what his neighbour or friend has, in spite of his best efforts.

Truly conceited people realise the distinctions between means and ends. Wealth and position are the means and not the ends of life. If one has a large amount of wealth, then some must be devoted to the benefit of the community and for altruistic purposes. The hoarding of wealth and the prestige of office are not to be used as means for self-aggrandisement or inflation of the ego.

4. Detachment

Detachment implies an ever increasing non-attachment to all things of a material nature. It does not imply renunciation or asceticism or indifference to the world in which we live. It implies devotion to duty and the performance of the chores of daily life. The Sikh serves the family and the community, but he does not get deeply involved in their problems. His attitude is that of a nurse attending a patient. She ministers to their care and comfort, but maintains her distance. Similarly, a Sikh has to live the life of a family-man* at the same time, he ought to adopt an attitude as that of a trustee in reference to his near and dear ones. Bhai Gurdas explains this attitude thus:

"Thue Sikh is the living yogi, for he lives unattached in the midst of Maya."[5] (Var, 29-15)

Guru Nanak has given the example of the lotus in the pond which is unaffected by the mud or the movement of the water. In the same way, the 'detached' individual keeps himself away from worldly things. They live in the world, but are not involved in worldliness. They keep their heads high and look to a more spiritual goal.

Here is a story which reveals how detachment is possible in normal life. A Ruler once asked a saint to tell him how he could practise detachment. The holy man told the king that he had just one week more to live, that his death would occur after that period. The king believed the holy man, and fearing death, led a good life, doing his duty, avoiding evil things and constantly thinking of his coming death. After the week when he did not die as forecast, the holy man returned to the king's palace and asked him how he has passed the seven days. The king replied that he had spent that period like a traveller in an inn. He had done his duties as usual, but his mind was not involved in the routine. He had avoided doing any thing wrong, fearing that God would call him to account after his end. He had also prayed as much as he could during this period. The holy man told the king that this was what was meant "practising detachment in life."

5. Humility

The individual alone, must overcome his own ego and pride. This is most easily done on the path of humility, regarding oneself as the lowest of the low and considering all others as being superior. The humble man, will serve others without material motive or the expectation of reward. He does this through his love of God and man. God is present in every living soul, and therefore to injure the feelings of another person is to hurt the God in him. Those who are vain and the haughty have an inflated ego and as such do not mind exploiting their fellow-men. Even some holy men are not free from pride and prejudice. Guru Tegh Bahadur warned pious people of that pride, which is subtle and unobstrusive.

Modesty is generally appreciated as a virtue. A tree laden with fruit bends downward. Humility is not depreciation of oneself, but rather a recognition of one's own faults and of how much one falls short of the ideal. It was a practice among the Sikhs before Guru Gobind Singh, to greet each other by touching the other's feet. This was an expression of the Sikh's humility. In the Sikh religion, the opportunity to touch the feet of saintly beings or even the dust of the feet of the congregation, is regarded as a great blessing. The Gurus in their compositions have called themselves 'unworthy and without merit.' This reflects their own sense of humility. Guru Ramdas says:

"O my Master. I am silly, save me, O my Lord-God!
Thy slave's praise in thine own glory!" (AG, 166)

CORRECTIVES / RESOURCES

In order to develop virtues, one must also utilize other resources, like self-discipline, moral reason, natural suffering and the company of saintly beings.

(i) Self-discipline

Forced regulation due to fear or guilt feeling cannot be called self-discipline. Self-discipline comes from within. It is natural and gentle and comes spontaneously like water from a spring. It emanates from creative love- the love of man for God. Jut as a child has his father as his ideal, so the seeker of "The Truth" has God as his ideal. He wants to be like Him! Truthful, Just, Generous and Compassionate, in short at one with His virtues. This all-embracing love leads man to think about the welfare of God's creation and the uplift of his fellow-men. The lure of material possessions is instinctive, but a seeker wants these things not for his own pride or display, but for sharing them with others. The sharing or giving principle is the essence of self-discipline. It is as natural as a child's love for his father or the sharing of sweets and chocolates with friends.' The Guru says:

> "With self-discipline and the control of desire, we forsake vice and see the miracle of man's perfection." (AG, 343)
> "Control your craving, and wisdom will dawn on you; this wisdom will express itself in deeds." (AG, 878)

(ii) Moral reason

God's divine essence in man manifests itself as moral reasoning. The popular word for it is conscience. The conscience is independent of any religion or belief. Even those who have no religion possess conscience; they know what is wrong and what is right. But this does not mean that religion is not necessary for an individual. Sikhism believes that man has both reason and conscience to guide him, qualities which other animals seem to lack. In the struggle between good and bad, it is man's inner voice which suggests him the correct course to follow. However, many people stifle their consciences or turn a deaf ear to it. The Guru says:

> "The mind knows every thing, and does evil wilfully;

116

How can one get peace, when with torch in hand, one falls into the well!" (AG, 1376)

Conscience is the guide to good character and noble action. The Guru says:

"Without developing a moral conscience. salvation can not be attained; the egoist wanders aimlessly like an insane person. He does not listen to his conscience; he does not lead a dynamic life. He talks a lot of logic and philosophy, and is stepped in sin. The voice of the conscience is the voice of God."

Undoubtedly, it is the conscience which enables us to lead a balanced and virtuous life. Good conduct and noble deeds go together. They give peace of mind and moral courage to the individual. The command of moral reason is the Will of God. According to Guru Nanak, the Will of God is ingrained in man, and if he follows it, he will be a man of righteousness. (Japji, 1).

(iii) Suffering

The law of Karma postulates that evil actions bring suffering. In certain cases, suffering like a purgative rids man of evil emotions. There is also another kind of suffering which we may call 'creative suffering.' Good and noble souls undergo this kind of suffering, not because of Karma or evil deeds done in the past, but for the purpose of countering inequality, injustice, tyranny and bigotry. The true martyr suffers torture and death, not for having done any thing wrong himself but for the fact that goodness has to be used as the means to conquer evil, in others. Many apparent tragedies in life are caused by this apparent waste of good to uproot evil. The sufferings of men when upholding high principle are not pitiable, but noble, inspiring and blessed. Even in normal beings, suffering is a means to encourage reform. Guru Nanak calls suffering a 'remedy,' because when we are in difficulties, we turn to God for help. As such, suffering has a positive purpose to serve in life. It is pain and tragedy which often goad man to endeavour for spiritual uplift.

(iv) Holy company

As mentioned earlier, the society of those who travel on the spiritual path is a great incentive for the seeker. He can get help and guidance from a God-oriented person—*Gurumukh*. The Gurus have stressed the value of association with saintly persons and the congregation. The Guru says:

> "Just as the castor plant becomes fragrant in the vicinity of the sandal-tree,
> In the same way, the wicked may become perfect if they remain in the company of the saints." (AG, 861)

In the company of the holy. the seeker gives up his defects and vices, and feels inspired to climb the steps of the spiritual ladder through good conduct and service.

VICES ACCORDING TO SIKHISM

The five major vices according to the Sikh faith are Lust *(Kam)*, Anger *(Krodh)*, Greed *(Lobh)*, Worldly attachment *(Moh)*, and Pride *(Ahankar)*. There are many minor vices like deceit, falsehood, back-biting, hatred, stealing, suspiciousness, profanity, vindictiveness, self-abuse through the use of intoxicants and drugs etc. but here, we shall deal only with the five major vices mentioned above.

1. Lust

Excessive sexual activity is harmful, physically, mentally and morally. It gives rise to many psychological problems. The common cause of divorce is adultery, which means infidelity to the marital partner. It leaves a bad impression on the children who feel insecure and neglected. Illegal sexual conduct is due to sex perversion. It produces disease, nervous tension and emotional outbursts. Guru Nanak says:

> "As borax melts gold, so do lust and anger consume the body." (AG, 932)

Moreover, lust creates feelings of guilt. Pre-marital and extra-marital sex produce emotional disorders and often involve lying, revenge and crime. It washes away the benefit of many good things done earlier often at his life's end, the lustful man feels repentant for the misery he has brought to himself and many others. For the momentary pleasure of satisfying his own passion, he aggressively tramples over the sensitivities and rights of others. Some people take a sadistic satisfaction in inflicting injury and punishment in orgies with their partners. Some times unnatural and beastly acts are committed by the lustful men. Homo-sexuality, lesbianism and prostitution are some of the more frequent manifestations of lustful behaviour. All these practices are forbidden to Sikhs. Immodesty in thoughts, word or deed is to be shunned.

2. Anger

Anger is another form of self-indiscipline. It is a spontaneous emotional reaction to insult or frustration—actual or imaginary—which leaves its mark on both the angered and the victim The Guru says:

"An angry man frets and fumes, abuses and suffers humiliation."
(AG, 1288)

Anger leads to quarrels, violence and victimisation, An angry man becomes impatient, peevish or sullen. At the time a person's mental faculties are lost in the excitement and explosiveness of the situation. Anger may be a symbol of emotional imbalance, of conceit or of mercurial temper. The Guru preached that God is present in all, and therefore to be angry with another is to reject the God in him. Sweetness of speech and courteous conduct are recommended in Sikhism.

A small measure of anger may be necessary for maintaining discipline or correcting one who is at fault. Righteous indiguetion for purpose of reform is excluded from the ambit of anger. Anger is the destroyer of social relations and harmony in society. Hatred and jealousy are often consequences of anger. As such, we should be vigilant and keep both our patience and composure.

3. Greed

Greed is the excessive love of money or possession. A greedy person grabs whatever he can whenever he can. It is not that he really needs the things, it is his excessive passion for acquisition and hoarding which makes him rapacious. Generally a greedy person is selfish, discontented, untrustworthy as he runs hither and thither to collect whatever he can. The Guru says:

119

"A greedy man is like a mad dog who wanders in different directions;
He devours both lawful and forbidden food." (AG, 50)

This quotation tells us that a greedy person's mind is restless and excited, and that he often takes what is prohibited to him, this resulting in his anti-social behaviour as he misappropriates for himself that which belongs to others. Greed is a major sin; it creates an instable condition of mind and leads to inhuman behaviour. A greedy man cannot be trusted and as such his company is to be avoided.

4. Worldly attachment

Attachment to the fleeting and the perishable is called *moh*. This attachment does not only relate to wealth and possessions, but also to near and dear relatives. Man is caught in the illusion of the importance of mundane things, he feels that their possession will give him peace and joy. For example, in order to express his attachment to his family, men often do many foolish things and often get steeped in vice. The Guru says:

"Give up attachment, for it leads to sin." (AG, 356)

This does not mean that one has to neglect the family or the care of one's dependents. What is implied by attachment, is that one does not "keep some distance" or draw a line between 'interest in the family' and 'deep involvement in family affairs.' A person must discharge his responsibilities, but at the same time must also think of the things of the spirit which alone can lead to his moral development. They should realise that all things will ultimately perish and therefore attachment to them, will bring only sorrow and despair in the end.

5. Pride

Pride is nothing but a reflection to self-esteem and arrogance. It is Ego, writ large. It includes touchiness, superiority complex and aggressiveness. Some people are proud of learning, youth, wealth, power and charisma. Others boast of the performance of religious duties and charitable works. Pride makes one blind to the merits of others. It produces a false sense of one's superiority and often sense of jealousy and domination. The proud man is foolish and mean in his relationship with others. By his ego, he creates enemies, and also falls in the estimation of others. A man of achievement should not blow his own trumpet; he should feel humble and grateful to God for what he has attained. Pride is both socially wrong and morally undesirable. The Guru says:

"A person who gives up pride in the company of saints is supreme;
He who considers himself as low is regarded as the highest of all."
(AG, 266)

Guru Tegh Bahadur warns us against the pride of one's achievement:

"O seers! Renounce the pride of your spirituality." (AG, 219)

God does not like pride. Those who are proud of their spiritual attainment are rejected in God's Court. Humility is the passport to the Divine Mansion.

SOCIAL ETHICS

While personal ethics ensure the development of the body and the mind, social ethics pertain to man's relations with the community and his contribution to the uplift of society. Sikhism lays emphasis on social equality and the participation of the individual in projects of welfare and community development. The Free Kitchen (langar) is a forum of service and ensures equality of men and women. The King and the pauper eat the same food at the same place. This is a step towards the creation of a casteless and classless society.

Moreover, Sikhism did a lot towards the uplift of women in Indian society. The Gurus removed the age-old disabilities of woman like sex-segregation in worship, veiling of woman, female infanticide, widow-remarriage and *suttee*. Women were allowed to perform religious ceremonies like men. Adultery and divorce are prohibited among the Sikhs. The *Anand marriage* ensures the equality of the bride and bridegroom and their families. The Gurus favoured a compact family-unit. Moreover, self-regulation in sex became the accepted norm of married life.

Guru Gobind Singh laid down the fundamentals of social conduct for his followers in the following words:

"O Sikhs, borrow not, but if you are compelled to borrow, faithfully restore the debt. Speak not falsely and associate not with the untruthful. Associating with holy men, practise truth, love truth and clasp it to your hearts. Live by honest labour and deceive no one. . . . Deem another's property as filth (untouchable). Preserve your wife and children from evil company. Eat regardless of caste, with all Sikhs who have been baptised and deem them your brethren."[6]

Exploitation of labour in any form is forbidden in Sikhism. Every Sikh must help in the economic uplift of the community. The income of Sikh shrines and charitable institutions is to be used for the benefit of the poor, the needy and the sick or for projects of public welfare. The leaders of Sikh society, are also under an obligation to use public funds for welfare of the masses. Whatever a King or the Ruler has to do after the welfare of his subjects is to defend them from a country's enemies. In the case of war, civilians and wounded soldiers are not to be killed.

Universal brotherhood and respect for the followers of other religions is commanded by the Gurus. Sikhs run schools and colleges, where students belonging to other faiths also receive education. Sikh clinics and charitable institutions are not exclusive. A Sikh works and prays for the good of all humanity in his daily prayer (Ardas).

SIKH CODE OF DISCIPLINE

The first nine Gurus laid down the routine of a Sikh as follows: He should get up at dawn, take a bath and sit down for prayer and meditation. He should attend to his job or go out to work during the day. In the evening, he should offer prayers; he should read or recite the *Kirtan Sohla* before going to bed. Whenever possible, he should attend the Gurdwara or the congregation and participate in the service.

Guru Gobind Singh established the Khalsa Brotherhood in 1699 and gave additional instructions to his baptised followers which are summarised below:

1. Believe in One God, The Ten Guru and The Guru Granth Sahib.
2. The Mool-mantra states the basic tenet of Sikh Faith; the Gur-mantra is "Waheguru."
3. Daily recite The Five *Banis* (Japji, Jaap Sahib, Sawaiyas, Rehras-Chaupai and Kirtan Sohla).
4. Maintain the Five K's (Panj Kakaar).
5. Do not steal, plunder, gamble or exploit the poor.

122

6. Do not covet another's wealth or wife.
7. Do not use intoxicants like wine, hemp, opium, toddy, etc.
8. Commit no religious offence (Kurahit) like cutting your hair, using tobacco, eating *Halal* (ritual meat) or committing adultery. If a Sikh does any of these things, he has to be rebaptised, after due penance.
9. Celebrate no Hindu ceremonies on birth, death or marriage, no sacred thread, no *Havan* (fire-worship), no *pitris* (ancestor feeding), no worship of idols, graves, monasteries, tombs or muths.
10. Have no relationship with Minas, Dharmalias, Ram-Raias and Massands.

Besides the above, oral instructions were given to his followers and later compiled by them, in the form of Rahat-namas (Codes of conduct). These are also to be followed. Main points from the important codes are given below:

Rahat-nama Bhai Daya Singh

i. A Sikh should not practise any of the ascetic practices of Yogis and sanyasis; they should not engage in Tantra, Mantra and Jantra.
ii. A Sikh should solemnize his marriage and those of his children according to the Sikh ceremony called *Anand Karaj*.
iii. A Sikh should not give his daughter in marriage to a *Patit* (apostate).
iv. A Sikh should not have any faith in Brahamanical, Vaishanava or Shiva deities.

Rahat-nama Bhai Desa Singh

i. A Sikh should give one-tenth of his income to religious and charitable causes.
ii. He should keep away from characterless men and women.
iii. He should not use money from temple offering or charitable institutions for himself. If he is a *Granthi* or *ragi*, he should take only what is absolutely necessary for his needs.
iv. He should disassociate himself from Patits (apostates).

Rahat-nama of Bhai Chaupa Singh[7]

i.   A Sikh should marry Sikh.

ii.   He should teach his children how to read the Guru Granth Sahib and also explain the meaning to them.

iii.   He should not dye his hair or beard or pull out the hair from the body.

iv.   He should not break his word or promise or commit perjury or treachery.

v.   He should always use the Sikh greeting: Waheguru Ji Ka Khalsa, Waheguru Ji Ki Fateh.

Rahat-nama of Bhai Nandlal

i.   A Sikh should comb his hair twice daily and tie his turban afresh every time.

ii.   He should not listen to vulgar and filthy songs or poems.

iii.   He should cover his head while going out, and while he takes food.

There is another composition called *Tankhah-nama* of Bhai Nandlal which details the minor lapses called 'Tankhah' (literally meaning fine). Some of these lapses are mentioned below:

i.   No talking or gossiping during hymn-singing, recitation of prayers or sermons.

ii.   No unequal distribution of Karah Prasad (sacred pudding).

iii.   The drinking of liquor or alcohol is forbidden.

iv.   The casting of evil glances or making gestures to women in the congregation, or the withholding or the misappropriation of the money of one's daughter or sister is forbidden.

v.   Non-contribution of Daswand (tithe) is a *tankhah*.

vi.   Slander and gambling are prohibited.

Shromani Gurdwara Parbhandhak Committee, Amritsar, issued instructions to the Sikh community in a booklet called *Sikh Rahat-Maryada* in 1945, as a result of the deliberations of a representative Sikh Board. This pamphlet contains a fairly comprehensive code of Sikh practices and way of life. Some of the major points mentioned therein are listed below:

1. A Sikh should base his life on the teachings of the Ten Gurus, Guru Granth Sahib and other scriptures and teachings of the Gurus

2. Sikhs should believe in the *oneness* of the Ten Gurus, that is a single soul or entity existed in the Ten Gurus.

3. A Sikh should have no dealings with caste, black magic or superstitious practices, such as, the seeking of auspicious moments, eclipses, the practice of feeding Brahmins in the belief that the food will go to one's ancestors. Ancestor-worship, fasting at differing phases of the moon, the wearing of sacred thread and similar rituals.

4. The Gurdwara should serve as the Sikh's central place of worship. Although the Guru Granth Sahib is the focus of Sikh belief, non-Sikh books can be studied for general enlightenment.

5. Sikhism should be distinct from other religions, but the Sikh must in no way give offence to other faiths.

6. It is the duty of a Sikh to teach Sikhism to his children.

7. Sikhs should not cut their children's hair. Boys are to be given the name ending with *Singh,* and girls the name of *Kaur.*

8. Sikhs should not partake of alcohol, tobacco, drugs or other intoxicants.

9. Sikhs should live on money that has been honestly earned.

10. Sikhs should not commit adultery.

11. A Sikh should live his life from birth to death according to the tenets of his faith.

12. Any clothing may be worn by a Sikh, provided it includes a turban (for males), and shorts or similar garment.

The above instructions can be divided into two heads, namely religious or social. The religious commandments are meant to preserve the Sikh tenets and practices, while the social instructions are intended to make the Sikh a responsible citizen. The idea behind the above instructions is to make a Sikh both a religious person and a sensible member of the country. Breaches of these instructions or vows taken at *Amrit (Kurhats* or *tankhah)* are subject to punishment.[1] The offender must publicly apologise to the congregation and perform whatever penances is suggested by five chosen members of the congregation. This wherever possible should be some form of manual work. The penance must be accepted without questioning and *Ardas* (Supplication) is recited immediately after its declaration.

THE SIKH CHARACTER

The Sikh character has evolved during the last five hundred years. The examples were set by the Gurus and those prominent Sikhs who have moulded Sikh history. They were the warriors on the battle-field, who would still appear humble when doing their daily chores. By their manliness and spirit of service, they have succeeded in situations where others have failed. They faced a lot of persecution in the eighteenth century. Even during their holocausts, the Sikhs only strengthened their resolve to stand firm against tyranny and fanaticism. Their stories of valour and exemplary conduct are a matter of history. They have received compliments from their adversaries. Qazi Nur Mahommed, the Muslim historian who came in the retinue of Ahmed Shah Abdali to India in 1762, wrote about the Sikhs thus:

"Do not call the Sikhs 'dogs,' because they are lions, and are brave like lions in the battle-field, they never kill a coward and do not obstruct one who flees from the field. They do no rob a woman of her gold or ornaments, be she a queen or a slave-girl. Adultery does not exist among these 'dogs.' None of them is a thief . . . the 'dogs' never resort to stealing and none of them is a thief. They do not keep company with any adulterer or thief."

The Sikhs are generally well-behaved, open-minded and cheerful. They are not afraid of facing new challenges and crises. They stood the shock, atrocities and killings at the Partition of India in 1947 and soon rehabilitated themselves by dint of hard work, perseverance and courage.

The Sikhs are known for their initiative, enterprise and industry. They easily adapt themselves to changes in climate, environment and situation. They know how to maintain their dignity and self-respect and the honour of their women-folk. They are admired for their patriotism and devotion to duty. The Sikhs are good farmers and sturdy soldiers. During the last forty years, they have taken to the learned professions with great eagerness and have made their mark both on the regional and national levels. Many of them are working as physicians, engineers, teachers, mechanics and technicians not only in India, but also in many foreign countries. Their success in the Far East, Kenya, Great Britain, Canada and the United States of America has not only helped the Punjab economically, but also added to the affluence of the countries where they have settled. Whereever they have emigrated, they have set up their religious,

126

cultural and educational institutions and also helped various community projects for the welfare of the local people. It may be noted that about 10 percent of the total number of Sikhs live abroad. In recent years, the Sikhs had to face many new problems, particularly the political and linguistic issues and the future of the Punjab. After partition, they met the pressure of the growing population of the Punjab by a Green Revolution which resulted in the increased out-put of food grains and milk. By sheer hard work and determination, they made Punjab the most prosperous province of India. They have rightly earned the distinction of being the best farmers and the best soldiers of India.

Notes

1. Minor sins are called "Tankhah," and call for award of penalties.
2. Major sins are called "Kurahit," and requireRebaptism (Amrit)
3. Sattee is the practice of a widow burning herself on or after the death of her husband.
4. See Anand Sahib.
5. Maya is the name of the Hindu goddess of wealth or materialism.
6. Macauliffe: The Sikh Religion, Vol V, p. 105.
7. Many of the Rahat-namas repeat common instinctions; these have been excluded.
8. Sikh Rahat-Maryada, Shromani G.P. Committee, Amritsar, Publication 1978, p. 34.

IV

Sikh Scriptures

A. Guru Granth Sahib

Its Compilation

Guru Amardas had declared the distinctiveness of Sikhism as a new Faith. He had established a *Manji* order to initiate the disciples into Sikhism. He also prescribed ceremonies for birth, marriage and death. Guru Ramdas established the *Massand* system in 1977 and established the new township of Ramdaspur, later to be known as Amritsar. He also had the tank excavated, residential quarters and shops constructed. Guru Arjan built the Harmander Sahib (Golden Temple) in the middle of the tank in 1589, also undertaking a preaching tour in the Punjab. His eldest brother Prithichand, through jealousy, miscopied some of the compositions of the Gurus, adding the word 'NANAK' to spurious poems to suggest that they were original compositions, which they were not. It is said that as one of the court-singers—*Rababis*—sang a hymn composed by Prithichand's son Mehervan, Guru Arjan was much surprised. He then decided to set the true compositions into the form of an authorised book for the benefit of all Sikh devotees; he sent his devotees to various places to bring back compositions of Indian saints and mystics, for inclusion in a universal Scripture.[1]

Guru Arjan travelled to Goindwal to collect the *Mohan-Pothi* of Guru Amardas. Then he took Bhai Gurdas to a quiet spot on the outskirts of Ramdaspur and dictated to him the compostions of the previous four Gurus and his own. To these he added those of fifteen Indian poets and some court-bards. Guru Arjan rejected those compositions of mystics which did not agree with Sikh doctrines. It took about a year to complete the new Scripture. The new volume was then bound and ceremoniously installed in the Harmandar Sahib, in 1604, Bhai Buddha being appointed as the first ever reader (Granthi) of the Adi Granth. The original copy is now preserved at Kartarpur.

The contributors are, the first five Gurus, Fifteeen saints (Bhagats) in the following chronological order, Farid, Jaidev, Namdev, Trilochan, Parmanand, Sadhna, Beni, Ramanand, Dhana, Pippa, Sain, Kabir, Ravidas, Bhikhan, Surdas, Eleven minstrels (Bhatts) namely Kal, Jalap, Bhikha, Sal, Bhal, Nal, Bal, Gayand, Mathura, Kirat and Harbans. Three minstrels (rababis) Mardana, Satta and Balwand, the grand son of Guru Amardas, Sunder.

Its arrangement

Guru Arjan was a proficient and vigilant editor. He numbered all the compositions to avoid the risk of interpolation. The order of compositions is as under:

(i) Compositions of *Nitnem* (daily prayers): Japji, Rehras, Kirtan Sohla (pp.1-13) A full note on Japji will be found later in this chapter. Rehras which means the correct path is the evening prayer. Kirtan Sohla which means the song of praise is the bed-time prayer. It contains five hymns of different Gurus.

(ii) Raga-wise, the compositions begin with couplets, then quatrains, then octets, These are followed by the longer poems and ballads (Vars), then the compositions of Bhagats (Bhagat-vani) pp.14-1352.

(iii) There are the Ragaless compositions of Gurus, Bhagats and Minstrels (Bhatts)-pp. 1352-1429.

(iv) Finally Ragmala—pp.1429-30. The total number of hymns is 5894, the largest number being of Guru Arjan: 2216.

The litho-graphed diction of the Adi Granth contains 1430 pages, with a list of contents, The compositions page-wise are as under:

	Pages
1. Japji	1-8
2. Rehras	8-12
3. Kirtan Sohla	12-14
4. Sri raga	14-93
5. Manjh	94-150
6. Gauri	151-346
7. Asa	347-488
8. Gujri	489-526
9. Devgandhari	527-536
10. Bihagra	537-556
11. Wadahans	557-594
12. Sorath	595-659
13. Dhanasri	660-695
14. Jaitsri	696-710
15. Todi	711-718
16. Bairari	719-720
17. Tilang	721-727
18. Suhi	728-794
19. Bilaval	795-858
20. Gaund	859-875
21. Ramkali	876-974
22. Nutnarayan	975-983
23. Maligaura	984-988
24. Maru	989-1106
25. Tukhari	1107-1117
26. Kedara	1118-1124

	Pages
27. Bhairav	1125-1167
28. Basant	1168-1196
29. Sarang	1197-1253
30. Malar	1254-1293
31. Kanra	1294-1318
32. Kalyan	1319-1326
33. Prabhati	1327-1351
34. Jaijawanti	1352-1353
35. Salok-Sanskriti	1353-1360
36. Gatha	1360-1361
37. Funhe	1361-1363
38. Chaubole	1363-1364
39. Salok Kabir	1364-1377
40. Salok Farid	1377-1384
41. Swayyas Guru Arjan	1385-1389
42. Swayyas Bhatts	1389-1409
43. Saloks Gurus	1409-1426
44. Salokas Guru Tegh Bahadur	1426-1429
45. Mundawani	1429
46. Ragmala	1429-1430

The total number of each contributor's works are as follows: Guru Nanak: 974 hymns, Guru Angad: 62 Salokas, Guru Amardas: 907 hymns, Guru Ramdas: 635 hymns, Guru Arjan: 2216 hymns Guru Tegh Bahadur: 115; *Bhagats:* Beni: 3, Bhikhan: 2. Dhanna: 3, Farid: 134, Jaidev: 2, Kabir: 541 Mardana: 3, Namdev: 60, Parmanand: 1, Pippa: 1, Ramanand: 1, Ravidas: 41, Sadhna: 1, Sain: 1, Satta and Balwand: 8, Sunder: 6, Surdas: 1, Trilochan: 4, *Bhatts:* 123.

There are three rescensions of the Adi Granth: the first original one prepared by Guru Arjan called *Kartarpur-vali-bir*, the second an un-authorised copy (containing two additional poems) prepared by Bhai

Banno called *Khari-bir,* the third prepared by Guru Gobind Singh called *Damdame-vali-bir.* Numerous copies of the third edition were subsequently prepared by devout Sikhs as a labour of love and supplied to various Gurdwaras in the country. The first litho-garphed edition was prepared in 1904. The most authoritative edition is the one published by the Shromani Gurdwara Parbandhak Committee, Amritsar.[2]

The following distinctive aspects of the Adi Granth deserve attention. Dr. Trumpp called it "the treasury of old Hindivi dialects": Apabhramsa, Sanskrit, Prakrit, Santbhasa or saint-language, Hindi, Sindhi, Arabic and the Persian language, each have added to the richness and variety of its contents. The writers belonged to different parts of India and came from different centuries (from twelfth to the sixteenth). If we examine the prosody, we find flexibility and variety in both rhyme and rhythm. Hymns are classified according to the number of *padas* (verses). In addition, we have Salokas, Chhants, and Swayyas, there are special compositions like Patti (acrostic), Bawan-akhri (alphabet). Bara-mah (calendar), Pahary, Allahuni, Ghorian and Vars. The imagery of the Adi Granth is remarkable. The Gurus used images from nature and activities of daily life like farming, hunting, trading, fine arts and sports. The images from Nature refer to flora, fauna, and sky-scape, Changes of the seasons affect the moods of the seeker of truth. *Bara-mah* includes many images from the seasons:

> "When the Lord. her Master comes to her,
> Then is spring seemly, she becomes enraptured," (AG, 1107)
> "As the winter's snow freezes the sap in the tree and bush,
> So an absence of the Lord kills body and soul.
> O Lord; Why comest Thou not?" (AG, 1107)

There are many similes and metaphors which impress us by their originality.

> "You are the cage and I am your parrot,
> What can *Yama* (death)—the cat—do to me? (AG, 323)
> "Life is the bride, death the bride-groom,
> Who will take then in marriage?" (AG, 1377).

The idea behind the use of images is not so much to beautify the poems, as to emphasise the moral:

"Maya is like a wicked mother-in-law, who will not let me make a home,
Or let me meet my Lord and husband." (AG, 355)

Mythological references are only illustrative and do not indicate any Guru's belief in mythological personages or their actions.

A unique feature of the Adi Granth is its intertwining of Revelation and Raga. Guru Nanak wrote of his revelation- during his disappearance form Sultanpur for three days—in a hymn as under:

"The minstrel(Nanak) was called to the presence of the Lord,
On him the mantle of divine praise was conferred.
God bestowed his nectar in a cup,
The sustaining substance being "Nectar of Truth." (AG, 150)

Guru Nanak did not claim divinity, only that he was a messenger of God:

"As the Lord sends me His Word, so I deliver it." (AG, 722)

The Gurus understood power of music in men's minds, it was for this reason that they conveyed their message in sacred and devotional music. This sublime music inspires the disciple to higher spiritual goals. This sacred music, called Kirtan promotes spiritual vision, and is quite different from ordinary wordly music that is meant for entertainment:

"People consider it only as song, but in fact it is a means to meditating on Divinity:" (AG, 335).

The Gurus mentioned the benefits of Kirtan in the Adi Granth:

"Kirtan is like a price-less diamond; it is an ocean of bliss and virtue." (AG, 449)

Kirtan creates an environment of peace and spiritual ethos. It can lead to communion with God. Many people who have experienced this *rasa* (relish) of Kirtan have felt blissful. The Kirtan-experience may link one's consciousness with the Universal Reality, for the divine light lives in the mind, to which the senses are only servants. All cooperate to create the ecstatic state which Guru Arjan describes in the following lines:

"Within him (the disciple) a torrent of nectar uniformly rains.
As the soul drinks, hears and reflects on the Holy Name,
So it rejoices and delights, day and night, and sports with the Lord
for ever." (AG, 102)

According to the Guru, the disciple while engrossed in his reflections of
the glory of God, unconsciously realises his own identity with the Lord,
and by singing His praises, imperceptively unites with the object of his
glorification.

It may be noted that the hymns, though sung in the Hindustani
classical raga with the appropriate or indicated rhythm(tala), create
devotion in the singer and the listener. That is why, when the Guru was
asked about his best raga or favourite melody,he answered:

"Of all the ragas, brother, that one is the best,
Which attracts your mind to the Lord:" (AG, 1423)

Any raga or hymn is good if it strengthens the spirit of devotion and
holiness.

The compositions of the *Granth* are classified according to the list
of ragas mentioned earlier. Raga Jaijawanti was added by Guru Tegh
Bahadur. Ragmala at the end mentions the families of eighty four ragas
and raginis out of which only twenty four are actually used, while the rest
are outside the classification. No difference is made in the Granth
between a *raga* and a *ragini*. Some musical instruments, like the Rabab,
Vaja, Khartal (cymbals), Pakhawaj, Mridang are mentioned in the
Granth. The Gurus encouraged the participation of the sangat (congregations) in chorus-singing.

Its Contents

The Guru Granth Sahib begins with a statement of basic creed,
which defines God. It is called the *Mool Mantra;* it is also written at the
beginning of each raga. Guru Granth Sahib ends with a hymn by Guru
Arjan in which he sums up its contents as of Truth, Contentment and
Wisdom—all of which if practised by the individual in daily life, will lead
to salvation. The last verse is a prayer seeking God's grace, as under:

"I cannot earn your grace; you alone have made me worthy of you.

I am virtue-less and without merit: you have been kind to me;
Out of your compassion, You have blessed me and enabled me to
meet my True Guru.
Nanak says, "I live on His Holy Name, it nourishes my body and
soul." (AG, 1429)

It is difficult to do justice to the contents of the Guru Granth Sahib
in few lines. It is a guide to the Sikh way of life. Its goal is of the ideal man,
who attains perfection by linking himself with God. The Guru observed
that the divine Spark in man, is strengthened through prayer and public
service. Frequent remembrance of the Holy Name may produce godly
qualities and rid man of selfishness and vice. The Granth rejects the old
methods to spiritual attainment, such as by fasting, pilgrimage, penance
and ritual sacrifice. It supports normal family-life and social commitment. It promotes the freedom and equality of all human beings and
universal brotherhood. It recommends leading of a pure life whilst
fighting temptations and imperfection of this world. Keeping company
with holy persons is of a great value to a disciple because he learns from
them how to conduct himself. Such people are beautifully described by
Guru Nanak in the following lines:

"In this world, rare are the persons who the Lord tests and then
welcomes to His Mansion.
They rise above caste and colour, they forsake wordly love and
greed.
They are imbued with the Lord's Name and are like purged pilgrim-
spots, free form the filth and disease of ego.
Nanak washes the feet of those, who by the Guru's grace, adore the
Lord." (AG, 1345)

The message of Guru Granth Sahib is not limited to the achievement and liberation of the individual. It includes in its compass the
perfecting of the qualities of a human being and the ushering in of a golden
age for all mankind. It is important that an individual, through his own
efforts, works to improve his family and community, so acting as a
catalytic agent in the amelioration of the conditions of society as a whole.
His example, altruism and sacrifice could eventually transform the
quality of life for the average man and the tone of society. Such an
achievement, though difficult, should be the goal of a Sikh. Guru Arjan
declares:

"An ideal man is liberated while striving for the salvation of others. Nanak says, I bow with respect to such a person." (AG, 295).

The Guru Granth Sahib clarifies many of the basic concepts of Sikhism. Its concepts of God and the Guru are fundamental. God is the Eternal Unity, Unique, Infinite, Perfect, Formless, Timeless, Omnipotent, Omnipresent, Omniscient, Transcendent and Immanent. There is also a personal God whom one can love and adore. The spiritual connection between man and God is compared to a Bride's longing for and devoted to her husband. It is impossible to know the extent of His creation or power. Whole of the creation is a play of the Lord. The world is a great arena in which God tests the potential of human beings.

The concept of Guru is also very significant. A Sikh Guru is not God in human form, but a messenger or prophet sent by God, for a specific mission. A guru is therefore that ideal person who by example inspires individuals with sublime thoughts and noble actions. A Guru guides the disciples in both secular and spiritual tasks. He teaches a devotee how to link his own consciousness to the Holy Name. There evolves an intimate relationship between Guru and Sikh. Guru Ramdas even equates the two in the following line.:

"The Guru is the Sikh, and Sikh is the Guru." (AG, 444)
Guru Gobind Singh called his Khalsa "Guru-Khalsa".

Another important clarification in the Guru *Granth* Sahib is its concept of "Ego" or *Haumai*. Man's selfishness and aggressiveness are the causes of most of his motivation and action. Self-conceit or I-am-ness gives rise to five main vices: Lust, anger, greed, attachment and pride. An egoist thinks only of himself and his own interest and does not care about others. Hence exploitation, violence and wickedness. How can man be free from self-centredness? The scripture speaks of the cure:

Self-centredness is to be replaced by God centredness. Service to God is also service to man. Only then will man start to think more of his duties than of his rights. He performs acts of charity and benefit for others, so that improves the link between God and himself.

The Guru declares:

"By shedding his Ego, man may unite with God." (AG, 750)

The ancient Hindu doctrine of *Karma* is accepted in Sikhism. It make sense of life and makes man feel responsible. The Guru says:

"The body is a field for action; action is a seed sown by the body; Man has to reap the consequences of his own actions." (AG, 78)

So think first, for one's deeds, produce results. Man has a limited free-will and with it he must do his best even under adverse circumstances. Man has no control over his own heredity, but has a restricted power over his own environment. Man has a mind and a conscience which can guide him in his choice of action. Stifling his own conscience is the same as acting contrary to its advice; he alone can suffer, through the law to *Karma* which is also subject to Divine Grace. Guru Nanak says:

"Births take place through Karma, but salvation is only attained through Grace:" (AG, 2)

The Guru *Granth* Sahib illuminates other current religions. It offers constructive criticism on their practices. It explains their deviation on account of the malpractices of their priestly class and the ignorance of the believers. The Gurus admonished the begging preachers and the Yogis because, by pretending holiness, they became parasites. The Gurus wanted man to put up a constant struggle to face life's challenges, only then would man be able to build up his strength and character. The Guru *Granth* Sahib emphasises "honest means" as the source of earning one's living. Some materialistic and secular activities may also have moral and holy aspects. The Guru *Granth* Sahib also stresses the overcoming of one's ego through humility and voluntary service. Physical well being is necessary, because the body is a temple of God. The acceptance of normal comforts and amenities does not constitute a hurdle on the spiritual path. A spirit of detachment will enable a disciple to do his daily chores, without tenseness or worry. The Gurus believed in an individual transformation through character-development and spiritual uplift. To them." Greater than Truth is Truthful conduct," for it demonstrates a respect for human values.

The Guru *Granth* sahib also stresses the need for keeping of good and holy company as a way of reform for the individual. The Guru says:

136

"Just as a bitter Arinda plant, being next to a sweet-smelling
sandal-wood tree becomes fragrant like its neighbour,
So a sinner, who associates with saints may become a saint," (AG,
861)

No poet can be a stranger to his own age. The period of the Gurus
was one of social decadence and moral degradation. Ignorance, superstition and violence were the way of the times. Higher classes exploited
lower classes. The Guru wrote:

"Greed is the King, sin his minister, falsehood the officer, and
Lust the lieutenant who is called and consulted." (AG, 468)

Even the learned and the virtuous became victims to this mammon and
hypocrisy:"

The foolish Pandits show wisdom in argument, themselves love
riches. . . .
The ascetics having lost their way now wander about and forsake
their families,
All think themselves perfect, none consider their own deficiencies.
(AG, 469)

It was caste-pride and the desire for exclusiveness that led to the
exploitation of the under-privileged sections of society. Even the Yogis
begged food from door to door and then cast lustful glances at those
women who gave them alms:

"They have filth within which is not cleansed, by wearing the garb
of an ascetic." (AG, 525)

Moreover, the priests and ascetics prescribed costly rituals and
sacraments to cheat the people, though they themselves often led immoral
lives. The Gurus exposed their machinationas and advocated the direct
approach to God. God does not need or want incense or flowers or coins,
given as offerings. He only wants devotion and compassion. The Gurus
also rejected the deification of dead rulers, both reflected flattery and sub-
servience. For their bold stand against current evil practices and for the
innovations made by them, they had to face continuous opposition from
the various vested interests. The enemies of Guru Amardas filed a

petition, before Emperor Akbar, that their own religious practices were endangered. The emperor listened to the Guru's defence and then rejected the complaint. The Gurus initiated enlightened modes of worship and service; they started the Free Kitchen, established new townships and constructed wells and tanks. Prayers and voluntary service were linked together to provide a better quality of life for the people. The Guru *Granth* Sahib recommends selfless service or anonymous contribution in cash or kind for public welfare schemes:

> "Voluntary service without any expectation of reward,
> Is a path to spiritual attainment." (AG, 286)

The Guru *Granth* Sahib was formally given the status of Permanent Guru by Guru Gobind Singh and renamed the GURU *GRANTH* SAHIB. According to Sikh belief, The Guru, is not a person, but the divine light within him. Bhai Nandlal, the poet-laureate of Guru Gobind Singh's Court, has given a three-fold interpretation of the word "Guru." He quotes the words of the Tenth Guru as under:

> "Of me as Guru, there are three forms, listen Nandlal carefully,
> Nirgun (God), Sargun (historical Guru), Guru-sabad (Gurbani),
> I hope this explanation is enough."

The light of the Word that shone in the Ten Gurus was their real *Guru personality*. God speaks to man through the Guru:

> "God abides in The Guru and through him proclaims the Sabad (revelation)" (AG, 1279)

The Guru is an encyclopaedia of spiritual knowledge and wisdom:

> "This Scripture is an abode of God!" (AG, 1226)

A prophet is immortal, because he lives in the *Word* and in God. That is why Guru *Granth* Sahib is so revered as a perpetual embodiment of the historical Gurus. When any one bows to the *Granth*, it shows his respect for the message of the Gurus which is enshrined therein, as "The Word."

The Guru *Granth* Sahib is not only a book of synthesising different moral philosophies, but also a universal Scripture due to the catholicity

138

of its outlook and its respect for different religious traditions. Emperor Akbar examined it carefully and found its teachings so commendable that he bowed to it with great reverence and made it an offering of gold coins. It is a repository of many centuries of Indian religious heritage. It is a book of Divine Wisdom and Sublime Thought.

Many non-Sikh writers and philosophers of international status have expressed an appreciation of the Guru *Granth* Sahib. Prof. Arnold Toynbee wrote: "The Guru *Granth* Sahib is a part of mankind's common spiritual treasure. It is important that it should be brought within the direct reach of as many people as possible. In the coming religious debate, Guru Nanak's Sikh religion and its Scripture The Guru *Granth* Sahib will have something of special value, to say to the rest of the world." Miss Pearl Buck, the Nobel Prize Winner, who wrote an introduction to an English translation of Guru *Granth* Sahib expressed her appreciation in the following words: "The hymns in Guru Granth are an expression of man's loneliness, his aspirations, his longings, his cry to God and his hunger for communication with that Being. I have studied the scriptures of other great religions, but I do not find elsewhere the same power of appeal to the heart and mind, as I find in the Guru *Granth* Sahib. It speaks to me of life and death, of time and eternity, of the temporal human body and its needs, of the mystic human soul and its longings, of God and the indissoluble bond between them." The late Dr. S. Radhakrishnan, an eminent philosopher, wrote admiringly of the Guru *Granth* Sahib as follows:

"We find in the Guru *Granth* Sahib a wide range of mystical emotion, intimate expression of the personal realisation of God and rapturous hymns of divine love.

As long as mankind lives, it will derive peace, wisdom and inspiration from this scripture. It is a unique treasure, a noble heritage for the whole human race.

B. DASAM GRANTH

Its Compilation

Guru Gobind Singh was a prolific poet. At Paonta Sahib, where most of his literary activity took place, he employed 52 poets who worked for him in creative writing and translation. Being so occupied by his wars with the hill-chiefs, the Moghul emperor, and local governors, he had no time to compile a book of his own compositions. Later, when some one suggested that he include some of his own hymns in the Adi Granth, he rejected the suggestion, saying that his compositions were not his serious work, that he was merely experimenting with poetry and music, this humility being responsible for the non-incorporation of his hymns in that Scripture. Much of his own literary work and that of his court-poets was lost during the crossing a flooded Sirsa river during his escape from Anandpur fort in 1705.

Mata Sundri, the widow of Guru Gobind Singh once asked Bhai Mani Singh to compile a volume of the Guru's poetry. She handed over to him all the copies she possessed of his poems. Bhai Mani Singh also collected copies from others. Bhai Mani Singh, who was a relative and had been a close companion of the Guru, spent many years sifting the materials and finally compiled a volume known as The Granth of the Tenth Master or the "Dasam Granth," in 1721. There are three well-known editions of this Dasam Granth, one in the custody of Sardar Gulab Singh Sethi of Delhi, another in Gurdwara Patna Sahib, and the third at Sangrur. Interestingly the sequence of composition differs in these three editions. Having had the privilege of examining six of the hand-written copies of the Dasam Granth at Gurdwara Takhat Sri Hazur Sahib, Nander, the author noticed one discrepancy: in some editions there were 32 Swayyas and not 33. So it should appear that some research is necessary to comfirm the authenticity of the text in these Dasam Granths. A work that could best be done by University Departments or the Guru Gobind Singh Foundation, Chandigarh. The present standard edition, contains 1428 pages and 17155 verses.

Controversy started soon after the compilation of the Dasam Granth as to its contents and authenticity. Some Sikhs suggested that certain compositions attributed to Guru Gobind Singh were actually works of his court-poets. According to Kahan Singh,[5] this particular controversy was settled after Bhai Mani Singh's death, when Bhai Mehtab Singh returned safely to Damdama Sahib in 1740. Earlier it had been agreed that if Metab Singh returned home after the killing of Massa Ranghar, the Muslim Chief who had desecrated the Harmandir Sahib at Amritsar, then the extant Dasam Granth would be treated as being the authentic work of Guru Gobind Singh. On this basis Bhai Mani Singh's compilation was regarded, as the authoritative one. However, today, there are two schools of thought—one which accepts Bhai Mani Singh's edition, and the other which excludes the compositions of Pakhyan Charitra and Hikayat as being the work of court-poets. Generally speaking, the Sikh Panth accepts the Bhai Mani Singh edition as authentic. The object of the Guru in writing verses was to inspire Sikhs to defend the freedom of worship by martial arts and to follow the moral and spiritual path.

Its contents

1. *Jap Sahib:* This contains 199 verses which praise the attributes of God. More than 900 names have been used for the Lord; some are positive, others are negative. For example, the first quotation contains both positive and negative aspects of God, while the second contains only negative ones:

(i)   "I salute that God who is Unborn:
      I salute that Lord who is most Beautiful." (21)

(ii)   Formless, Peerless, Beginningless, Birthless,
      Bodyless, Colourless, Desireless, Dauntless." (30)

ii. *Akal Ustat:* This is one of the finest works of the Tenth Guru. The title— "Akal Ustat" means "Praise of the Immortal Lord." Here, the Guru uses new names for God like Sarabloh (All-steel), Sarab-kal (All-death), Kharag-ketu (with a banner decorated by the imprint of the sword). This God is the embodiment of fearlessness and courage. The Guru rejects the idea of any chosen people, that is any group being favoured by the Lord— The Jews, The Muslims, the Christians. The Akal Ustat includes Ten Swayyas found in the *Nitnem.* The Guru rejected idol-worship and also the traditional marks or symbols of holiness. He emphasised repeatedly the brotherhood of man and the need for serving our fellow-men:

    "All have the same eyes, ears, body and form,
    All are made of earth, air, fire and water;
    Allah and Abhek are the same; the Puran and the Quran are the same.
    All are created by God!"

iii. *Bachitra Natak:* The title means 'The wonderful drama,' it is a 'Drama of Life'. It includes details of the Guru's life and wonderful performances of legendary deities and popular heroes. The Guru begins the work with an invocation to "The Sword"—one of his Symbols for God.

"I bow with love and devotion to the Holy Sword;
Let it assist me, that I may complete my work."

This composition is divided in to three parts: the first contains an autobiographical account of the Guru's dynastic history and of his battles. No other Guru or religious leader has written his autobiography, as Guru Gobind Singh has done. It reveals his character through his actions. It also provides a beacon for the Khalsa to follow. Dr. Mohan Singh wrote: "It is a model of the art of self-portrayal and self-estimation, for its self-awareness, its simplicity of statement and its frugality of affectation." The battle of Chandi with the demons and is known as Chandi Charitra; the second part of the Bachitra Natak deals with twenty-four incarnation of Vishnu, seven incarnations of Brahma and two incarnations of Shiva. Though the Guru considers these incarnations, he does not worship them. He declares:

"From the beginning I have not worshipped Ganesh.
Neither have I meditated on Krishana nor Vishnu;
I have heard about, but do not know them;
I meditate only on the Feet of the Lord!" (Krishan Avtar)

iv. *Chandi Charitra:* This details of battles of Chandi with various demons. Apart from the standard version of Chandi in Bachitra Natak which is based on Bhagwat Puran, there are two other versions in Hindi, based on Markande Puran.

v. *Chandi-di-var:* also called *Var Sri Bhagwati Ji Ki* is in Punjabi and contains 55 verses. It is regarded as the first *Var* of its kind in Punjabi.

vi. *Gian Prabodh:* this contains stories from the Mahabharata and also some pithy sayings and aphorisms. It is a book of practical wisdom, explaining the essence of *Raj-Dharam* (political morality), *Dan-Dharam* (the principles of charity), *Bhog-Dharam* (the principles of family-life), and *Moksh-Dharam* (the code for salvation).

vii. *Chaubis Avatar:* Though technically a part of Bachitra Natak, it is also treated as an independent composition. Here are given the 24 incarnations of the Hindu god Vishnu. There is also a supplement called *Mehdi-Mir-Badh,* which gives an account of the Saviours who came to uphold truth and justice.

viii. *Brahma Avatar:* Like *Chaubis Avtar,* but dealing with the seven incarnations of Brahma followed by descriptions of eight kings. It contains 343 verses.

ix. *Rudra Avtar:* Deals with the two incarnations of Indra, namely as Datta Avtar and Paras Nath Avtar.

x. *Shabad Patshashi Dasvin:* This is a collection of ten hymns (Shabads, also called Shabad Hazare. They are for singing in the classical raga indicated for each Shabad. They deal with the futility of asceticism, idolatry and attachment. One hymn in the *Khayal* tells us of the Guru's condition after escape from Chamkor to the Machiwara jungle. In this, Guru declares his faith in the essentiality of God, to care for the Children.

> "Go, tell our Beloved (God) about the condition of the disciples.
> . . .
> Without Him (God), the warmth of blankets is a painful malady.
> A house-holder's life is like dwelling with serpents."

xi *Sri Mukh Vak Swayyas:* These are 32 quatrains on God and current religious practices. The Guru rejects the ritual and hypocrisy of all priestly classes:

> "Dropping oil in their eyes to induce wetting,
> They (ascetics) show people a flood of tears.
> When they know a follower to be a rich man,
> They serve him with dainty dishes." (30)

xii. *Khalsa Mehma:* These are verses in praise of the Khalsa brotherhood.

xiii. *Pakhyan Charitra or Charito-pakhyan:* These are 404 stories in verse, illustrating the noble and wicked sides of life. Some deal with bad women, some with their virtue and valour. The total number of verses is 7558. The stories have been culled from ancient Indian epics like Mahabharata, Ramayana, Panch-Tantra, and Persian works like *Bagh-o-Bahar* and *Char Dervesh* and folk-lore of the Punjab. Some critics feel

143

that Guru Gobind Singh could not have written the lewd stories as he was a saintly person. However being a poet, he was also aware of the seamy side of life, and his purpose in telling these stories was to warn people against the temptations and vices of society. Moreover, there are also stories of true lovers like Sohni-Mahiwal and Heer-Ranjha, in which the Guru praises the lovers. Nowhere does the Guru commend the wiles of evil women or men. The epilog, known as Chaupai Benti contains 24 stanzas, forms a part of the Sikh evening prayer.

xiv. *Sri Shastra Nam Mala:* This is a list of armaments, and deeds of those who used them well. The names of the weapons are spelt in the form of riddles.

xv. *Zafar-Nama:* It is actually the reply of Guru Gobind Singh to Aurangzeb's letter to the Guru to meet him at the Moghul Court. It is written in Persian verse and in two parts, the first being an invocation to God to seek His blessing, and the second, the actual reply to Aurangzeb. The Guru gives a fair criticism of the emperor, mentioning both his good and bad qualities. Outwardly, the emperor was a pious Muslim, but at heart he was cruel and fanatical. With the blood of his brothers and the persecution of his father on his conscience, he could stifle his guilt and talk of peace and negotiations to lull his opponents into inactivity. The Guru emphasised the moral law that all who are hypocritical and violent will eventually get their just punishment, for the wheel of providence grinds slowly and exceedingly small.

xvi. *Hikayat:* These are eleven stories in Persian verse, each with a moral lesson. Some of the stories are the same as in Pakhyan Charitra. These stories begin with the praise of God.

SOME ASPECTS

The Dasam Granth embodies the philosophy and mission of Guru Gobind Singh. It is a gospel of the "Holy Name," which the Guru explained to Pir Buddhu Shah of Sudhura as follows:

"You are born of The Spirit. The ego is not the Spirit. The Spirit gets involved within the senses, it is this that ties it to falsehood. We can only rid ourselves of falsehood with the help of "The Truth." The Truth is of His Will in you. His Will and Grace are the two sides of The Truth. His Grace flows when you obey His Will, it is then that falsehood vanishes and you move into the orbit of Truth."

The Guru's philosophy has both positive and negative aspects. On the positive side, it declares the supremacy of God and His moral law. He uses, the power of the sword against the negative forces, of tyranny, violence and bigotry. His heroic poetry is meant to inspire, not entertain. It is a poetry of higher ethics, aesthetically fulfilling and spiritually gratifying. Above all, it gives a clear picture of the real world, without any gloss or blackening. In the opening scene of *Hussaini Jung* (1695), his words are like the blows of a hammer:

"Goaded by the tumultuous booming of drums,
The doughty warriors gave a thunderous roar.
They jumped and leapt with their zeal afire and all intent.
As they plied their weapons with great excitement, inflicting grievous wounds." (Bachitra Natak)

On the other hand, the Guru's caustic criticism of meaningless ritual, greed and hypocrisy of so-called holy men; is vivid and compelling:

"If one begins to serve a Massand, he says, bring all your offerings to me;
Whatever money and property and have, present it to me at this moment." (29)
"Like ascetics, they close there eyes, heron-like and make a show of meditation to the public.
Like a huntsman they lower their heads, their fixed gaze putting even a cat to shame." (31)

The diction and imagery in the Dasam Granth show that the Guru had a great mastery over different languages. The phrases are neat and the symbols perfect. The word points for sound-effect:

"You discover yourself in battle, the ground heaves under your feet, the guns blast, swords strike metal."

There is both imagery and resonance—an aesthetic vibration, which goes far beyond the literal meaning of words. Just look at the following

145

poem in praise of the sword, in the beginning of Bachitra Natak:

"You (the Sword) are the subduer of countries, the destroyer of armies
And of the wicked. On the battle-field,
You adorn the brave. . . .
You are infrangible; Your lustre is splendid,
Your radiance and brilliance dazzle even the sun."[6]

The heroic strain—*Bir rasa*—ends in the tranquillity of the *shant-rasa* (feeling of peace). The Guru's insight into the psychology of lovers in the portrayal of Radha's mind bypasses the traditional erotic detail. "Man's nature has an exterior world and also an interior world that lies within him. With his outer or conscious personality, man deals with the empirical world, with his inner personality, he struggles with the problems of his own individuality; few men know more than a few fragments of their inner world which is the unconscious, or of lying in the darkness of unknowing. The un-conscious part of human nature is the source and origin of the conscious, of all created things and manifestations, even of creation."

Perhaps some men wonder why the Tenth Guru wrote about the tricks and wiles of women. As a realist, he could not turn a blind eye to the 'goings on' of his age—the intrigue and lewdness and the seraglio, the perversions of widows, the sickly neglected children, the dabbling in necromancy, ghoulish tricks with corpses and above all, the unending procession of astrologers magicians, clowns, vagabonds, drug-addicts, all posing as priests or preachers.

Guru Gobind Singh was a fine singer and musicologist. He used new ragas like Adana, Kafi and Paraj, which were not included in the Adi Granth. His use of *Khayal*[7] was also an addition to Sikh Sacred music. The Guru patronised musicians. Buddhu and Saddu who were *rababis* sang the Asa-di-var in his court. He used poetry for both secular and spiritual purposes. His heroic poetry was intended to end the traditional concept of non-violence—*Ahimsa*—then forced on people by both king and priest. Now the voice of conscience should inspire people to fight for freedom and justice. His devotional poetry was intended to inspire the people for spiritual attainment. One writer has remarked:

"He gave us musical form that was martial and hymnal, sacred and secular, simple and complex. In him, we find a saint singing spiritual songs, a soldier listening to martial music, a householder singing of the virtue, of leading good life and of a painter creating wonderful sound pictures in music."

Finally, as the bulk of Guru Gobind Singh's poetry in the Dasam Granth is in Brij-bhasha, he is considered as a great poet not only in Hindi literature but also for his achievements in Punjabi and Persian poetry.

C. Some Important Sacred Compositions

(a) Japji Sahib

Japji Sahib contains the whole essence of Sikh philosophy. It contains the basic teachings of Guru Nanak. For these reasons it occupies the opening place in the Guru Granth Sahib. It is a treasury of secular and spiritual wisdom and deserves detailed study. It is difficult to say precisely when it was written. According to *Puratan Janama-sakhi*, it was stated by Guru Nanak, soon after his Divine revelation and benediction. Macauliffe[1] however felt that it was the mature work of Guru Nanak, in advanced age, after he had settled at Kartarpur in 1521. Other biographers believe that the verses were written by the Guru at different times and later collected together as a basic prayer, for the benefit of his followers. Japji is written in the *sutra* or *mantra* form, like the ancient Indian sacred texts and contains concentrated thought expressed in the minimum words. It is this economy of words and brevity of expression which distinguish this composition from all others. The expressions used are both pertinent and pithy.

The whole prayer concerns itself with the problems of ordinary people. Its theme covers a suggested course of training for an average family-man that would enable him to attain spiritual perfection. It does not recommend passive contemplation or living an isolated life. It favours man's participation in the affairs of the world, combined with an integration of wisdom and selfless activity. In the very first verse, Guru Nanak states its whole theme in question form:

"How can one be a man of "The Truth"? How can one break down the wall of falsehood?" He supplies the answer very briefly in the following line. The goal is to elevate ordinary people to the mystic vision of God. Prof. Seshadri explains it thus: "The quest is inward and the goal, God-realisation! The sacred shrine is within the heart

147

of man, but the essential precondition for the success of man's earthly pilgrimage is to overcome his own Ego. Hence the need for *Dharma* and the discipline of morality."[9] There is a constant inner urge of the human soul for Oneness with God, for every person has a Divine Spark within himself.

Japji describes the basic concepts of Sikhism: Firstly, Bhakti or Simran (devotional worship) is given as the best way to God realisation. The best time for devotional prayer or meditation is during the ambrosial hours—about dawn. Secondly *"Hukam"*—Divine Law or Will—that which controls and governs the universe, sometimes also thought of as "Cosmic Law." This law brings grace as the fruit of good action, and divine retribution as that for bad action. Man's effort to live a holy and virtuous life may be rewarded by a divine grace which may lead to his salvation. Grace does not come merely by doing good deeds. Devotion and the singing of God's Name and His praises are also essentials for deserving this grace or blessing. Thirdly the concept of the Creation, which the Guru explains, is the result of God's command or word (and the world came into being instantly). No one knows the expanse of the Lord's creation. There are millions of lower and upper worlds. The infinity of the creation and manifestation, is beyond count or measure. Finally, Guru Nanak describes the five planes of spiritual progress by which man may come to God's abode—in the realm of the Eternal. The last Verse (Salok) of Japji is repeated by Guru Angad in his *Manjh-ki-var* on page 146 of the Guru Granth Sahib.

The overall excellence of the Japji is not structural or literary, nor is it the step-by-step progression of an argument for a planned thesis. Its unity is obtained by its consistent drive toward a basic vision or goal. Its stanzas are clustered in groups which then lead to unity of idea. The groups of stanzas deal with one topic at a time, for example, Listening to the Holy Name *(Suniyai)* in stanzas 8 to 11, Faith in the Holy Nams *(Mannei)* in 12 to 15, the discipline of Yoga in 28 to 31, or the steps of spiritual ascent *(Khands)* in stanzas 34 to 37. However each stanza varies in its number of lines and rhymes. Such variations are necessary in order to break up uniformity and regulate the flow of thought and rhythm.

Consider the message of the Japji by taking the clusters of verses serially. Examine how these leads to total achievement of their goal. In the *Mool-mantra* (the introduction) we are told of the qualities of God. This is the basic corner-stone of the Sikh Religious Path. Then, in the first verse, the Guru rejects all the traditional methods of spiritual uplift which

148

rely on ritual purity, silence, fasting, speculation and worldly wisdom. His path to spiritual liberation is by obeying God's Divine Will as expressed by one's conscience. Verses 2 and 3 deal with the glory of God's Will: how each individual has his own way to express his wonder and admiration. Many people however, fail to recognise His glory through their own limitations.

Verses 4 to 7 speak of God's Love and Grace which are infinite and eternal. How can we win God's love? The Guru says that best way to earn it is to contemplate His greatness, in the calm and tranquillity of early dawn, Praising God through singing and reflecting on His excellences, trying constently to "live in His presence" are also methods suggested for communion with Him. God is not found in idols, temples or places of pilgrimage or by performing sacramental rites, but by one's own love and surrender to Him, at all times, every where. Verses 8 to 11 deal with the attentive listening and the contemplation of holy books on spiritual lore. The understanding of holy teaching brings honour and joy to all seekers of "The Truth." Verses 12 to 15 emphasise the importance of faith and total acceptance, of the Guru's message and of Divine Will. This is the process of confirmation and conviction in the Guru's teaching. Through reflection on the Holy Word, people establish also preference for the inner peace and joy which it brings. Verse 16 deals with the stage of spiritual uplift, namely Dhian or Nidhayasan or concentrated contemplation, through which the disciple may discern or learn the true significance of things and find inner enlightenment. He may begin to understand the basis of God's creation; to comprehend the laws of social harmony which are based on every one doing his duty and not interfering with the work of others. A good social order brings righteousness supplemented by compassion. How 'Enlightened persons,' are able to express God's powers! The next three verses (17 to 19) deal with the variety of God's creation; some people become good and wise, others bad and foolish. Some people ask: 'Why has God, who Himself is good and compassionate, created evil?' The Guru answers that that is part of His divine play—Lila. There is a need for a 'Villain', who will try to corrupt people. Only such a challenge can bring out the virtue and courage, latent in all people.

In verse 20, the Guru explains how God's Name—The Holy Spirit, the perfect Purifier—alone, can cleanse man's heart. Man's sin causes a corruption of the heart which can only be washed clean, by His Love and Grace. In verses 21 to 25, Guru Nanak tells us that God's Creation is Infinite. That no one could ever praise it enough. Whatever little we came to know or adore it is only His Grace which reveals it to us. We are all subject to the same human limitations as such we cannot of ourselves come to know the Infinite. He is the only Giver; He gives to us, even before we make any demand. All must be grateful to Him for His Generosity.

In verse 26, we are told that God's Glory excels all things. He is beyond comprehension and words. He is inexpressible. Where is His Mansion from where He watches and controls the universe? The solar systems and galaxies, all sustained by Him in harmony, glorify Him in their Universal Harmony. Our happiness comes from the acceptance of His Will—whether in joy or grief. In verses 28 to 31, we are told about 'True' Yoga, which itself is beyond physical appearance and symbols; it combines the sublime qualities of contentment, spiritual effort, contemplation, chastity and faith. Self-conquest is the highest of man's achievements. As 'The' Lord's agents—all other gods and goddesses of human origin, all work under His Will. He dwells in all the worlds and creations. All those who share in His work, adore Him because they find earthly bliss as they work for Him. In verses 32 and 33, the Guru declares that All Power is His: He is just and true. Any disciple who utters "His Name" in sincerity and devotion at every opportunity gently ascends the stairs that lead to His Mansion. Enlightenment comes not through endeavour, but only through His Grace.

Verses 34 to 37 are important, because they deal with the stages of spiritual progress. The first stage is called the Realm of Duty *(Dharam-Khand)*. The world is regarded as an inn—*Dharamsal*—where man has a temporary stay. As the world is only one stage in man's spiritual journey, he should react to it dispassionately, in a spirit of detachment. Human birth provides the opportunity for man to fulfil his social, moral and spiritual duties. He has to work with his family and others—all temporary links, which make up this environment. Think of the many types of persons whose names and temeraments are quite different, but each unique in his own way. The Guru's disciple must be courteous and polite to all. Secondly, the world is governed by the law of *Karma,* where every action produces consequences. Actions done repeatedly, form habits, and habits form charecter. So beware of your actions for they affect you as well as others; be tolerant and fair to all. 'Remember that the relatives for whose sustenance and welfare, you may commit selfish or evil deeds, will not be there to share your ultimate punishment with you.

"We shall be judged according to our actions;
The Lord is True; His court is Just. . . .
In His Court, the good will be separated from the bad." (34)

The second stage of one's spiritual ascent leads to the Realm of Knowledge *(Gian-Khand)*. For this, all seekers have to learn of the extent, variety and depth of God's creation. God has not only created the world in which we live, but also numerous other solar systems and beings. Sir James Jeans, the great physicist, has mentioned that just as it is impossible to count the number of plants and trees in our world, it is equally impossible to count God's worlds and His animate and inanimate creations. There are as many other earths and stars as there are different kinds of water, air, fire, and beings and different capacities and qualities. Apart form a basic knowledge of the arts and sciences of this world, there is also higher knowledge,—*para-vidya*,—of various cultures, philosophies, religions and mystic traditions. This higher knowledge is obtained through reflection and intuition. It opens up fresh vistas of wonder and of new approach to Divinity. It is only when man realises his own ignorance and insignificance that he can lose his self-conceit and narrow-mindedness, only then he can start to appreciate the inter-dependence of secular and spiritual knowledge and the need for establishing harmony between the two. His new extending horizons fill him with joy and ecstasy, as he then realises how!

> "Many the Indras, Suns and Moons;
> Many the stellar and earthly regions;
> Many the Siddhas, Buddhas and Nathas;
> Many the gods, demons and sages!" (35)

He becomes thrilled by his new understanding of the glory and extent of God's creation and begins to praise God's vastness and infinitude.

The third stage concern the Realm of Effort *(Saram-Khand)*. Some refer to it as the stage of "righteous action" or region of "inward orientation." In fact after gaining the new knowledge of the second stage, the seekers become inspired to take further steps to make the life richer and nobler. They exercise increased self-control and actively cultivate moral virtue. Through their new found patience and perserverance, their mental power and emotional potentiality are redirected. They are able to direct their thoughts, desires and emotions towards spiritual advancement. This stage requires sustained endeavour on the part of all seekers to probe within themselves, to cast away their egocentricity and replace it with God-consciousness, to become a sort of a super-person whose

151

comprehension, discernment, intuitive cognition and understanding are refined and perfected:

"There is moulded in their now discerning mind a recognition and understanding.
Of the consciousness of gods and mystics!" (36)

The fourth stage of spiritual progress is called, The Realm of Grace (*Karam-Khand*). Man's spiritual efforts on their own end, without God's grace cannot come to fruition. He is always a seeker and a devotee whose hope is to receive ultimate recognition by the Lord:

"Death or frustration can no longer affect those,
In whose hearts, dwells the All-pervading Lord!" (37)

Only if he ever becomes graced by God's approval could he become a Bhagat or Saint. In this realm exist the heroes who suffered martyrdom for worthy causes or died fighting on the battle field of life with God's Name on their lips. They are rewarded by God's blessing and are then beyond this world's turmoil and tension.

Noble souls are fearless souls, full of power and grace; they show their love of God by working for the public good. They do not mind dying to protect others from tyranny and fanaticism. They are also delighted if they can guide the novice on to the spiritual path. They are constantly awake of the presence of the Lord within themselves

The ultimate stage is of the Realm of Truth (*Sach-Khand*), where God is always present. Sach-Khand is not a region. It is a state of mind in which the seeker and God are now linked.

"In the Realm of Truth, abides the Formless one.
He watches over all he has created with bounteous eyes!" (37)

Here God and His devotee are joined in harmony, like melody and rhythm. This is The State of Achievement, with all its splendour and bliss. The devotee now becomes the Saint, in tune with Infinite. It should be realised that this stage of bliss is attainable during one's ordinary life. The stages need not be sequential. They may be simultaneous. They occur when seeker, while living in the world and doing his daily chores, gains this higher spiritual knowledge and then so disciplines himself that he wins Divine favour and becomes graced by God.

Verse 38 summerises all five stages and additionally examples the achievement of the seeker, to the minting of a gold coin. The process of smelting, refining, moulding and stamping is vividly brought out. In a factory of self-control, where patience the gold-smith beats out the golden ore of life on an anvil of understanding with a hammer of wisdom, the gold then purified, of by the fire of austerity, blown by the bellows of discipline, thereafter the molten gold is pounded in the crucible of love, and cast in the mould of immortality. In this way the gold coin is finally stamped with the Guru's Name, in the "True Mint." This is the way God favours those who win His grace and so come to supreme bliss. This transformation of human clay into gold in not within man's choice. Only those who completely surrender to His Will are given the chance to be moulded in this Mint of Truth.

" If you wish to play the game of love with me,
Then enter into my Path in humility and
With your head held in your hands." (AG,   )

In the "Salok" (epilogue) Guru Nanak stresses, the performance of good actions, for they are essential to spiritual uplift. Only by altruistic actions coupled with the remembrance of the Holy Name can one hope to win Divine Grace. Our life gives us opportunity. We either do our best to achieve the goal or fritter it away in useless pursuits, this is our own choice. It is possible for people to attain their goal in this life or the next. Those who reach their goal are like pole-stars which give light and direction to those who still live in the world's darkness. Such torch-bearers, inspire many others to cross the ocean of life successfully.

The message in Japji has inspired many seekers of "The Truth." The late Prof. Puran Singh was spiritually awakened through the recitation and message of the Japji. He wrote: "Japji has in it the inimitable rhythm of life, in Nature; it encourages man to flow as a "fountain of the milk of human kindness." Japji is a text for the art of living in unison with Nature and with God Nature. Those who carry the likeness of God within them, dwell in their inmost circle of the family that is Nature. Is it not crude to speak of 'one's own family' and not to be of all families? What is the court-yard which knows not the moon or the mountains within its small expanse? It Is miserable to be small. I wonder we do not suffocate in mental misery because of our ignorant exclusiveness. But by its rhythm, Japji lifts us to great heights. We clasp the stars in one hand and the roots of life in another. In its vision swing many universes. In its sound, live many beautiful gods and goddesses. In its movement there is the thrill of the silvered steps of the myriad dancers in the sky. In its repetition is the assonance of the choir heavenly and the companionship of liberated souls. It teaches no philosophy, but imparts the spark of life. Be it true or false, in its chant is the secret of the future esoteric religion of all mankind."[10]

(b) Asa-di-var

Asa-di-var—means "A ballad of hope;" it is one of the basic sacred compositions for the Sikhs and is sung every morning in congregation in gurdwaras. The *Var* is an heroic ode which describes the brave deeds of a hero. It is generally sung to inspire armies going to battle or to inspire people with martial spirit. The *Asa-di-var* is normally sung in the Asa raga. It consists of 24 stanzas (Pauris) and 44 staves (Salokas) and was originated by Guru Nanak; later, Guru Angad added another 15 staves of his own. In congregation, the musicians sing this var along with Chhants (quatrains) of Guru Ramdas. The stanzas express the ideas in general, while the staves clarify them by example and detail. Social and religious issues are then related, to ordinary life.

The *Asa-di-var* does not tell a story, its theme is: "How to become a spiritual person"—a *devta*. In it, Guru Nanak also warns us against the rituals and tricks of priests and monks. The most important thing is how to build up one's character and how to remove the obstacles that lay in the path of a disciple, the most important of which is the ego, selfishness or conceit. Even holy persons, who are outwardly very good and kind, often suffer from religious pride. Sometimes so-called religious people, commit heinous crimes through self-righteousness and bigotry. It should be remembered that Ego in its pure essence is self-awareness or identity which when regulated is an essential, for it is the basis of one's character or moral nature. When regulated by right motivation and active service, it is positve and beneficial. But if uncontrolled through selfpride of position or riches, it becomes selfish and mean. The effects of the Ego are particularly contemptible and disastrous when disguised by the apparent holiness or tradition, which exploits ordinary people's ignorance and credulity. The practice of humility and love are the most effective qualities for keeping people away from sin, far better than all recitations and rituals of religion.

Initially, it is the fear of God's wrath or displeasure which inspires the seeker to offer worship and prayer. Over the years this fear should

154

become gradually replaced by love and self surrender, so that he loses his impatience with those who are imperfect; he is in sympathy with them, for they are like strayed sheep. Only by self-discipline and serving other people, can one become worthy of divine grace. Associate with holy persons and learn from them, the secrets of spiritual wisdom.

The *Asa-di-var* also deals with concepts like Guru, Grace, Egoism, pollution *(Sutak)* and falsehood. The Guru's personality and message transform the life of the disciple. Guru Nanak says:

"By meeting the Guru, The Truth, is realised;
He banishes Ego from the mind of man;
He gives insight in to supreme Reality.
Only The Guru can grant the gift of "The Holy Name." (AG, 465)

The Guru sets a course of life for his disciple, that of plain living and high thinking. Following this, the seeker's life-style begins to change:

"The good ones, who are absorbed in "The Truth," do service;
They do no evil;
They travel on the right path and do what is just;
They break worldly bonds. They eat and drink, little." (AG, 467)

There is also the concept of 'Self.' Our individual self is only a minuscule part of Universal Reality. It is only by understanding our own self-limits that we achieve the highest goals of our own existence. Through ignorance, we engage ourselves in selfishness and enjoyment, this will frustrate our hopes of a higher life. Man starts this life coupled to the background of his previous life. His past and present mould his future. We have self-will with which we can modify our own conduct. It is only when we attune our own will to the Supreme Will, that we can become super-men.

Now to a summary of the *Asa-di-var* in serial order. After explaining the role of a spiritual teacher (Guru) Nanak goes to tell us that divine wisdom is acquired through intellect. The Guru offers us a vision of a God whose whole presence in made manifest in Nature. The world is not a dream, but an impermanent reality. If people really observe God's creation, they will be filled with wonder. The entire Cosmos, follows Divine Ordinance or law; so should we. The Lord is not pleased by the theatrics of the so-called incarnates, but only by acts of love and devotion.

The religious teacher instructs his disciples to distinguish good from bad, true from false. However, the assertion of individual ego, is the great obstacle to the process of moral law. So that our self-assertiveness should be replaced by self-surrender. By submission to His Divine Will, one may win the favour of the Lord.

Secular knowledge or scholarship does not prevent us from sinning. Ultimately we will be judged not by our learning or status, but by our conduct. Arguing, hair-splitting over sacred texts, the performance of rituals and traditional offerings or the wearing of symbols or other marks of holiness, are of no avail. What counts is self-control, purity and compassion. God knows our inner selves and cannot be cheated by any so-called holy practice. He reads our hearts and is not affected by only recitations of holy texts, markings on the fore-head with sandal-wood paste, cooking food within plastered squares, offering of choice dishes and libations of water, or by the barley-rolls and leafy platters, served to priests for the benefit of the dead. These things are done to win popular acclaim or to appease priests.

Guru Nanak exposed the maladies of his time. Both Hindu and Muslim have strayed from the path of their religious preceptors and practised greed, falsehood, extortion and tyranny. The Guru rejected the 'Transfer-theory' of Brahmins, that offerings given to them, were of benefit to the ancestors of the donors. God will ultimately punish them for deceiving and exploiting ordinary people. Guru Nanak also exposed any idea of pollution, being connected with the events of birth and death. These two are natural events being ordained by God. Real pollution is selfincurred; it comes from greed, lust, lying and slander, all of which corrupt the mind. There is nothing wrong with food and drink. Impurity does not exist in matter, but in one's ego, indifference to God and other people.

Guru Nanak also warned us against lust in sex. In his age, women were neglected and held in contempt by men. Both Hindus and Muslims, ill-treated their women. The Guru praised the role of woman in family-life. Prof. Puran Singh wrote in this connection:

"The Guru transcends sex through sex. Women, says the Guru, are the centre of life here on earth and in heaven. Man is born of woman; he is wedded to women. How can woman be outside the spiritual court, she who gives birth to the geniuses of this world? Talking slander, as is done of woman, is to slander one's soul."

156

Women are equally responsible to God for their actions. There is no reason why we should conduct ourselves so foolishly towards each other. If we are learned, we should not call any one low or inferior. Let there be no rudeness or discourtesy between one person and another. People who are over-bearing and haughty only harden their own hearts. All people are equal and human. It is not right for any one to pass judgement on or vilify others.

The True seeker of "The Truth" welcomes all that comes from God—both good or ill—as a blessing. He does not criticise Him or rail at Him. A love of God cannot live in the heart that loves only itself. Servants of God must content themselves by only obeying God's will and ask for no reward or bonus. If they abide by His will, they will be content and filled with compassion of others. They will not feel disturbed, if others appear to be more fortunate. They constantly endeavour to put their wills in harmony with Divine Will.

Summing up the *Asa-di-var's* message we can summarise it under three headings ethical, social and metaphysical. Under ethical teaching, we find the Guru's emphasis is on overcomings one's ego by humility, truth, virtue, holy living and keeping the company of saints. Even though the Guru also puts a premium on discrimination—Bibek-Budhi—learning to sort good from bad, he emphatically refutes any belief that austerities like fasting, bathing, ritual worship have spiritual merit. The social teaching of the Guru relates to the current trends of the age; caste pride and prejudice, bribery, greed, hypocrisy, the tyranny of kings and rulers and priestly class as all of which were accepted as a matter of course. The Guru pointed to the need of improving of the conditions of the poor and under-privileged. The metaphysical aspect of the *Asa-di-var* emphasises Divine Ordinance (Hukum), God's grace, the wonders of Nature and the pervading spirit of God in all His creation.

The style of the language of the *Asa-di-var* is crisp, and pithy. Some of the lines form proverbs which need to be treasured. A few are given below:

"Suffering is a remedy, pleasure a disease (for in pleasure God is forgotten)."
"Sweetness of speech and humility are the essence of virtues."
"Ego is a deep-rooted disease, but in it lies its own cure as well."
"Learned fools are those in love with scepticism and doubt."

157

(c) The Sukhmani Sahib (The Song of peace)

The Sukhmani is probably the greatest composition of Guru Arjan. It is said that he wrote it in response to request from a devotee who was suffering form physical pain and mental anguish; it restored him to calm and health. The word 'Sukhmani' means the psalm of equipoise or jewel of bliss. It is reported that Wazir Khaq, the Governor of Lahore, whose real name was Hakim Alleem-ud-din Ansari, was suffering form a chronic stomach disease. He came to Amritsar for treatment and also visited the *Harmandar Sahib*. As Baba Buddha pressed his stomach, his condition became normal. When he met Guru Arjan, the latter told him to listen to a recitation of the "Sukhmani Sahib" daily, to gain inner peace. Wazir Khan then engaged a Sikh to recite this to him every day. By and by, he memorised the text and became a healthy and happy man.

The Sukhmani Sahib has structural unity. It has 24 staves *(Salokas)*, one of which begins each canto. There are 24 cantos, each dontaining 8 stanzas. Each stanza has ten lines, that is five couplets. There is also the unity of theme: the perfection of man mentally. morally and spiritually. The stave of each canto gives the gist of the stanzas that follow.

Let us now examine the thought and contents of each canto briefly. The first canto sums up the benefits of contemplation and meditation. It tells that all physical pain and sorrow may vanish through the sincere remembrance of God's Holy Name and that man becomes physically healthy and morally strong. Such people find the inner strength to devote themselves to the public good and develop the endurance to overcome all worldly obstacles. The second canto tells us that "practising holiness" reduces man's propensity to sin. It also provides an escape from the hardships of life. He comes to inner peace and spiritual joy. In the third canto, the Guru states that any study of holy texts, the performance of austerities and various religious practices as giving away much in charity, cannot compare with the benefits obtainable by reading or listening to the Sacred Word. Meditation and nobility of conduct can provide a passport to the Divine Court. Canto four stresses the need for good behaviour, Man is a thinking animal and should think ahead to consequences of his actions. Learning and cleverness can not hide a filthy mind. Keep away form stealing and slander. Give up greed in all its forms and remember that all worldly things come to an end. In canto five, we learn to thank God for all his various gifts and treasures which He gives us. Man should compare himself to the less fortunate. Canto six examples God's gifts to man: a healthy body, delicacies to eat, silks and jewels to wear and pleasant music to hear. Should we not thank the Lord for all His gifts by singing of His glory?

Canto seven dwells on the attributes of the saints: their self control, their love and compassion, their solicitude for the welfare of other people. Joining their company brings hope and peace, they never turn any one away empty-handed. Similarly an appreciation of the God-oriented man—the *Brahm-giani*—is found in canto eight. He is kind, patient, humble and care-free. He offers help and support to all without any inhibition. He is the refuge of the forsaken and the lost whom he accepts and treats like the members of his family. In canto nine, Guru Arjan defines the various types of holy persons like the Pandit, Vaishnav, Bhagwati and touch-me-not, of these the best is the *Jivanmukt*, the liberated one who has acquired immortality while still alive. Canto ten deals with the various types of people and substances, both good and bad. How the conceited men blindly follow their basic nature, while the seekers and seers who win God's grace, attain the goal of this life. Man's powers are limited; the more he knows, the less he knows. In canto eleven the Guru tells us that the meek and the humble win God's love, while the haughty and the vain find no peace or joy. Man's desires are limitless as his cravings are beyond appeasement. It is only when his time comes that he may join the company of the holy and then he gets a glimpse of his light, within. Such a man knows True happiness for such a vision is powerfully blessed. Canto twelve dwells on the lot of the boastful and the arrogant. Self-indulgent money-grabbers waste away their lives in eating and sleeping. If an egoist performs good deeds, he all too often only inflates his conceit. Pride and mental peace never go together.

Canto thirteen tells us of the need to associate with saintly people and of avoiding their slander. A slanderer is spiritually insolvent and a corruptor of all. However, if the saint blesses him, he will get peace of mind and benediction. Canto fourteen points out that mortals, by their very nature, are fickle and way-ward; so no reliance can be placed on them. On the other hand, the holy ones are extremely helpful and convey to their disciples a true understanding of life and its goal. Canto fifteen tells us that just as darkness is dispelled by light, and a track in the wilderness is illuminated by a flash of lightning, so the Guru's instruction opens up our inner consciousness and reveals the hidden mysteries of spiritual life. This enables the seeker to throw away the garbage of worldliness and gather specially good merchandise which will bring both profit and honour. In canto sixteen, the Guru refers to God as the Director, Play-wright and Actor in His own plays, who assumes any role at any time and at any place. He also assigns parts in His play for individuals to act out. In canto seventeen, the Guru emphasises the qualities of a true servant of God, namely obedience and humility. A good master is pleased with a person who obeys him and is loyal to him. So a good and sincere disciple will be able to win the grace of God. Canto eighteen stresses the characteristics of a Seeker of Truth. He must give up his ego and surrender his mind to the Guru. The Guru will then enrich his mind with compassion and spirituality. The Guru will remove his tensions and sorrows and give him wisdom and joy.

In canto nineteen, Guru Arjan warns of the distractions of life. Why one spends all of one's life amassing wealth, which will ultimately be of no use? Or worldly knowledge and possessions which will be left-here on death. People should think of the things that will be helpful to them in the hereafter. Canto twenty deals with the need of efforts for spiritual progress. Meditation is a progressive step on the road to Divinity. A love of virtue, goodness and a remembrance of the qualities that we associate with God, will make one noble and blissful. In canto twenty-one, the Guru tells of the pre-creation state. Before creation, there was a great void. Then God by His own will manifested Himself in His own creation. So the Universe came into existence, where different peoples play out their various roles. In canto twenty-two, there is a short list of God's attributes. He is the fountain of generosity and goodness. He selects people according to what he wants from them. He gives special protection to some but those who turn away from Him come to harm and grief. Canto twenty-three tells us of the omnipotence of God. He created the fabric of the universe; He controls the stellar bodies. Mankind will be forever unable to understand their complexities, as he gropes for clues to their unravelment. True Seekers stand lost in wonder at God's power and excellence. In canto twenty four, the benefits of the Sukhmani are expounded. The true devotee will be rewarded with health, culture, wisdom, peace and enlightenment through the sincere recitation and understanding of this Psalm of Peace. He will be crowned with glory both in this world and in God's Court.

The *Sukhmani* is a gem of spiritual wisdom. Many philosophers and eminent writers have expressed their great admiration for it and Prof. Puran Singh was much influenced by it. He wrote: "I had no sleep for many nights. I thought I was going mad. Such was my condition. The clouds came, the cold wind from the north came. I laughed. My eyes closed. I took up the hymn of *Sukhmani* and began reading it. I went on, it gave its own lilt to my soul. It lent a sweetness to my voice. My face that had been overcast by the dark stain of the sin of untunement began to glow. The stains disappeared. I felt light and gay like a bird, as I realised the singing of the Sukhmani was a great cure for human falling out. That insane mind into which business worries had driven me also comes to nations; they lose their tempers and go to war, killing millions. Before they lose their temper, were they to bathe in this lyrical river of Guru Arjan Dev, the world could be set right. . . . . The whole psalm flows in an ambrosial stream of hope and light from the bosom of the Guru. The glory of the day-break symbolises the great illumination that like a holy numbus, pervades this hymn."

(d) Anand Sahib

The Anand Sahib of Guru Amardas is a literary masterpiece of devotional poetry; its aesthetic and symbolic elements will please the literary critic; its special literary qualities will be mentioned later in this section.

Some biographers have tried to make the Anand Sahib a historical document by stating that it was composed in 1554, soon after Guru Amardas's grandson—the son of Mohri was born, and to whom he gave the new name of 'Anand,' in place of the pet-name (Sidh-yogi). This story appears improbable because the composition contains no reference to any event or the child. It is a purely religious composition and needs no peg to hang on. Its theme is of man's true goal and his spiritual illumination. The word 'Anand' means bliss, so it is a song of man's spiritual achievement, or of being in tune with the Infinite. In a metaphysical sense, this stage is known as harmony, equipoise or *Sahaj*.

Every man desires happiness and joy, but he tends to seek it in things either apart from himself or which pertain to his sense organs. He does not realise that these things at best can only give him temporary or unstable happiness. Firstly, man seeks to do better than his neighbour or colleague. He wants more wealth, power and position. The human rat-race increases both avarice and greed, it inflates the ego and often leads to domination and exploitation. Even after gaining what he has set his mind to, he is afraid of losing what he has obtained. This fear of a possible loss creates tensions in his mind, so that he becomes unable to enjoy that which he already has. Additionally there is the fear of some one doing better, so he tries to keep others at bay. All this destroys his peace of mind and sense of achievement, so that in spite of his power and position, he inwardly feels dissatisfied and sullen.

Man's desires and doubts cast a shadow on his efforts to gain joy. Even if some joy is experienced, the spectre of its short duration haunts the mind and creates anxiety and neurosis. After a while, this condition appears openly when his friends and relatives feel that he is mentally disturbed and unhappy.

The *Anand* is both inspirational and philosophical in its content. It details the pilgrim's progress and the obstacles that lie on the way. The ultimate goal is for union with the Supreme Reality. It is called *Sahaj, Nirvana, Mukti, Sangham.* Sahaj is a mental state which encourages the living of a normal family-life and a concern for social commitment. The requirment is one of detachment; all that one possesses, is to be regarded a kind of trust and used for good and altruistic purposes. Similarly, one's senses directed to higher goals and not only to worldly enjoyment. Regard your body as a chariot, your mind the charioteer, your soul, the owner of the chariot, while your senses are the horses and desire is their road. The soul symbolises divinity; man cannot realise his divine element without seeing through the veil of *Maya.* Normally he regards himself as separate from God, it is this obvious duality or fallacy that the Guru removes. Through the Guru man may realise his divine nature, then he becomes *Gurmukh* or *Sunmukh.* Those who remain worldly-wise and follow their own ego, they are called Munmukh or Bemukh. Their senses—eyes, ears, tongue etc. lead them to mundane and evil pursuits, not towards spiritual effort (Sadhana). So self-discipline and obeying of the Guru's directions is the way to spiritual progress.

The obstacles on any spiritual path are many and difficult. They include human cleverness, intellectual hair-splitting, family attachments, the taboos and rituals of traditional religion, conformity to custom and convention, the unending chain of desire, hypocrisy and 'ad hoc means' for the purpose of compromises with ideals and principles for personal gain, and the many other compulsions of expediency. The disciple in to overcome such obstacles by obeying the instructions of the Guru. The blessing of the Guru will support and enable him to progress, on his spiritual path. Any association with godly people or of doing of acts for the public good and social welfare, also help on the spiritual journey.

The pattern of the *Anand* projects a development of thought. Stanzas one to five mention that Bliss obtained through the Guru, after his instructions are followed. Stanzas six to twenty deal with the various obstacles and difficulties that one may face on the spiritual path. Stanzas twenty-one to twenty-five tell us about the two types of human beings: the ego-oriented and the God-oriented. Stanzas twenty-six to thirty-four mention the various desires that hold man back from his inner quest. Stanzas thirty-five to thrity-nine deal with the correct functioning of the human body and its senses. Stanza forty deals with the benefits of sincere recitation and singing in particular of the *Anand.* These benefits are enlightenment, a realisation of the blissful state and the ultimate union with Divinity. In short, Bliss may be attained through self-discipline and the development of one's own personality through purity, morality, contentment, poise, compassion, wisdom, a loving understanding of others and spiritual harmony.

The *Anand* belongs to the sixteenth century and contains words from *"sant-bhasa"* (saint-lore). It represents the idealism of the Guru and his vision for man's ultimate achievement. Its large canvas covers the realities of contemporary life—including a description of the paraphernalia of organised religion, which ironically disguises the hypocrisy and egoism of its practitioners, under the veneer of outer correctness and cleanliness. The diction of the *Anand* suited to its theme and musical fom—Ramkali raga—leaves a subtle and powerful impression on the mind of the disciple. The diction is powerful, with 'winged' words and 'felt' phrases, which make a great impact on the listener. The 'loaded' text deals with some of the basic concepts of Sikh religion like *Sahaj, Karma, Hukam, Shabad* and *Maya,* words which in addition to their semantic nuances, also reflect the spiritual states of the Third Guru. Consider the polarised juxtapositions, like *Sahaj* and *Sansa* (18),[12] *Sach* and *Koor* (19), *Nirmal* and *Maila* (19), *Sanmukh* and *Bemukh* (21&22), *Sachibani* and *Kachi-bani* (23&24), *Punn* and *Paap* (27), *Har-ras* and *Un-ras* (32). These contrasts all add to the beauty of the composition.

The *Anand* reassures every one that they can experience both joy and bliss, without sacrificing the normal comfort and pleasures of life. Bliss is the destiny of man, Pain and suffering, though unavoidable, do not disturb the inner peace of that person who leads a purposeful and pious life, by obeying the Guru's discipline.

Notes

1. Kesar Singh Chibber: Bansawali Nama, 96.
2. Three English Translations are available, one of Dr. Gopal Singh and the other by. S. Manmohan Singh, and the third of Gurbachan Singh Talib.
3. "Teen roop hai moh ke suno Nand chitt lai, Nirgun, Sargun, Guru-

Sabad, kaho tuhi samajhai."
4. According to S.S. Gandhi, the number of poets and scholars was 99. (History of the Sikh Gurus, p. 592)
5. Mahan-kosh in Punjabi, p. 616.
6. "Khag Khand bihandang, Khal dal khandang. . . ."
7. Khayal is a fixed form of Hindustani classical composition.
8. Macauliffe; The Sikh Religion, Vo I, p. 196.
9. H.S. Shan, Guru Nanak's Masterpiece, Japji.
10. Puran Singh; The Spirit Born People, p. 76.
11. Sahaj; means equipoise, peace of mind.
12. The figures in the brackets refer to the number of stanza of the Anand.

V

Sikh Worship

Concept of worship

Worship is an act of adoration, or of respect, to God or other deity. Different religions prescribe different forms of worship. In Sikhism, however, worship is not of the Guru but of God, of "the Word" or "Nam." Guru Nanak says: "Without `The Name' there is no worship." (AG, 439). In the same vein, Guru Arjan remarks: "I am the worshipper only of the Holy Name." (AG, 209). Some people think that the Sikhs worship the Scripture—Guru Granth Sahib, but in reality it is the reverence shown to "The word" of the Gurus in the *Granth*. The Gurus did not approve of the traditional Indian modes of worship of idols or of holy places. They rejected the practice of burning incense, of lighting candles or of earthen pots with lights, the blowing of horn, even the offering of flowers and coins. Worship is due only to the Supreme Reality (Almighty God), He who is the Creator, the originator of the world. Worship is due only to that Lord who is All-pervasive, not to the multiplicity of gods and goddesses, angels or other supernatural beings. The Gurus criticised the paraphernalia and the material ingredients used in worship. Ravidas says:

"The milk that you offer to the deity has been polluted by the licking of the calf,
The flowers that you shower have already been touched by the bee and the butter-fly;
The water you sprinkle has been spoilt by the fish." (AG, 525)
How can God be pleased by the things which are polluted and defiled!

There are hymns in the *Granth* which clearly indicate the Gurus' insistence on the adoration of the Formless and Timeless God *(Nirgun)*. At Jagannath Puri, Guru Nanak sang the song of true worship—the *Aarti*—in which he mentioned the glorification of God as evidenced by the moon,

165

the stars and the winds, not of the earthen lights (AG, 13). Similarly Ramanand rejected the worship of idols by washing them with milk, applying sandal-wood paste. He declared:

"One day, it came to my mind to see God,
So I took many flowers and fragrant sandle-wood paste with me,
To the temple, to worship the Lord there, but I would not find Him.
The Guru then revealed His Presence within me;
Now wherever I go, in water or stone, I know His Abode." (AG, 1195)

It may be mentioned that Gurus did not approve of the current practices of Hindu devotees like the application of *Tilak,* the obvious use of a rosary, rituals recitations, fasting, oblations to fire, the feeding of Brahmins for the benefit of one's own ancestors or the difficult penances and tiring pilgrimages. For Gurus, true devotion, was the practice of love and service to one's fellow-men. Real worship is inward and outward, internal and external. The seeker has to initiate the intense search within in order to discover the God in him, while on the outside, his efforts in noble conduct become an act of prayer in the service of God's creation. He finds God in the outer and inner world. This gives him a sense of peace and joy.

Sikh worship takes two forms—private and public. Private devotion is done at home through the understanding recitation of daily prayers and readings from Gurbani. Some Sikhs also do Kirtan at home and meditate for short periods at convenient times. Public worship is done at the Gurdwara with the sangat (group of disciples or congregation). The history of the institution of the Gurdwara and the later enlargements of its role, indicate the numerous activities of Sikhs, both in the religious and social fields.

(a) Temple Worship: The Gurdwara

During his missionary tours, Guru Nanak attracted many seekers of "the Truth" who later became his disciples (Sikhs). He established sangats (Congregations) in many centres under the guidance of local devotee, who in turn, held religous gatherings from time to time. After settling at Kartarpur, Guru Nanak held prayers in his own house where his followers gathered, both morning and evening. His house became a Dharamsal (forum for the practice of *Dharama* or righteousness). Such

166

was the beginning of the Gurdwara (Guru's door). Here, hymns in praise of God were sung by Guru Nanak while Mardana accompanied him on his rebeck. *Japji* was recited in the morning and Sodar in the evening. Such congregations were later held in the homes of his followers.

The hymns of Guru Nanak remained in the possession of his successor Guru Angad and were sung in turn at his house in Khadur. Guru Angad simplified the original script and so originated the Gurumukhi script as in use today. He also started teaching Punjabi to those who attended the congregation. This was the beginning of both literary classes and religious instruction. The Guru also taught physical culture and arranged tournaments, for games and sports, particularly wrestling, in this way physical training and education became part of the Gurdwara activities.

Guru Amardas established the Free Kitchen (langar) as part of a Sikh Gurudwara. A place for cooking and serving meals to the congregation, was to be provided in every temple. Guru Arjan asked the massands (missionaries) to collect offerings and the voluntary contribution of Daswand (tithe of one's income) for the upkeep of the Free Kitchen and the construction of wells, rest houses and other charitable purposes. Guru Hargobind organised military training as an additional activity for the Sikhs. He knew that difficult times would come for the Sikhs, so they should be trained for armed struggle. Guru Har Rai opened a clinic at Kiratpur for providing medical treatment for the sick and handicapped. Guru Gobind Singh made the learning of martial arts, compulsory for the Khalsa. Putting all these things together, by the time of the Tenth Guru, the Sikh temple fosterd a number of Sikh activities: prayers, hymn-singing, the learning of Gurumukhi and Gurbani, training in horseman-ship, swordsmanship and medical assistance.

Due to the hostility of the eighteenth century rulers, the Sikhs left their temples in charge of *Mahants, Udasis* or *Nimalas'* and themselves sought refuge in the jungles. Through this, the scope of the Gurdwara became limited to prayers and feeding the poor. During the time of Maharaja Ranjit Singh, in the first half of the nineteenth century, many new Sikh Gurudwaras were built and old ones renovated.

The real incentive and momentum to Sikh religious devotion, came in the seventies of the last century with the emergence of the Singh Sabha Movement, the Gurdawara Reform Movement and the Akali agitation of the twenties of this century which brought the historical Gurdwaras, under popular control. The Shromani Gurdwara Prabandhak Committee, Amritsar, was formed for the administration of these Gurdwaras under the

Gurdwara Act of 1925.

The main features of a Gurdwara today, are as under:

i. It is a place where a Guru Granth Sahib is maintained and is open to all people who wish to offer prayers at any time. Small Gurdwaras have limited times, sometimes of only a few hours. Gurdwara is open to all, irrespective of caste, sect or sex. Similarly, *Kirtan, Katha, Path* and lecture may be done by Sikh.

ii. The Gurdwara is a place for the performance of Sikh ceremonies like the Naming of Sikhs, marriage (Anand Karaj), death and the celebration of Gurprabhs (festivals). Some times Sikh youth camps, debates, conferences and seminars are held in the Gurdwara premises.

iii. It is a place for learning the Punjabi language and the Gurumukhi script, also Kirtan, if a trained musician is available. Normally, a Gurdwara has a small library of books on Sikh religion, history and culuture, in different languages.

iv. It offers free food and shelter to the poor and the needy. It generally has some accommodation for travellers and pilgrims.

v. If funds are available, the Gurdwara will provide a clinic for the care of the sick, the handicapped and the aged. It will also provide facilities for games, sports and physical culture.

Religious services in a Gurdwara are generally held twice a day. In the morning, the ragis (musicians) or the Granthi, will sing the *Asa-di-var,* followed by *Anand Sahib, Ardas,* the *Hukam* and distribution of *Karah Parsad.* In the evening Rahras-Chaupai is recited, followed by the singing of hymns by musicians or congregation in chorus. Then the Ardas, Hukam and the distribution of Karah Parsad. It is not essential that the Karah Parsad be prepared twice daily. Langar is optional, as far as the daily routine is concerned. Only on Sundays and special occasions like *Gurprabhs* (festivals) is langar prepared. In addition, special programmes are run for important *Gurprabhs,* these may take the form of reading an *Akhand-Path, Kirtan Darbars* (Hymns-singing by professional musicians) or Kavi-Darbars (poetic symposia). Practised speakers are then generally invited to deliver lectures suited to the occasion.

168

Gurdwara should be kept open all day, then the worshippers can come at any time suited to them for prayers. Most Sikhs bathe early in the morning and then visit the Gurdwara. They take off their shoes at the entrance, then wash their hands (and feet) in running water provided near the gate. Then they enter the actual prayer-hall where the Guru Granth Sahib is kept on a raised platform under a canopy. As they come near to the Guru Granth Sahib, they kneel before it with reverence, make an offering in cash or kind, and bow before it, after which they sit in the hall. Those who do not wear a turban cover their heads with a handkerchief or cloth. This is as a mark of respect to the Guru Granth Sahib. No one is allowed to take any kind of tobacco or intoxicant inside the hall. If he has any such thing, he must leave it outside with the care-taker.

All the worshippers sit on the floor (generally carpet-covered), however handicapped or aged persons who cannot sit comfortably on the covered floor, may sit on cushions or stools which they may bring for their use. There are no clergy (in the Christian sense). Any one may lead the prayers. However, for convenience, a *Granthi* (reader of the *Granth*) is generally employed to hymn-sing and recite Gurbani. Some Gurdwaras have paid care-takers (Sewadars), while others, have musicians on their pay-roll. The paid musicians play for the daily *Kirtan,* they also teach Kirtan and gurbani to those who are interested. After the service is over, any one may read the Guru *Granth* Sahib.

The congregation generally elects a Managing Committee to run the day-to-day administration of the Gurdwara. Funds are raised through subscription, offering and donation, surplus being used for religious and charitable purposes. After the religious service, the Sikhs amy discuss any problem facing the community or hold a special meeting for the purpose. The congregation has the power to punish infringements of the Sikh Code of conduct which are called Tankhah. These are minor lapses which are purged by a penance or service of some kind. For this purpose, the congregation will nominate or select the Five Beloved ones (Panj Piyaras) who will call the offender before them, discuss the case and suggest some punishment (as award), usually in the form of voluntary service (Sewa) or fine. Their recommendation is then placed before the congregation, which usually conveys its approval by the shout of the Sikh greeting— *Bolay so nihal, Sat sri akal*. The offender then accepts the award.

Extended Role of the Gurdwara

Due to the migration of Sikhs, outside Punjab, particularly after the

Partition of India in 1947, at least 15 percent have settled beyond the borders of the Punjab. To accommodate the change of living style, the role of the Gurdwara has been modified. Firstly, the religious services are generally held during the week-end, generally of Sundays. Sunday however is not a Sikh holy day it is used for convenience, as it is a non-working day and provides both time and leisure for religious and social activities. Parents appear to find little time to tell their children about Sikh values and teachings of the Gurus in the new system. Sikh youth in particular finds itself insecure in local surroundings and feel the lack of a sense of identity and a direction for their values in life.

The life of the West and lack of discipline in schools and training institutions, constantly challenges them. In a state of confusion, it is necessary to provide them with information on the Sikh way of life and its moral values. To meet this need, Sikh associations and Gurdwaras have to pool their resources to form a "Resource Centre" which could provide the necessary facilities for their Sikh youth. These facilities should include accommodation and equipment for various youth activities, lectures, discussion-groups, seminars, workshops, competition in the literary field and tournaments, in major games and sports. Premises allocated to this use could be used as a Community Centre. Its facilities should be available to the entire community. As Gurdwara premises are utilised only one day a week, there is no valid reason as to why they should not be utilised for the remaining days for the holding of children's Kirtan, Ladies *Satsang*, in addition to providing a play-area for indoor games, the learning of self-defence or Sikh exercises like *Gatka*. Many welfare projects for the benefit of the community could be taken up if the funds were consolidated. Some welfare-projects have been taken up by a few Gurdwaras in England. The Gurdwara at Woolwich (Greater London) offers the following services:

i.   A Senior citizens club which includes a library and reading room.

ii. A Legal advice and Assistance Centre for questions on immigration, housing, property etc.

iii. A Youth centre for activities like debates, plays; indoor games (eg. badminton, billiards, table-tennis), self-defence training in karate and judo; and major games like indoor hockey and foot-ball.

iv. A general assistance program to cover employment, social security benefits, pensions, form filling and certificates of support.

Perhaps some big Gurdwara, a group of Gurdwaras or the Federation of Sikh Organisations should consider taking up the protection of civil rights for Sikhs abroad. Funds could be raised for help to the victims of discrimination, for organising rallies and demonstration for mobilising public support. In this, it could be advantageous to collaborate with other minorities or ethnic groups, for protection of civil liberties.

In regard to the reform of Gurdwara Management, it is difficult to assess whether democratic election on party lines for Gurdwaras committee selection has proved successful, since in many places, the election-system has generated factionalism and in-fighting. Why not try the system of Panj Piyaras (five Khalsa Sikhs) in a few Gurdwaras, the results then being compared with those managements established on the elction-system, to see which system seems to be the more effective for the Sikh community.

The present system of Gurdwara management, based on caste or class affiliation like *Jat, Ramgarhia, Malwa, Bhatra, Manjha*. etc. is open to question, as this kind of management has promoted disunity and discord in the community.

Also for consideration must be the question as to whether religious services in Punjabi should be continued in Gurdwaras in foreign countries. Religious services in Punjabi may be good enough for part of the audience; but most young Sikhs born in foreign countries are not sufficiently well versed in Punjabi to understand it properly , so that they are not attracted to the Gurdwara. They feel that time spent in the Temple could be better utilised in some other occupation—even in the Langar (Free Kitchen) which they understand and appreciate. Gurdwaras are also visited by many non-Punjabis who are also not conversant with Punjabi. Restricting the service to Punjabi means that doors are virtually closed to non-Punjabis, so accentuating misunderstanding and prejudice by the host community. Were the religious service to be held in the local language then the host community and our own young would get a better chance of appreciating our worship, so coming to a better understanding of Sikh character and values There is a case, for making our religious services bi-lingual or for holding separate services in Punjabi and the local language. This holds good for all Gurdwaras like those situated in other parts of India, and in Malaysia, Thailand, Singapore, the Far East, Great Britain, Canada, U.S.A. and Kenya. A beginning should be made now, and the results compared later. Another way of overcoming

171

prejudice and hostility of the host community is to invite its prominent members to the Gurdwara and to acquaint them with Sikh worship and culture, provided we can find the Sikhs who are able to do this. Such an exercise is not to satisfy curiosity, but rather help others to understand the customs and beliefs of new settlers. New publications should be brought out for the information of foreigners like "Who are the Sikhs." "What can Sikhism contribute to world peace", "Relevance of Sikhism to modern life", "Sikhism as a World religion," and so on—preferrably in "English English" or "French French," and not 'Indian English' or 'Indian French.'

2. Sadh-Sangat

The word 'sangat' has already been mentioned earlier. It means society, congregation or associa;tion, for the social amd moral uplift of Sikhs. Such sangats have existed in different parts of India since the times of the Gurus. They fostered welfare projects for the community such as the establishment of inns, water-supply and the relief of the poor and distressed.

The word 'sadh-sangat,' has a special and restricted meaning. It mean a "Company of holy men." These are spiritually evolved persons willing to raise the tone not only of their friends and neighbours, but of society as a whole. Their example and training can improve that disciple who learns to work selflessly and also guide others on the moral path. The Gurus regarded joining Saintly Company, as extending a school where the seeker learns to imbibe godly virtues. All saints have been at one time disciples, who by self-discipline and *Sadhana*[2] progressed on the moral path. As they are transformed, so also are those who enter their company. Gradually the disciple acquires instruction, from his spiritual guide. The five vices which are normally very powerful will then come under control. He now avoids doing any thing which bring a sense of shame or guilt. His heart and mind become purified, and he extends his love to one and all.

3. Kirtan

Prayer can take many forms. One of the more powerful forms is that of hymn singing. Guru Nanak regarded Kirtan (hymn singing) as a distinct and easy way of linking one's consciousness to God. The first prayer-centre that he established at Kartarpur was also known as a Kirtan-ghar

172

(house of devotional music). Though the Gurus maintained professional musicians, they encouraged the disciples to sing hymns with the simplest of tunes and in the form of choral singing.

Kirtan is defined in many ways, but basically it is the singing of the praises of God in melody and with rhythm. Though most of the compositions in the Guru Granth Sahib are classified for singing in the classical ragas, we also find hymns can be set to be sung, to folk-music. So it is not necessary for a devotee to be a trained musicians to solo-sing or to appreciate the music for he can joining in the chants, or repeat-items of lines of the song, after the musician's solo. What is important in Kirtan is this devotion and not the excellence of voice or melody. The prime requirement behind hymn-singing is to glorify God and to realise His Presence and thereby enjoy the peace and bliss which He alone can give to the heart. Vocal or instrumental excellence or permutation in rhythm is not the criterion of good Kirtan. What really matters is the sincerity of the feeling and the love of God which it evokes, through the song. There should be no egoism or feeling of pride for being able to attract large audiences and winning their applause and respect. Some Kirtaniyas become arrogant through their vocal achievement or personal charisma. They try to exploit a sangat's love to listen to Kirtan by their excessive demands, in terms of money or special facilites. Such musicians were not approved by the Gurus, because money or fame is not the objective of Kirtan. Mammon and spirituality do not go together. Kirtaniyas lacking character and devotion were rejected, in spite of having melodious voice. Musicians who sing *Gurbani* in film-tunes or imitate a disco style and rhythm should find no favour with congregations. The Shromani Gurdwara Prabandhak Committee has recently banned the use of film-tunes for singing hymns in Gurdwaras.

Songs which only entertain or evoke erotic passions are never 'Kirtan.' Even the love-songs attributed to gods and deities, are outside the ambit of Sikh sacred music. Only music inspired by spiritual goals and moral purpose can be regarded as Kirtan. In the Guru Granth Sahib, the spiritual evocation and inner bliss of Kirtan is emphasised: "People think that Kirtain is just ordinary song, but in fact, it is a meditation on Divinity." (AG, 335)

The Gurus popularised Kirtan for it touches the heart of ordinary people. They also used it as an instrument for national integration. Both Hindus and Muslims sang hymns together in praise of God. The Guru's musicians included Muslim singers called *rababis* who sang their sacred compositions in classical or folk tunes. The Gurus themselves patronised professional musicians of good character. They also warned these professional musicians against exploitating people and of their need to cultivate tolerance and humility.

Most of the Gurus were musicologists of a high order. They also used ragas in the Karnataki style under the heading of "Dakhni." They experimented in different styles of singing and using varied rhythms. Guru Arjan laid down guide-lines for singers of sacred music as follows:

"The Lord's singer, imbibing a love for the One, sings His melodies of the only God.

He abides in the service of His One God and shows others, the way to the All-pervading God

He visualises the One God and serves his Lord who he knows through the Guru.

O! praiseworthy, praiseworthy is such a Kirtaniya!

He sings the praises of the omnipresent Lord, and leaves his attachment to material things.

The five virtues' he uses as his flat notes and following the Lord's love, his pure notes.

As renunciation of personal pride becomes his drone,'

So the avoidance of duplicity becomes his 'discord'.

He ties "The Name" to his skirt and so escapes the rounds of transmigration!" (AG, 885)

The Gurus popularised musical instruments like the *Sarinda, Sarangi, Dhadh* and *Khartal*. Normally, the singing of each line of a hymn is followed by playing the same tune on instruments. This custom gives breathing time to the singers and also keeps the listeners busy in humming The Kirtaniyas are trained in classical music and are acquainted with the appropriate hymns for the various Sikh ceremonies and *Gurpurabhs*. The correct pronunciation of the word of Gurbani is essential. The use of extra words or interpolations in not permitted. The singers must try to recreate the ethos, the mood and the spirit of the hymn they sing.

4. *Ardas* (Supplication or General Prayer)

The *Ardas* is the general prayer of the Sikhs. It can be said when one is alone at any time or in a congregation. It can also be recited for a specific purpose or a special celebration. Many people think that God knows of all our needs and wants and therefore it is not necessary to ask for any thing special for oneself or one's family or a group in a prayer. But this attitude is not approved by the Saints. They say that as God is our father; we should ask Him for all things. In the Guru Granth Sahib, Dhana Bhagat declares:

"If I cannot pray when I am hungry;
It is better that God takes away my rosary!" (AG, 656)

He suggests that God must supply his needs, and solve his problems, so that he can better devote himself, whole-heartedly to prayers.

The *Ardas* is written in three parts. The first part requests God and the Gurus blessings for the disciples. The second part deals with the history of the post-Guru period and the numerous sacrifices made by the Sikhs to maintain the principles of their own faith and freedom of worship, for others. Their strength of their faith in the face of torture gives inspiration to all men. The third part deals with request for an understanding of the True Name (the Holy Spirit) and the victory of good over evil. The disciple asks for God's blessing to be granted the gift of humility, high thinking, for the welfare of all mankind. The Sikh prayers does not ask for the destruction of one's enemies or the defeat of any opponent of the Sikh faith.

Sikhs generally offer prayer, every day and also when starting any new project or business. Even when in a hurry, they will stand and offer a short prayer. If they have enough time, they will think over their actions and reflect on the past, then ponder on the means by which they can best be inspired for their future. The reading of the Scripture or the reading of *Gurbani* is considered a a prayer. There is no liturgy or set composition, as such, to express one's devotion. Reading the *Granth* provides both instruction as well as inspiration for spiritual development. Prayer can change man's life and character, provided it is sincere. Routine ritualistic daily prayers are a mechanical exercise, but real devotion can transform the life of any seeker of The Truth. Prayer has a potent and cleansing effect on the mind. It purges man of evil inclinations and thoughts. Sinners have become saints through prayer and repentance. Just as lighted match will set fire to a pile of rubbish, so sincere prayer may destroy one's evil inclinations and offset any prospective punishment for bad things done. Prayer also has a psychological effect, and gives both hope and courage. It confirms to conviction that God is All Pervading and will hear any one's requests and will offer His help, when asked for insincerity, for it is His nature and prerogative to support His devotees.

5. Langar and Pangat

The equalness of human opportunity is foundation of the Sikh faith. The Gurus insisted that the Sikhs should pray and eat together. Guru Nanak established a *Dharamsal* at Kartarpur for this purpose. Guru Amardas made it obligatory for the Sikhs and visitors to a Sikh congregation to eat first, in the Free Kitchen[4] and then join in prayers. The reason for this directive was that many Hindus who were willing to join in the prayers would not eat in the presence of men of other castes or religions. They were obsessed with the idea of pollution by any proximity of some one not of their own caste. It was the Guru's intention to rid them of this sense of pollution. It was for this, that all sat together in rows to eat the same food. The Guru said:

"All food and drink is holy; the Lord has given these to us for our subsistence." (AG, 472)

The temple of bread and of worship formed the Gurdwara. The words *pangat* (meaning, sitting in a row and sharing meals) and *sangat* (meaning worship as a congregation) became popular among the Sikhs. The sharing of free food was made possible by the voluntary contribution of tithes by all Sikhs under the advice of Guru Ramdas. The tradition of langar was continued by Guru Arjan and his successors and maintained from the offerings and donations made by their followers. Guru Gobind Singh further strengthened the system of the Free Kitchen by asking his Sikhs to start individual langars, to meet the growing needs of his numerous followers. The Guru himself, incognito, visited the various 'langars' to find out whose langar was best and most satisfactory. The Guru's instructions in this matter have been included in the *Rahat-namas*, later compiled by his devotees. He also ordered that quotations from Gurbani should be recited before and after meals.[5] He also started and encouraged the use of mobile langars during his travels to the North and South of India. Though donations to the Free Kitchen were at times inadequate to meet their needs, he continued their practice and ensured regular supplies and funds. He thought, it was a most important practice in Sikhism.

The langar is also a forum for practising the Sikh doctrine of service. It gives the chance to any disciple to show his love of God by service to his fellow men. Sikhs are required to do physical work in the service of the people and so cultivate humility. Sewa in Free Kitchen has become such a popular practice among Sikhs, that they wait for their opportunities at all religious or social among Sikhs, and when this opportunity does not occur, they open Free Kitchens during droughts, floods or other calamities in whatever part of India. The Sikhs believe that feeding a fellow-being is the same as putting food in to the mouth of the Guru. As such, the contributions to langar are generally more than its requirements. Surplus food is distributed among the poor, the aged, the maimed, the handicapped, or given away to animals and birds.

The practice of langar has helped in the creation of a democratic and sane society. In India, it has become a means for national integration and unity. It promotes a spirit of cordiality and cooperation among different peoples. This in turn is a simple and effective method of developing sense of fellowship, caring and philanthropy.

6. Social Responsibility

The Guru not only aimed at the reform of the individual but improvement of society as a whole. Society however being still nothing more than groups of individuals, it became the duty of each individual to contribute to the common good. The Gurus favoured social interaction and community-cohesion. They organised projects for the welfare of all people. In the post-Guru period, Sikhs continued this tradition and promoted charitable projects for the benefit of different communities and countries. Altruism has no barriers or frontiers or forms of Charitable organisations run by Sikh organisations and Trusts, which include orphanages, old peoples homes, homes for the handicapped and chronically ill, in the Punjab and other Indian States as well as abroad. Some of the outstanding welfare institutions of the Sikhs are *Pingalwara* (Home for the seriously ill and crippled), Amritsar, The Guru Nanak Hospital Kanpur, The Guru Nanak Hospital for Handicapped Children Ranchi (Bihar), The Guru Nanak Niketan, Thakur Nagar (West Bengal), The Dashmesh Hospital and Medical College, Nander (Maharashtra), the Guru Nanak Engineering College Bidar (Karnataka) and the Guru Nanak College, Madras (Tamil Nadu). Many other Sikh Trusts are also operating in other States of India.

The idea behind social service and public welfare is to give a practical shape to the doctrine of "The service of God's creation," in one form or another and the elimination of ego or selfishness in the individual.

177

Many people restrict the notion of "doing social good" to the welfare of their own families and relatives. But the fundamental reason. for Sewa service is to make apparent one's love of God by serving His family—which means every one. The Sikhs consider that their over-flowing and unbounded affection covers not only the people of India, but also of other countries. Wherever Sikhs settle, they take up projects of welfare in their host country, working in cooperation with local people and other local charitable institutions.

(b) Home-Worship

1. Every home a temple

Guru Nanak first set up a temple in his own house at Kartarpur, and so did many of his disciples. In time congregations were later held in new Gurdwaras set up by the different Gurus. After the compilation of the Adi Granth by Guru Arjan, several devotees set up prayer-rooms in their homes, where the Sikh Scripture was kept. Early in the morning, the whole family, including the children sang hymns or the *Asa-di-var* or recited Gurbani. After an *Ardas* and a *Hukam,* each one would go to their own studies, work or business. During the day, any member of the family could go to the prayer-room for recitation, reading of Guru Granth Sahib or meditation. In the evening, the family again came together to recite the *Rahras* and *Chaupai.* On family birthdays and on Gurprabhs, the family would invite friends and relatives to join them in prayers in their own prayer-room. The closeness of family-members and the communal sprit of devotion and service, improved their inter-action and resulted in a greater sense of mutual responsibility and trust. This strengthed the natural bonds of love and respect.

Many people fail to understand the role and purpose of individual prayers in a family environment. They take it as a display of piety. However, it must not be forgotten that such prayers require time and effort. They also demonstrate humility and meekness in the individual, in their attempts to communicate with God as they seek His Divine Grace. However, sincere prayer does not require the mechanical repetition of a hymn or *mantra.* It provides the opportunity for man to discover the inner spiritual self and for his sincere endeavour to develop it. Prayer prepares one for moral activity and altruistic action. The Guru says:

"Let devotion to God be your service, and faith in Him your

178

occupation." (AG, 596)

2. Meditation: Chracter-building through prayer.

How is character developed through prayer ? Prayer is the attempt of man to search for God and the foundation for Him to do his best to become God-like. Meditation or the remembrance of the attributes of God, serves the same purpose. By constantly reflecting on the qualities of God—Truth, Goodness, Beauty, Compassion, Forgiveness etc. one begins to realise their importance in life and the need to cultivate them in day-to-day activity. Man also comes to realise the mystic presence of God and His All-pervading power. He feels he is in the care and watch of God, as such, he should not do any thing which may deprive him of His love and care. This awareness helps him keep apart from evil or wicked ways. He can then better control his thoughts and actions. Meditation or Gurbani or hymn-singing brings its own reward, for it provides joy and bliss.

Meditation is not only reflection or contemplation. It is done by word, thought and action. Meditation by words includes recitation, chant and hymn-singing; meditation by thoughts, means concentrating on the Presence and qualities of Divinity; meditation by action implies service in charitable projects and altruistic deeds.

The best time to meditate is in the morning or late in the night, because there is an environmental calm and quietness. During the day, one is involved in the chores of living. But the disciple, like the lotus in the water, tries not to be disturbed by its worldly ripples; he lives in the world, but is not worldly.

3. Social evolution and individual development

The moral tone of any society depends on the quality of its members or constituents. If individuals are below average, society does not go forward, so that individual development must come first. For the uplift of individuals, we need good men and great leaders from among the group, who by their own example may encourage a better quality of individual. The role of prophets, saints and heroes, who are born into the world from time to time is to inspire such individuals. who like them may become better people. This is what the Gurus did in their time. Just as a lit cantle can kindle another candle, in the same way, a holy man can inspire another person to strive to be as holy as he is. The Guru has given the example of engrafting a stem of superior quality on a plant of inferior quality, for a better fruit.

"All kinds of plants are grafted in the gardens of holy men;
All of them bloom, none are without good fruit. " (AG, 385)

Therefore the burden and responsibility for the uplift of society falls on noble men and women who through integrity, love and character, win the individuals to their way of living and change them into better people. For this are needed individuals who are keen to learn and who can profit from following the instructions of society's moral leaders. This can be mutually rewarding for as people individually improves themselves, their leader strengthens the moral fibre of the groups or the community as a whole. So it becomes possible for more people to be the great or noble. As there is always chaff in a bag of grain, if we can find ninety percent grain, then all will be happier. It is individual uplift that leads to community evolution as a rule.

Notes

1. *Nirmalas* are a branch of Sikh celilate missionaries.
2. For such special words see the glossary at the end.
3. The Five Sikh virtues are; Charity, Patience, Contentment, Detachment, Humility.
4. Some people use the word 'refectory' for langar. Refections or meals are served in Christian cenvents and monasteries in the dining hall, which is known as 'refectory.'
5. Macauliffe; The Sikh Religion, Vol. V, p. 109.

VI

Sikh Rites and Ceremonies

Some ceremonies of special occasions are mentioned in almost every religion. Some of them are simple, others complicated, some inexpensive and others costly. These special occasions are for events like birth, initiation, marriage and death. There are differences between rituals and ceremonies. Rituals are performed by the priests who read certain prescribed texts, prayers or *mantras* connected with the particular occasion or event. Secondly, ceremonies are fixed and traditional, and are based on a need at the time of their inception, even though they may have no significance or relevance in a letter age or changing set or circumstances. Fortunately, the Sikhs have no ordained priesthood and as such are free form the corruption of clergy as is to be found in some other Faiths.

Sikh ceremonies are simple but significant. They must be held in the presence of Guru Granth Sahib. They are devotional in substance and congregational in character. Prayers or hymns appropriate to the occasion are sung or recited as friends and relatives join the conegagrtion in bonds of unity and fellowship.

The original Sikh rites and ceremonies took shape when Guru Amardas declared the distinctiveness of Sikhism as a new religion. An important step in this direction was taken at Goindwal with the digging and construction of a *Baoli Sahib*—a deep well—for supply of public water. It is said that this was brought about, because the orthodox Hindus resenting the non-observance of caste restrictions by the Guru and his followers, desired to teach them a lesson. They broke the water containers of those Sikhs who came to the village-well to draw water.[1] Guru Amardas realised then the need for a alternative water-supply and so started the digging of Baoli Sahib, so that all at Goindwal would have clean water. He also set up Manjis (centres or the assignment of missionary work) for the initiation of his followers into Sikhism.

The Sikh Naming ceremony was also initiated by Guru Amardas. When a grandson was born to him,. the infant was presented to him after a few days. His father—Mohri—had given him the name Sidh Yogi, but Guru Amardas was of the opinion that a proper Sikh[2] name should be given to the child. He therefore gave him the new name of Anand (Bliss). Macauliffe[3] mentions that Guru Amardas also composed the Anand Sahib for that occasion, but this appears to be improbable, because there is no reference to any birth or child in this composition.[4]

Guru Amardas initiated the Sikh Anand marriage Ceremony which required the recitation of "The *Anand* Sahib" for the marriage of his daughter Bhani to Bhai Jetha in 1553. The new ceremony "constituted a distinct break with Hinduism." Later on, when a Sikh complained to Guru Ramdas that a Brahmin had refused to solemnise the marriage of his daughter as he could not afford to pay him a high fee, the Guru composed his *Lavan* (wedding song), and made it part of the Sikh ceremony. Sikh marriage was given statutory recognition by the Indian Legislature in the Anand Marriage Act of 1909.

The beginning of the Sikh funeral ceremony was authorised a by special directive of Guru Amardas. According to his grand-son—Bhai Sunder—the Third Guru ordered that only hymns in praise of God should be sung after the death of a Sikh. No Pundit, no lamps, no offerings, no immersion of the ashes in a holy river were necessary at the death ceremony of a Sikh. Lamentations and wailing were also prohibited at the time of death or after, as death is a natural and inexorable event for all people. The Sikh ceremonies have developed over the centuries and have been codified in the *Rahat-Maryada* and authorised by the Shromani Gurdwara Parbandhak Committee, Amritsar and published in the form of a booklet.

1. The Naming Ceremony

No ceremony is necessary immediately after the birth of a child in a Sikh family, but as soon as the mother and child are well enough, they and the family should go to the Gurdwara for the naming ceremony. There are no taboos attached to the birth of a female child. Friends may join with the family at the Gurdwara at the date and time fixed by the parents. There the mother carries her baby to the Guru Granth Sahib.

The *Granthi* or any Khalsa Sikh may then put sugar—puffs or sugar crystals into a bowl of water and stir it with a Kirpan (sword) while reciting the first five verses of the Japji. If there is a singer or musician available, he may sing the hymns of Gurbani. The Ardas (General Prayer) is offered, to invoke Gods's blessing on the child. Normally, it will include the

182

following words:

"O true King! I present to you this child. With your grace,
I give him /her your nectar to drink. May he/she be a true Sikh and
obey his/her parents,
May he/she serve his/her all people and his/her country
May he/she live a long and healthy life
May he/she be inspired with a devotion to God"

Thereafter a *Hukam* is read from Guru Granth Sahib. The first letter of the opening line of the *Hukam* read, is the letter according to which the name of the child is to be given. If the initial letter is "G," the name may be Gurpreet. The suffix "Singh" is added to the name of a boy and "Kaur" to that of a girl. Generally a *Rumala* is presented to Guru Granth Sahib by the parents at this time. A few drops of the sweetened water (nectar) prepared earlier, is then put on the tongue of the child, while the remainder is given to the mother to drink. Karah Parsad is then distributed. Guests may bring sweets and distribute them among those present. Langar (community meal) is optional. In some cases, the Naming ceremony is held in the prayer-room of the parents' home. The procedure is the same, but the gathering is small. Sikhs are not required to add their caste or village names, after Singh or Kaur.

2. Baptism Ceremony

In the beginning, the initiation into Sikhism was very simple. Guru Nanak accepted his disciples by giving them *charan-amrit* (foot-wash) and asking them to practise his teachings in daily life. There were *three rules,* for the Guru's disciples: To do honest labour, to share their food with others, to pray and meditate on God. The Tenth Guru modified this form of baptism to *Khanday-da-amrit.* He initiated the Five Beloved Ones (Panj Piyare) at Anandpur and called them *Khalsa.* The ceremony is mentioned in detail in the section dealing with the life of Guru Gobind Singh. However, more details are given below:

The baptism ceremony can be held in any Gurdwara or any quiet and clean place. At least six Khalsa Sikhs who are Amrit Dhari must be present, in addition to those who are to be baptised. One of the Khalsa is required to attend the Guru Granth Sahib, and read it, while the other five are required for preparing the Amrit. Both the Panj Piara and the recipients of Amrit. must have a full bath and wash their hair before the

183

ceremony. Only those Sikhs can administer *Amrit* who are physically fit, in no way handicapped and are themselves Khalsa having taken *Amrit* and wear the Five K's. There is no maximum age for receiving amrit, but the recipient should be able to understand, and perform his duties and responsibilities. The recipents should wear their five K's and have their heads covered. Those who are apostate and are receiving baptism for the second or third time, must confess their broken vows and be given an appropriate award or penance. Non-Sikhs taking Amrit may be given a Sikh name at their own request.

One of the five administrators of *Amrit* then stands up and explains the rules and obligations to the recipients, namely that they must pray to the One God, read the Scriptures, live according to the Sikh Code of discipline and serve their country and mankind in general. After the recipients have given their consent to these instructions and duties, one of the officiants will offer *"Ardas"* for the commencement of the preparation of the *Amrit* and then read a *Hukam*.

The *Amrit* ceremony begins with the five officiants sitting around a steel bowl containing clean water and some sugar crystals. They sit in the heroic posture—kneeling on the right knee with the weight of the body on the right foot, and the left knee raised. Then they recite *Japji*, the *Jaap*, then The *Swayyas*, the *Benti Chaupai* and the first five and last verse of the *Anand*. After which one of the five offers an Ardas. All the recipients sit in the heroic posture mentioned above, with cupped hands to receive the nectar; as they are given the nectar, they utter the Sikh greeting—"Wahegure Ji Ka Khalsa, Sri Wahegure Ji Ki Fateh." and drink it. Then the nectar is sprinkled five times on their eyes and five times on their hair. Any remaining nectar is then shared by all the recipients, all drinking from the same bowl as they recite the *Mool-mantra* together.

One of the five officiants declares the duties and obligations of the baptised Sikhs as under:

"From now on, your life as an ordinary individual has ceased; you are now a member of the Khalsa Brotherhood. Your religious father is Guru Gobind Singh, and your mother is Sahib Kaur. Your spiritual birth place is Kesgarh Sahib (birth-place of the Khalsa) and your home is Anadpur Sahib (the place where Guru Gobind Singh was installed as the Tenth Guru). Your common spiritual parentage makes you all brothers, you will forsake your previous names and surnames, and previous local and religious loyalties. You are to pray to One God alone, through the Scriptures and teachings of the ten Gurus. You should learn the Gurmukhi script, if you do not know it already and recite daily the Five Prayers of Japji, Jaap, Ten Swayyas, Sodar-Rehras and The Sohila.You should hear and read Guru Granth Sahib."

Only Amritdhari Sikhs constitute the Khalsa Panth. Khalsa Sikhs must maintain the Five K's through out their lives and should not commit any of the following four misdeeds:

i. Smoke or use tobacco or take any form of intoxicating drugs

ii. Eat the meat of any animals killed by ritual slaughter (for example Halal or Kosher).

iii. Commit adultery.

iv. Cut or remove hair from any part of the body.

Any one who breaks these Khalsa vows becomes *Patit* or apostate and will have to take Amrit again, after undergoing suitable penance in case of deliberate contravention. All baptised Sikhs male and females are not to associate with the following:

i. The followers of Prithicand, Dhirmal, Ram Rai and other breakaway groups

ii. Those who oppose Sikhism, practise infanticide or use alcohol, tobacco or intoxicating drugs.

iii. Those who wed their children for monetary gain

iv. Those who perform any ceremony contrary to Sikhism.

v. Apostates who have discarded the Five K's.

Then the *Ardas* is recited and the *Hukam* read. If there is any candidate for *Amrit* whose name was not earlier chosen according to Sikh practice, he must be given a new name from the Hukam of the scripture. Karah Parsad is then distributed and the newly baptised eat it from a common dish.

Those who have broken their previous Amrit vows and become Patit or apostate agree to undergo whatever award or penance is ordered by the Panj-Piyara. This generally takes the form of voluntary service or the additional reading of Gurbani. After the penance has been accepted by the defaulteran. Ardas is offered.

3. Marriage Ceremony (Anand Karaj)

Sikh Marriages are generally arranged by the parents. Nowadays, the young tell their parents of their preferences who can then arrange to meet with the other parents to discuss the matter. The young can then meet under some sort of supervision to get to know each other better. The girl is normally discouraged from going out with a boy alone. It is the duty of parents to look for a suitable match. Sikhs are expected to marry into Sikh families. This is necessary because similarity of upbringing and background and also for their own children's upbringing. There is no actual bar to marrying outside one's caste or class, if there is understanding in the families. However, (Amritdhari) Sikhs, should marry into Sikh families as their wives should also embrace Sikhism. Sikhs do not consult horoscopes in the matching of partners. Tne voluntary consent of the young is required before any marriage is finalised.

The confirmation of any marriage proposal is normally siginified by a betrothal ceremony. Here, the bride's representative or relatives and the bride-groom's family, exchange presents for the bride and the groom. The betrothal ceremony is confirmed by an *Ardas* to invoke the blessing of God on the persons betrothed, this ceremony is not compulsory and can be dispensed with. When the proposal of marriage is confirmed by both families then the date and venue of the wedding is fixed. Any day convenient to both parties is in order because Sikhs do not believe in auspicious days. The marriage ceremony is generally held in a Gurdwara; but can be held in the bride's residence or at any other clean and open place according to the convenience of the parties. The solemnising of marriages in clubs, hotels and restaurants is discouraged on account of the uncongenial environment.

On the day of the wedding the bride-groom with his relatives and friends go to the venue of the wedding ceremony. The bride's party should reach there first in order to welcome the groom's party. Then the two families exchange greeting and presents. This meeting is called a *Milni*, which means "get-together" and is prelude to the wedding. At this time, both the families and their friends sing the following hymn:

"Friends have come to our house,
The True One's favour has brought us togehter to confirm a union
of hearts
That is always pleasing to God." (AG,764)

Afterwards an *Ardas* is offered for God's blessing on the Union.
Wedding ceremonies are generally held in the morning. Friends and
relatives sit down and listen to the hymns sung by singers. The bride-
groom takes a front seat facing the Guru Granth Sahib. The bride then
takes her seat to the left of her groom. The officiant may be any one who
knows how to conduct the ceremony, for there is no ordained priesthood
in Sikhism. He confirming for the consent of all parties, then asks the bride
and groom and their parents to stand up. An *Ardas* is performed in which
the name of the boy and girl who are to be married are specifically
mentioned.

The musicians then begin the ceremony with a hymn seeking
divine blessing:

"Before undertaking any task, seek the grace of God for He will
ensure its success.
The True Guru stands witness to this
The True teacher will enable you to relish His ambrosia.
O Compassionate Lord,
Destroyer of fear please bestow your grace on your servant:" (AG,
91).

The officiant then explains to the couple the role of a married life
in the attainment of life's goal. He also tells them of their individual
duties. It is only by fulfilling their marital obligations that their married
life will be peaceful and happy:

"There is only one way to the heart of the beloved
Be humble and loyal and obey his command.
It is only in this way that a blissful union may be attained." (AG,
788)
"Let humility be the code -word,
Resignation the offerings, and yours
Tongue the mant of sweet speech.
By adopting these habits, dear sister,

You will have influence over your lord." (AG, 1384)

The officiant then seeks the consent of the couple to the acceptance of these duties. After they signify their consent, he asks the bride's father or guardian to place the groom's scarf in the bride's hand or attach it to a part of her dress.

The wedding song of four stanzas called *Lavan* is now recited. As soon as the first stanza is finished, the couple stand up, bow to Guru Granth Sahib and then walk round the Granth in a clock-wise direction,as the musicians repeat the first stanza (Lavan). This verse stresses the performance of house-hold duties and the acceptance of moral obligations, by the couple. The couple finally bow to the *Granth* and then return to their original palace. The officiant then reads the second stanza and again the couple walk round the Guru Granth Sahib and return to sit down. This verse stresses selflessness and purity of heart which should be practised by the couple. Then for a third time the couple go round as the third stanza is read. This emphasises the value of detachment and the importance of joining holy company. Finally and for the fourth time the couple again go round the Guru Granth Sahib while the final verse is being sung. This expresses the real joy of union and the attainment of bliss. As soon as fourth *Lavan* is completed, the musicians sing the *Anand Sahib*, the song of Bliss. This, completes the marriage ceremony. The whole congregation

then stands for an *Ardas*. After which a *Hukum* is read and *Karah Parsad* is distributed. The couple and their parents are then congratulated by their friends and relatives, and presents are given to the bride and bride-groom. The ceremony generally is followed by Langar or refreshments, for those present. There may also be a reception for the guests if desired by the couple, at a later date.

The "Anand marriage" is monogamous. It is a sacrament and such a marriage cannot be dissolved. Under Civil Law there can be a judicial separation or divorce by the courts. The ceremony is the same for the legally divorced, widows and widowers. Sikhs do not follow the old-fashioned custom of refusing to take food at their married daughter's home. The payment or acceptance of a dowry is discouraged, and any presents that are exchanged, should not be formally displayed on the occasion of the wedding. Baptised Sikhs should encourage their partners to take Amrit, if they are not already baptised.

4. Death Ceremony

When a Sikh is about to die or dies, his relatives and friends will assemble by his side and recite *Gurbani*. No crying or mourning is permitted by the Sikh religion, for death is a natural event (like birth) and eventually comes to all. No rituals based on other religions or any other source should be performed on the death of a Sikh. Solace should be sought through the recitation of *Gurbani* and hymn-singing. Suitable hymns from the Guru *Granth* Sahib like the one given below are to be read, recited or sung:

"The dawn of each knew day is the herald of its sunset:
This Earth is not your permanent home; for life is like a shadow.
As all your friends have departed, so too, must you go " (AG, 793)

Sikhs believe in the soul's immortality. A devotee should have no fear of the pangs of death. He should face death willingly, this summons by God is to be accepted with resignation, looking forward to a vision of the Supreme Being. It is only an evil person who dreads death, for he fears punishment and future cycles of birth and death.

The dead body of a Sikh is bathed and dressed in clean clothes. The Five K's are left on the body which is then placed in a coffin or on a bier. The funeral procession is to a cremation ground. The mourners singing hymns on the way. If there is a Gurdwara nearby, the mourners will stop there and offer an *Ardas*. Ladies do not accompany the procession. On reaching the cremation-ground, the body is placed on the top of a firewood platform and covered with logs of wood. The pyre is lit by the nearest relative and all join in singing the appropriate hymns. In the case of using a crematorium, the body is consigned to the flame as the hymns are sung. Finally the *Kirtan Sohila* is read and the *Ardas* recited. The mourners then return to their homes, take a bath and change their clothes. The second part of the death ceremony consists of the death rites. The ashes of the deceased are collected from the cremation ground or the crematorium, and then disbursed into running water or the sea. Sikhs do not consider any river or palace of pilgrimage as being specially suitable for the disposal of the ashes. The erection of a memorial over any remains in any form is forbidden.

Prayers for the departed soul take the form of a complete reading of Guru Granth Sahib. Generally the reading is held over a period of ten days. Then friends and relatives of the deceased gather together for the ceremony of Final Supplication—The *Antim Ardas*. A Bhog ceremony is held, when the last few pages of theGuru Granth Sahib are read. The musicians then sing the appropriate hymns from *Gurbani*. The Ramkal Sadd (AG, 923) is then read, this stresses the value of the Holy Name for consolation to the bereaved family. Then the Final supplication is recited, after which a *Hukam* is read and *Karah Parsad* is distributed. *Langar* is optional. Finally, any donations are given to charitable instituations or religious organizations. When the Head of the family dies, the senior-member of the family is declared as the successor, as a turban is presented to signify the assumption of becoming head of the family. This is known as a Dastar-bandi or turban-tying ceremony.

5. Path And Bhog (Complete Reading of Guru Granth Sahib)

(i) Sahaj/Sadharan Path (Normal reading of Guru Granth Sahib)

Sikhs are expected to maintain a separate place or room for the reading and studying of the Guru Granth Sahib. They should read a hymn or lesson (Hukam) from the Granth before taking their morning meal. If they cannot do so,they should do the reading at any time before going to bed. If on account of difficult circumstances, they cannot do so, they should not feel guilty or ashamed. They should gather the family when commencing to read the Sahaj Path. Before beginning the Sahaj Path, the first five verses and last verse of the *Anand Sahib* should be read followed by an *Ardas* and a *Hukem*. The reading of the Guru Granth Sahib should commence with *Japji*.

(ii) Akhand Path (Non-Stop Reading of Guru Granth Sahib) And Bhog (Completion Ceremony)

An Akhand Path may be held to celebrate any occasion of joy or sorrow. A complete reading of the *Granth* takes at least 48 hours and is done by relays of readers. Generally, five persons are necessary, four for reading and one for attendance and any emergency. An electric torch or extra light is always kept to hand in case of any light failure. Any ceremonial lighting or endless burning of joss sticks or ringing of bells is forbidden. The placing of water or coconut near the Guru Granth Sahib or bowing to pictures of the Gurus is forbidden. As far as possible, the reading of the Scripture should be done by members of the family and their friends. The reading by professional readers is discouraged. No other book should be read, while the Path is being read or recited. Traditionally no Kirtan and *Katha* are permitted at the same time as the Akhand Path is being read in the same place. This is necessary so that the reading of the Scripture is undisturbed. Before starting an Akhand Path, the first five and the last verse of the Anand Sahib should be recited. Then follows an Ardas, a Hukam and the distribution of Karah Parsad. Now the Akhand Path can begin, Those who assist in the reading of the Guru Granth Sahib should be offered food and refreshment.

Bhog means the reading of the last few pages of the Granth. The reading of The Rag-mala is optional. Generally, new Rumala(Cloth-Covering) is donated and placed over the Guru Granth Sahib when its reading is completed. The final readings of the Anand Sahib, Ardas and Hukam are followed by the distribution of Karah Parsad. Performing a Langar (Community-meal), is optional. Generally, any donations to charity are announced by the person sponsoring the Akhand Path.

Notes

1. I.B. Bannerjee: Evolution of the Khalsa, Vol I, p. 173.
2. The word Sikh literally means a disciple or follower of the Ten Gurus. According to the Sikh Gurdwaras Act, 1925, Sikh is defined as a "person who has faith in one God, the Ten Gurus and Guru Granth Sahib and its teachings. He also believes in the necessity and importance of *Amrit* and must not profess any other religion." It may be noted that a Sikh is excepted to follow the Sikh Code of Conduct (Rahat-Maryada). A Sikh is known by his turban and his unshorn hair. Those who maintain the Five K's, and have taken *Amrit* (Initiation) are known as the *Khalsa*.
3. Macauliffe; The Sikh Religion, II. p, 117.
4. The Sikh Times (Maryland) December, 1983.
5. Tara Chand: History of the Freedom Movement in India, II, 396.
6. G.S. Mansukhani; The Quintessence of Sikhism (1965) p. 233.
7. Adi Granth, p. 923.

VII

The Important Sikh Festivals

Their Significance

Religious festivals are intended to focus their followers' attention to a revival of their faith and devotion by its historic linking to the past and to its project for the future by way, for example of community uplift and public benefit. It is at such times that Sikhs take stock of their religious performance during the past year and analyse their success or failure. During the celebration of Sikh festivals, good speakers and professional *Ragis* with their instrumentalists are asked to sing special hymns for the occasion. Some time *Kirtan Darbar* (professional hymn-singing session) and *Kavi-Darbar* (poetic symposium) may also held.

Sikhs regularly celebrate "Sangrand," (the first day of the Indian lunar month). On that day, the appropriate verse for the month from the Barah-mah (Calendar) of Guru Arjan Dev (AG, 133-136) is read. The Sikh calendar begins from the month of Chet (Mid-March) and ends with the month of Falgun. The Baisakhi festival—the day on which Guru Gobind Singh established his Khalsa Brotherhood—falls on 13th April. All festivals which celebrate the birthdays or deaths of the Gurus, or events of special significance like Diwali and installation of Guru Granth Sahib, are called *Gurprabhs* (holy festivals). During such festivals, there are mass-prayers, meetings and personal rededication to the ideals of the Gurus. Special celebrations as for the centenary celebrations of births of the Gurus (some of which occurred recently) have led to the establishment of new Foundations dedicated to the dissemination of that Guru's teachings, and also to the initiation of new public welfare projects.

The celebration of *Gurprabhs* held in India differ in many ways from those held in foreign countries where large numbers of Sikhs are now settled. In India the celebrations are held on the actual day of the Gurprabh, while outside India, on the nearest sunday or other public holiday. In India, festivals are held in spacious places or in the open air, save in the hills, while in cold countries like Great Britain and Canada,

192

Nankana Sahib, Gurdwara, Birth Place of Sri Guru Nanak Dev Ji. (Now in Pakistan).

Gurdwara Punja Sahib, at Hasan Abdaal, Near Rawalpindi (Pakistan).

The Golden Temple, Amritsar: (Kar Sewa April, 1973)

Gurdwara at Anandpur (Punjab).

The formation of the Khalsa.

A view of Langer.

Hola Mohalla Procession, Anandpur Sahib (Punjab).

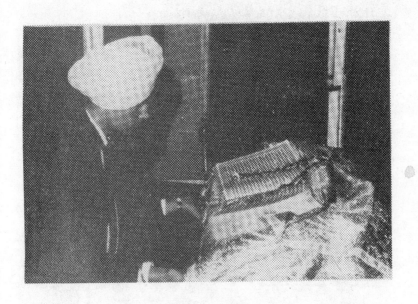

Reading the Guru Granth Sahib.

Mass Massacre in Lahore (Now in Pakistan).

Bhai Ghaniya, the founder of Red Cross in Sikh Religion.

The Great Warrior- Baba Jassa Singh Ahluwalia in the battle field.

Soldiers (Sikh left) and (Gurkha-right) belonging to the *Fauj-i-khas*.

The *Fauj-i-khas*: Military Manual of Maharaja Ranjit Singh, (Ranjit Singh Museum, Amritsar).

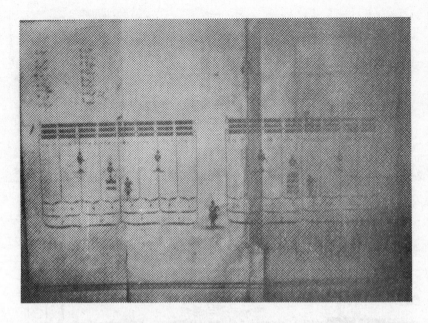

A regiment of the *Fauj-i-khas* on parade; Military Manual of Maharaja Ranjit Singh. (Ranjit Singh Museum, Amritsar).

Sikh Wedding Ceremony.

the celebrations are held indoors. No processions are held overseas on account of the uncertainties of the weather, but there are always *langar* arranged for the *Gurprabhs*, because people come from long distances for the celebrations. *Akhand Paths* which are easily done in India, are far more difficult to arrange abroad. So very few Gurdwaras can arrange them, as insufficient readers for the Guru Granth Sahib are available.

The following Sikh festivals are celebrated in almost all Gurdwaras in India and abroad:

1. Guru Nanak's Birthday

Though latest research has shown that Guru Nanak was born on 15th April, 1469, (hence also Guru Gobind Singhs primary reason for his selection of Baisakhi day for his Khalsa) the normal birth-anniversary by tradition and based on the Janam-sakhi of Bhai Bala, is celebrated on Kartik Poornima (in November) both in India and abroad. The actual day varies from year to year, as its calculation is based on the lunar calendar. The birth-place of Guru Nanak was at Nankana Sahib, (now in Pakistan) about thirty miles N.W. of Lahore. Even so, Sikh pilgrims go there in large numbers from all over India, to celebrate the Guru's birthday. They assemble at Amritsar three or four days before the birth-date, then go by special trains or coaches from Amritsar to Nankana Sahib under the leadership of the Shromani Gurdwara Parbandhak Committee. They are escorted from the border by the Pakistan authorities to Nankana Sahib. The number of visitors differs from time to time as allowed by the Pakistan government, which is responsible for their care and safety. The group arranges its Akhand Path two days prior to the birth-date. The Bhog is held on the actual morning of the birthday. Both Sikh and Pakistani singers join in the celebrations which are relayed by Radio Pakistan. A Free Kitchen is run for the entire period of the celebrations. After the function is over, the pilgrims may visit other places like Panja Sahib, Dera Sahib at Lahore with Pakistan Government permission. Recently, The Nankana Sahib Foundation, incorporated in United States of America (with its headquarters in Washington has made an arrangement with the Pakistan government that Sikhs settled abroad, can visit Nankana Sahib and other Sikh shrines at any time, when visas will be granted to them as required. Indian Sikhs however, do not enjoy the same facilities, they must go in groups for specified festivals, when permitted by the Pakistan government. The general supervision and care of the Sikh shrines in Pakistan is in the hands of the government-controlled Wakaf Board.

The celebrations of Guru Nanak's birthday by important Gurdwaras and Sikh organisations in India and abroad, last for three days. Sometimes, two or more Gurdwaras situated in the same town may hold joint celebrations, and so split the functions that the individual Gurdwaras will host one or the other programmes which all the people will attend. There will be a joint procession, the Akhand Path will be read at one Gurdwara, while Kirtan, lectures and Kavi-darbar may be held in another. On this festival, Amrit ceremonies are also held as a part of the celebrations, if it is requested.

Normally, the reading of the *Akhand Path* will begin two days before the birthday in the morning, the Bhog will be held 48 hours later on the actual birthday itself. In some cities, Prabht-feris (morning hymn-singing rallies) will be arranged to generate a greater awareness of the celebration-schedule.

Big processions are a colourful feature of these celebrations. In some places, the procession will be organised a day before the birthday, while at others, it will be arranged for the birthday itself, most probably in the evening. The processions are led by two Sikhs, smartly dressed, each holding *Nishan Sahib* (Sikh flag) followed by the *Panj Piyara* in orange robes, and the *Palki* (palanquin) containing the Guru Granth Sahib. This is normally carried on a motor-truck or in a handcart pulled by devotees. There will be brass-hands and singers from local schools and colleges. Boy-scouts and girl-guides will join the function, as also women, singing hymns in chorus. Sometimes Gatka (sword-stick) players, will demonstrate their expertise en-route. At some important places, the procession will halt a while, to enable the organisers to address it and the spectators, and give them details of the celebrations. The procession will pass through streets which will be decorated with flags, flowers and bunting. There may be numbers of ornamental and floral floats specially decorated for the occasion. Food, snacks and soft drinks are served free to the participants as they march through the streets. The procession usually takes three to six hours on its journey to reach its destination, usually a Gurdwara or place, where the main celebrations are held.

On the birthday itself, after the Bhog ceremony in the morning, Asa-di-var will be sung by *Ragis*. This will be followed by lectures, sermons and recitation of poems composed by Sikhs especially for the celebrations and referring to the life and work of whichever Guru whose birthday is being celebrated. At lunch time, *Langar* will be served. Sometimes, the programme continues, as people leave in batches to eat their food. In the evening, there may be hymn-singing by different

194

groups—possibly of women or students until late in the night. Sometimes a Kirtan-darbar and Kavi-darbar is also arranged as a part of the celebrations. At night, Fire-works display with the Gurdwara being illuminated by coloured lights and other decoration. Traditionally, Guru Nanak was born between 1 and 2 A.M., and therefore the celebrations run on until about that time in the morning. In small Gurdwaras or in remote villages, they will hold only one-day celebrations. In foreign countries, Sikhs invite local people and tell them about the work and message of Guru Nanak. The birthday is celebrated on the nearest Sunday to the actual day.

2. Guru Gobind Singh's Birthday

Guru Gobind Singh's birthday is celebrated with the same enthusiasm and devotion as that of Guru Nanak. Guru Gobind Singh was born at Patna in December 1666. His birthday falling in December or January according to the lunar calendar. This celebration lasts for three days generally, and the programme is similar to that for the birthday of Guru Nanak. The *Akhand Path,* procession, and full-day schedule with lectures, sermons, hymn singing and poetic recitals. All of which generate a lot of interest and respect, for Guru Gobind Singh's mission. Sikhs who are unable to join in the Gurdwara celebrations for one reason or another have Kirtan, Ardas and Karah Parsad in their own homes inviting relatives and friends to join them in the function. In the bigger celebrations in major cities, an Amrit Ceremony (Baptism) is also arranged for those who desire to join the Khalsa Brotherhood.

3. Installation of Guru Granth Sahib as Permanent Guru

Before his death, Guru Gobind Singh declared that he had decided to end personal Gurship, and that after him, the Guru Granth Sahib was to be regarded as the perpetual Guru of the Sikhs. So on 3rd October, 1708, he held a special assembly at Huzur Sahib (Nander), where bowing to the Guru Granth Sahib , he invested it with the permanent status of "Guru." From that time on, this day is sacred as the installation day of the Guru Granth Sahib. Again celebrations are held for three days. In small towns or villages, it is celebrated for one day, with Kirtan, Katha, lectures, Ardas, Karah Parsad and langar. Special lectures being given on the contents and significance of the Guru Granth Sahib and the need to follow its teachings in daily life. Guru Gobind Singh nominated the Scripture—

195

this devotional hymnody—as the spiritual guide for the Sikh community for all time to come, so that, there was no longer any need for a human or *deh-dhari* Guru for Sikhs. that is why the Guru Granth Sahib itself is the focal point of any Gurdwara. Written expositions of the Guru Granth Sahib are now available in Punjabi, Hindi and English. Some people keep these books in their own homes and study it in their spare time. The most important studies and translation of Guru Granth Sahib, are those of Dr. Sahib Singh and Amir Singh in Punjabi and of Dr. Gopal Singh and of S. Manmohan Singh and Gurbachan Singh in English. Many eminent writers and philosophers declare that the Guru Granth Sahib contains very remarkable insights which can contribute to the modern Inter-Faith dialogue and problems of world peace.

4. Baisakhi

Baisakhi or Vaisakhi, is the birthday of the Khalsa. It first became of interest to the Sikhs in 1699, when the occasion of its festival was first used by Guru Gobind Singh as being the most suitable time for his founding of the Khalsa Panth at Anadpur, where he initiated the baptism of Amrit or *Khanday-di-pahul* and prescribed the Code of Sikh Discipline. Baisakhi day, now the Birth-day of the Khalsa Panth is fixed on 13th April. Every 36 years, however, there is a difference of one day, so that then it falls on 14th April. Baisakhi celebrations generally last for three days with the usual programme of Kirtan, Katha, Akhand Path, langar etc. One special feature of Baisakhi celebrations is that of holding Amrit ceremony to baptise those who offer themselves as Khalsa. After baptism, they become Amritdharis and Khalsa Sikhs. Details of the baptism ceremony are given in chapter VI. In foreign countries, Baisakhi is celebrated on the nearest Sunday. Baisakhi has now also a political significance. On this day in 1919, the British General Dyer, had his troops open fire on a peaceful Sikh gathering in Jallianwala Bagh in Amritsar, and had killed some 400 unarmed men, women and children. An animal fair is also held on this day on the outskirts of Amritsar.

5. Diwali

Diwali (though also a Hindu festival) is celebrated by the Sikhs since the time of Guru Amardas. He ordered that Sikhs should assemble on this day at Goindwal to discuss matters of religious and social interest. The Sikh *manjidars* (missionaries) were also instructed to attend as it was a religious convention. There is also another special reason for Sikhs to celebrate it. It was on Diwali that Guru Hargobind reached Amritsar after his release from the Gwalior Jail, where he had been imprisoned by the Emperor Jehangir for some months. On his return to Amritsar, his Sikhs welcomed him back with rejoicing. This day usually falls in November. Gurdwaras then hold a one-day celebration with sacred music sessions and lectures, to express their joy for the Guru's release and freedom. They distribute sweets, burn candles and light oil torches. They also have a firework, display in the evening at Amritsar. There, Sikh treasures, relics and heirlooms of the Gurus and Sikh Chieftains are displayed to the public, both in the Toshakana (treasury) and also in the Harmandar Sahib.

6. Holla Mohalla

This is a local festival and it is not observed generally as other Gurprabhs are. Holi itself is another Hindu festival; on this day, Prahlad, child-saint of the Hindus was saved from the clutches of Holika, the demonic sister of his father—Harnakash. The festival falls in March, when the Hindus throw coloured water and powder on every one as a matter of fun and frolic. Some times, this sort of frivolity gets out of hand and leads to rioting. In order to give a healthy direction to this occasion of the victory of good over evil, Guru Gobind Singh held a fair at Anandpur on this day in 1680. Mock battles and competitions in archery, horseman-ship, wrestling and athletics were and still are held at Anandpur, to mark the occasion. The celebrations last for three days and include rural arts and crafts display and sales. This festival was given the name of Holla Mohalla.

7. Guru Arjan's Martyrdom

Guru Arjan the fifth Sikh Master who built the Harmandar Sahib (Golden Temple) at Amritsar became a victim of the jealousy and bigotry of the Moghul Emperor. On trumped up charges, the Guru was arrested and tortured in Lahore in 1606 under the Emperor orders. He died as a result of his tortures, on 25th May, 1606. The anniversary of his martyrdom falls during May-June every year. Generally, a one-day celebration is held, with the usual programme, but emphasising the life and work of the Fifth Guru. The main celebration is held annually at Dera Sahib, Lahore, where the Guru died in the river Ravi. Many Sikhs from India and other countries go to Dera Sahib to pay homage to the first Guru-martyr. A special feature of the celebration is the offering of cold water, sweetened milk-shake and syrup to the general public, distributed at the side of main roads, to remind local people of Guru Arjan's great sacrifice.

8. Guru Tegh Bahadur's martyrdom

Guru Tegh Bahadur was arrested under an order of the Emperor Aurangzeb in 1675. The latter offered him a choice, accept Islam or die. The Guru did not recant and offered himself as a sacrifice in the cause of Religious freedom, worship and conscience. His martyrdom stopped the forcible conversion of non-Muslims to Islam. He was tortured for many days to break his spirit, but he still refused to change his religion. He was then beheaded in Delhi on 11th November, 1675. His anniversary falls in November/December, each year according to the lunar calendar. Most of the Gurdwaras hold a one day festival. However, in Delhi, there is a three-day celebration of religious music and discourse, specially the singing of his own hymns in the Sisganj Gurdwara built where he was executed and also at the Rikabganj Gurdwara where his body was cremated. A Kirtan and Kavi darbar are also very prominent in Delhi celebrations.

198

Glossary

Adi: First, Original

Amrit: Water of immortality, nectar, the Sikh initiation/baptism ceremony

Ardas: The General Prayer of the Sikhs, the Supplication.

Avtar: Incarnation, rebirth

Baisakhi: Second month of the lunar Calendar (starts mid April) a Sikh Festival.

Bani: Hymn or composition included in the Sikh Scriptures

Bhagat: An exponent and practitioner of Bhakti, a devotee, a saint or mystic.

Bhog: The completion ceremony for the reading of Guru Granth Sahib.

Brahm-giani: God-illuminated human being, a perfect saint.

Charan-amrit: Literally water poured over the Guru's toes, used originally for initiation into the Sikh Faith.

Chauri/ Chaur: A fan of Yak hair or peacock feathers, waved over *Guru Granth Sahib* as a sign of respect, a symbol of authority.

Darshan: The sight of a holy man, a system of philosophy.

Dasam Granth: The Scripture containing the compositions of Guru Gobind Singh, the Tenth Master.

Daswand: Tithe, a one-tenth contribution to charity

Dharamsal: A place of worship, a hostel or hospice.

Dhyan: Concentration or meditation.

Fakir: A wandering mendicant

Gaddi: A seat or office of the spiritual preceptor, throne, succession

Grastha: The Life of a family-man, a house-holder.

Granthi: Reader of the Guru Granth Sahib.

Gurdwara: The Guru's Door, Guru's place, a Sikh temple.

Gurmukh: One who is Guru-oriented, an ideal Sikh.

Haumai: The ego, Self-conceit.

Hukam: Command, will of God, a random reading from the Granth.

Jivan-mukt: Liberated while still living, a God-conscious man.

Kam: Sexuality, lechery, lust.

199

Kes/Kesh: Un-cut hair—also applies to hair everywhere on the body.

Khalsa: The Pure in heart, the enlightened, one who has taken khanday-di-pahal.

Khanda: A double-edged sword, the Insignia of the Khalsa Panth.

Kirpan: A "Please help me" sword, one of the Five K's.

Kirtan: Singing the Guru's hymns to the accompaniment of suitable instruments.

Langar: Free Kitchen, Community meal or the refectory where it is eaten.

Lavan: Sikh wedding song, marriage hymn of Guru Ramdas.

Manji: A cot, an assignment of missionary office.

Manmukh: An egoistic person, an irreligious person, a conceited person.

Massands: Missionaries appointed by the gurus to be in charge of certain regions.

Maya: Materialism, worldly attachments, illusion.

Missal: Confederacy, a group of Sikhs under a leader, a Khalsa army group.

Mool Mantra: The basic creed of the Sikhs, starting from 'Ik Oankar through to Gur-Parsad,' the preamble of the Japji.

Mukti/Moksha: Liberation from transmigration, salvation.

Nam: The Holy Name, the spirit of God, the Power of God.

Nam simran: The Remembrance of God, meditation of the Word.

Nishan Sahib: The Sikh Flag, generally hoisted on a pole in front of a Gurdwara.

Nitnem: The Five Sacred compositions to be recited daily by a Sikh.

Panj-Piyara: The Five Sikhs who took the amrit at the hands of Guru Gobind Singh, the five administrators of amrit-ceremony, any five practising Khalsa appointed by the Sangat for a special task.

Panth: The Sikh community in general.

Parchar: Propagation of the Guru's teachings, missionary work.

Patit: An apostate, a Sikh who has discarded one or more of the Five K's prescribed by Guru Gobind Singh.

Pothi: A book of Sikh sacred compositions, a hymn-book.

Raga: An Indian musical pattern of melody.

Raj-yoga: Spiritual perfection in worldly glory and quality of life.

Sabad (Shabad): A hymn or sacred song or word.

Sadhana: Spiritual apprenticeship, following the spiritual path.

Sahaj: The Natural way, the serenity or bliss of a spiritual state.

Sangat: A Religious assembly, a congregation.

Sanyasa: Renunciation, asceticism.

Sewa: Selfless and voluntary service, service for the community without thought of the self.

Sidh: A hermit possessing mystic powers.

Takhat: Literally throne, seat of spiritual authority.

Udasi: Preaching tour, an order of monks founded by Baba Srichand, the eldest son of Guru Nanak.

Vairag/ Bairag: Renunciation, distaste for worldly things.

Var: Ode, ballad, a composition about the deeds of a hero.

Vedas: The Four Hindu spiritual Texts.

Waheguru: The Wonderful Lord, The Sikh descriptive name for God.

Wismad: Wonder, feeling of spiritual ecstasy.

Yoga: Union with God, techniques for obtaining control over one's own mind and body, also for developing mytic and occult powers.

A Short Bibliography

Archer J.C.: *The Sikhs in relation to Hindus, Christians and Ahmediyas;* Princeton, 1946

Bannerjee A.C.: *Guru Nanak and his times,* New Delhi, 1971.

Cole W.O: *Thinking about Sikhism,* Lutterworth, Guilford, U.K.

" *Sikhism and Its Indian Context* (1469-1708), Darton, London, 1983.

Cole and Sambhi P.S: *The Sikhs, their religious beliefs and practices,* Vikas, 1980.

Chhabra G.S: *Advanced Study in the history of Punjab,* 2 Vols.

Cunningham J.D: *History of the Sikhs,* Delhi, 1972.

Dalip Singh: *Universal Sikhism,* Bahri, Delhi, 1979.

Daljeet Singh: *Sikhism a comparative Study,* Sterling, Delhi, 1979.

Darshan Singh: *Indian Bhakti Tradition and the Sikh Gurus,* 1968.

Duggal K.S: *The Sikh Gurus,* Vikas, Delhi, 1980.

Fauja Singh: *Guru Amardas,* Sterling, Delhi, 1979.

Field Dorothy: *Religion of the Sikhs.*

Gandhi: S.S: *History of the Sikh Gurus,* Delhi, 1980.

Gopal Singh: *A History of the Sikh people* (1469-1988), Delhi, 1988.

Greenless D: *The Gospel of Guru Granth Sahib;* Madras, 1972.

Grewal J.S: *From Guru Nanak to Maharaja Ranjit Singh,* 1970.

Gupta H.R: *History of the Sikh Gurus,* 1973.

Harbans Singh: *The Heritage of the Sikhs, Bombay, 1964*

" *Perspectives on Guru Nanak,* Patiala, 1975.

Iyengar K.R.S: *Guru Nanak, a homage,* Delhi, 1973.

Jagjit Singh: *The Sikh Revolution,* Bahri, Delhi, 1980.

Jodh Singh: *Studies in Sikhism,* Ludhiana, 1960.

Jogedra Singh: *Sikh Ceremonies,* Chandigarh, 1968.

Johar S.S: *Handbook on Sikhism,* Delhi, 1977.

Khushwant Singh: *A History of the Sikhs,* 2 Vols., Delhi, 1979.

Kohli S.S: *Outlines of Sikh Thought,* Delhi, 1977.

" *A Critical Study of the Adi Granth,* Delhi, 1979.

" *Sikh Ethics,* 1975.

Macauliffe M.A: *The Sikh Religion,* 6 Vols., Delhi, 1978.

Mansukhani G.S: *The Quintessence of Sikhism,* S.G.P.C., Amritsar, 1986.

"	*Introduction to Sikhism,* Hemkunt Press, Delhi, 1988.

"	*Guru Nanak,* Apostle of Love, Hemkunt, Delhi, 1969.

"	*Life of Guru Nanak,* G.N. Foundation, Delhi, 1975.

"	*Guru Gobind Singh,* Cosmic Hero, Delhi, 1967.

"	*Guru Gobind Singh,* His Personality and Achievement, Hemkunt, Delhi, 1976.

"	Guru Ramdas, His Life, Work and Philosophy, Oxford, Delhi, 1979.

"	*Indian Classical Music and Sikh Kirtan:* Oxford, Delhi, 1982.

".	*Aspects of Sikhism,* Punjabi Writers Coop. Society, Delhi, 1982.

"	*Sikh Studies,* Part I and II, Singapore, 1986.

MeLeod: *Guru Nanak and the Sikh Religion,* Oxford, 1968.

Narang G.C: *Glorious History of Sikhism,* Delhi, 1972.

Narain Singh: *Guru Nanak Reinterpreted,* 1970.

Puran Singh: *The Book of the Ten Masters,* Patiala, 1980.

"	*The Spirit Born People,* Patiala.

Prakash Singh: *The Sikh Gurus and the Temple of Bread,* Amritsar,1971

Ranbir Singh: *Glimpses of the Divine Masters,* Delhi, 1963

"	*The Sikh Way of Life,* Delhi, 1980.

Sahib Singh and Dalip Singh: *Guru Nanak Dev and his Teachings,* Delhi, 1969.

"	*Guru Gobind Singh,* Amritsar.

Satbir Singh: *The Tenth Master,* Patna, 1970.

Sambhi P.S: *Understanding your Sikh Neighbour,* Lutterworth, Guilford, U.K., 1980.

Sidhu G.S: *The Sikh Woman,* Sikh Missionary Society, Southall (Mddx), U.K.

Sher Singh: *Philosophy of Sikhism.*

Talib G.S: *Guru Nanak, His Personality and Vision,* Delhi, 1969.

Taran Singh: *Teachings of Guru Nanak,* Punjabi University, Patiala, 1977.

Teja Singh: *Sikhism, Its Ideals and Institutions,* 1960.

Teja Singh and Ganda Singh: *A Short History of the Sikhs,* Bombay, 1950.

Trilochan Singh: *Guru Tegh Bahadur,* Delhi, 1967.

Verma S.C: *Guru Nanak and the Logos of Divine Manisfestation,* Delhi, 1969.

Translation in English

H.S. Doabia: *Sacred Nitnem*, Singh Bros., Amritsar, 1976.
Gopal Singh: *Sri Guru Granth Sahib* in 4 Vols., Delhi, 1978.
    " Thus Spake the Tenth Master, Punjabi University, Patiala.
Khushwant Singh: *Hymns of Guru Nanak*, G.N. Foundation, New Delhi.
Lou Singh: *The Nitnem and The Sukhmani Sahib*, Sterling, Delhi, 1980.
Manmohan Singh: *Guru Granth Sahib* in 8 Vols., S.G.P.C., Amritsar, 1981.
G.S. Mansukhani: *Hymns from Guru Granth Sahib*, Hemkunt Press, Delhi, 1980.
    " *Hymns from the Dasam Granth*, Hemkunt Press, Delhi, 1980
    " *Hymns from Bhai Gurdas*, Singh Brothers, Amritsar, 1988.
    " Premka Kaur: *Peace Lagoon*, San Rafael, California, 1971.
    " Puran Singh: *The Sisters of the Spinning Wheel and other Sikh poems*, Punjabi University, Patiala, 1977.
    " The Spirit of the Sikh, Vols. II and III, Punjabi University, Patiala.
G.S. Talib: *Selections from the Holy Granth*, G.N. Foundation, New Delhi.
    " *Selections from: Translation of Guru Granth Sahib*, 4 Vols, Punjab University, Patiala.
UNESCO: *The Sacred Writings of the Sikhs*, Allen and Unwin, London, 1960.

Journals

Journal of Religious Studies (Quarterly) Punjabi University, Patiala.
Journal of Sikh Studies, Guru Nanak Dev University, Amritsar.
Khera: New Delhi
Studies in Sikhism and comparative religion, Guru Nanak Foundation, New Delhi.
Punjab: Past and Present, Punjabi University, Patiala.
The Sikh "Messenger," London.
The Sikh Review, Calcutta.
The Spokesman Weekly, New Delhi.

Index

Abdali, Ahmed Shah 126

Abdullah, Nawab 61

Adi Granth, complication of 68, 69, 70, 79, 92, 122, 125, 178.

Akal Takhat 9, 10, 75

Akbar, Emperor 63, 68, 71, 138.

Alif Khan 89

Almust 75

Amardas, Guru 12, 46, 56, 63, 65, 68, 71, 111, 112, 128-30, 137, 161, 167, 181, 182, 196.

Amir Singh 196

Amrit 5, 7, 11, 15, 92, 125, 184, 191

Amritsar, development of 61-62, 64, 67

Anand. Acharya 36, 102

Anand, B.S. 102

Anand Sahib 161-63, 182, 191

Anandpur Sahib 82, 87

Angad, guru 37, 53-8, 63, 67-68, 130, 148, 167

Arjan Dev, Guru 9, 14, 46, 66-73, 88, 101, 128-34, 158-61, 165, 167, 174, 178, 192, 197, 198

Asa-di-var 154-57

Atal Baba 77

Aurangzeb 78-79, 83, 85, 87, 96-100, 144, 198

B

Babar 21, 22, 25, 36, 43, 47, 48, 102

Bagho-o-Bahar 143

Bahadur Shah 98

Bahlo Bhai 69, 70

Bahlol Dana 36

Bal 129

Bal S.S. 27, 102

Bala, 31

Balwand 129, 130

Balu Hasan 75

Banda Singh Bahadur 5, 98

Bangla Sahib 81

Bano Bhai 69, 131

Bannerjee, A.C., 95

Bannerjee, I.B. 85, 99, 191.

Baoli Sahib 58, 62

Beg, Shamas 76

Beni 129, 130

Bhaglhari 77

Bhal 129

Bhani 61, 182

Bhikha 129, 130

Bhikham 129, 130

Bhim Chand, Raja 89-90

Bidhi Chand 76

Bikhari, Bhai 70, 71

Birbal 68.

Buck, Miss Pearl 139

Buddha, Bhai

Buddhu 146

Buddhu Shah, Pir 76, 89, 100, 144

Bulaki Das 83

205

C

Chamba, Queen 82
Chandu Lal 9, 73
Char Darvesh 143
Chardy Kala 79
Chibber, Kesar Singh 163

D

Dadu 95
Daljit Singh 27, 102
Darshan Singh 19
Dasam Granth 12, 19, 104, 139-41,
    compilation 139-41,
    contents, 141-44
Dastagir, Pir 44
Daswand 45
Datu, Bhat 57, 62
Daulat Rai 99
Daya Singh, Bhai 7
Dayaldas, Bhai 83, 84
Daud 42
Dhana 129, 130, 175
Dharam Singh, 90, 91
Dhirmal, 185
Dhru, 120
Dhuru, 80
Dip Singh, Baba 95
Dyer, General, 196

F

Farid, 129, 130
Fakir Nuruddin, 22
Fetehchand, Raja 89
Five K's, 14-7, 91, 94, 184, 185, 189, 191

G

Gandhi, S.S., 164
Gangu, A trader, 60
Gayanand 129
Gani Khan, 96, 100
Ghosh, Sri Aurobindo, 98
Gobind Singh, guru 4, 6, 9, 10-4, 16, 17, 83, 84, 86, 87
    his message, 100; 104, 106, 115, 121, 122, 131, 135, 138, 139, 141-47, 167, 184, 192, 193, 195, 197.
God, Concept of 5, 8, 135
Gonda, 75
Gopal, Pandit 29
Gopal Singh, 27
Gopal Singh, Dr, 163, 196
Garewal J.S., 27
Gupta, H.R. 102
Gurbachan Singh 163, 196
Gurdas, Bhai 6, 8, 14, 69, 74, 104, 114, 128
Gurditta, Baba, 77
Gurditta, Bhai, 82
Gurmatta, 5, 9, 99
Gurmukh, 70, 71
Gurmukhi script, 54, 167, 168, 185
Guru concept of 5, 8, 135
Guru Granth Sahib 7, 12, 13, 18, 37, 128
    arrangement of 129-31; contents 133-39, 147, 165, 168, 169, 173, 175, 181-83, 188-91, 195

H

Hamayun, 55

206

Har Rai, Guru, 77-80, 82, 167
Harbans, 129
Harbans Singh, 19, 27, 121
Hardayal, Pandit, 30
Hargobind, Guru 9, 68, 73-8, 82,88, 167, 197
Hari Chand, Raja, 89
Haridas, 63
Harkrishan, Guru 80, 82
Harminder Sahib12, 67, 69-7, 75, 128, 158, 197
Harnakash, 197
Haumai, 135
Hayat Khan, 89
Heer-Ranjha,144
Himat Rai, 90
Hindal, 66
Hinduism, 11, 23
Holika, 197
Hukam, 5, 163
Hussain, Mir Munshi Ghulam 85

I

Iftikar Khan 83
Islam, 11, 23

J

Jaidev, 129, 130
Jairam, 31
Jai Singh, Raja, 81
Jaita, Bhai, 84
Jalap, 129
James Jeans, Sir, 151
Japji Sahib, 38, 147-54, 167
Jehangir, 71-3, 75
Jetha, 61, 62, 182
Joginder Singh, 27

K

Kabir, 129, 130
Kahan Singh, 140
Kal, 129
Kale Khan, 76
Kali, Goddess, 36
Kanahiya, Bhai, 45
Karma, 117, 136, 150, 163
Kartar Singh, 27, 102
Karoria, 48
Kennedy, J.F. 1
Kesgarh Sahib, 184
Khalsa Panth 6, 9, 12, 88, 94, 196
Khandey-di-pahul, 15, 91, 183
Khatri, Daya Ram, 90
Khusro, 72
Kirat, 129
Kiratpur, 76
Kirpa Ram, 84
Kirpal, Mahant, 89
Koer Singh, 27
Kohli, S.S. 27, 102, 103
Kurahat, 127

L

Labana, Lakhi Shah, 84
Labana, Makhan Shah, 82
Lal Beg, 76
Lal Chand, 89
Lalo, 33
Lane, Lord, 95
Langah, Bhai 71
Langar, 2, 45, 121, 171, 176, 177, 194
Latif, Mohammed, 21, 99, 101
Lahna, 37
Lodi, Bahlol, 20

Lodi, Daulat Khan, 21
Lodi, Sikander 21
Lodi, Sultan Ibrahim Khan, 22
Lohgarh, battle of, 75

M

Macauliffe, M.A. 27, 127, 147, 164, 180, 182, 191
Mahabharata, 143
Mahadev, 67
Mohan Singh, Bhai, 95, 97
Mahommed, Nur Qazi, 126
Mai Bhago, 97
Mani Singh, 15, 95
Mani Singh, 140-41
Majh, Bhai, 70
Manmohan Singh 163, 196
Mansukh, 35
Mansukhani, (Dr) G.S. 27, 102, 103, 191
Mardana, 28, 31, 33, 44, 46, 47, 120, 130, 167
Massa Ranghar, 140
Mathura, 129
Mati Das, Bhai, 84
Maya 163
Mcleod, 27
Mehervan, 128
Mehta, Kalyandas, 28
Mehta Singh, Bhai, 140
Mian Mir, 67
Mir Khan, 89
Mohakam Chand, 90
Mohan Singh, Dr. 142
Moreland, 25, 101, 102
Mukhlis Khan, 75
Murad, 78
Murtaza Khan, 73

N

Nabi Khan, 196
Namdev, 129, 130
Nandlal, Bhai, 7, 138
Nanak, Guru, 3, 6, 7-11, 13, 14, 20-54;
    as a teacher, 37;
    his message, 44;
    respect for women, 52; 58, 68, 85, 99, 100, 104, 113, 114, 117, 118, 131, 132,136, 147, 149, 153, 155, 156, 165-167, 193, 195
Nanki, 29, 31
Narad, 102
Nanu, Pandit 33
Nirmal Das, 180
Nishan Sahib 194
Nurshah , 46

O

Oberoi, J.P. Singh, 16

P

Painde Khan, 76
Panchtantra, 143
Pangat, 28, 176
Panipat, battle of, 22
Panj Piaras, 90, 169, 171, 183, 186, 194
Parmanand, 129, 130
Pardah, 25
Paro Jhulka, Bhai, alias Param Hans, 61
Phool Singh, 75
Pincott, 36
Pipa, 129, 130

Piri and Miri, concepts of 74
Phul, 79
Prahlad, 80, 197
Prema, 59-60
Prithichand, 67, 68, 128, 185
Puran Singh, Prof. 153, 156, 164

Q

Qutubuddin, 29

R

Radha, 146
Radha, Krishanan, Dr. S.,
106,139
Rahat Nama Bhai Champa Singh
124
Rahat Nama Bhai Daya Singh,
123
Rahat Nama Bhai Desa Singh,
123
Rahat Nama Bhai Nand Lal, 124
Rai Bular, 29
Ram Rai, 79, 80, 185
Ram Das, Guru, 6, 12, 28, 62-8,
115, 128, 130, 135, 176, 182
Ramayana, 143
Ramdas Sarovar, 61, 67
Ram Singh, Raja, 83
Rama, 61, 62
Ramanand, 129, 130, 166
Ranjit Singh, 6, 22, 167
Rattan Rai, 89
Ravidas, 129, 130, 165
Religion, role of, 17
Rikabganj, Gurdwara, 84, 198
Ruknuddin, 29
Rupa, 76, 77

S

Saddu, 146
Sadhna, 129, 130
Sadhu, 76, 77
Sahaj, 163
Sain, 129, 130
Sahib Chand, 90
Sahib Kaur, 184
Sahib Singh, Dr., 102, 196
Saif Khan 83
Salvation, 5
Sandli, 79
Sangat, 9, 28, 166, 172
Sangat Singh, 95
Santokhsar, 67
Santokh Singh, Bhai, 27
Sati Das, Bhai, 84
Satta, 129, 130
Satti, 59, 121, 127
Sayyad Khan, 96, 100
Seshadri, Prof. 147
Sethi, Gulab Singh, 140
Shabad, 163
Shah Jehan, 78
Shan Suhagin, 35
Shan, H.S., 164
Shikoh, Dara, 78, 79
Shivaji, 99
Shivnabha, 35, 102
Shujah, 78
Sikh, definition of 7, 191
Sikh army formation of, 75
Sikh code of discipline, 4, 14, 16,
93, 122-25, 196
Sikh Ethics, 3
Sikh Studies, objective, 3, 4;
scope of , 4-6
Sikhism, foundamentals of, 8;
its distinctiveness 8, 11

Sin, concept of, 106
Sohni-Mahival, 149
Soma Bhai, 65, 66
Srichand, Baba, 75
Sulkhani, 31
Sulhi Khan, 68
Sukhmani Sahib, 158-61
Sunder, 129, 130
Sundri, Mata, 140
Surdas, 129-30
Suri, Sher Shah, 55, 56

T

Tagore, Rahibdra Nath, 101
Taimur Lung, 20
Takhat, 5
Takhat Sri Hazur Sahib, 98
Tankhah, 169
Tankhah nama, 124
Tara Chand, 191
Teg, Bahadur, Guru, 14, 69, 81-87, 101, 115, 130, 132, 198
Toynbee, 23, 139
Trilochan, 129-130
Trilochan Singh, 27,102
Trumpp, Dr. 131
Turu Singh, 15

U

Udasis, A sect. 75

V

Vir Singh, Bhai, 27
Virtue, Sikh Concept of, 4, 104

W

Wazir Khan, 96-8
Wazir Khan, governor, 158
Whitehead, A.N., 1
Women, uplift of, 121; status of, 156
Worship, concept of, 165

Z

Zafarnama, 97, 144
Zakir Hussain, Dr., 99

Errata

Page	Line	Incorrect	Correct
15	30	weaving	wearing
16	5	permit	permits
17	35	a	as
19	7	indicate	indicates
21	14	nineteen	fourteen
37	32	forward	for
38	25	this	His
39	10	natur	natural
41	1	Forg	Frog
41	12	of	(delete)
42	25	loses	lose
52	29	idanlised	idealised
53	1	(missing)	What
54	34	word	work
55	16	his	(delete)
56	13	tis	this
57	34	effects	effect
58	15	wore	were
60	23	the needy	(delete)
63	35	was	were
64	19	Sikhism	of Sikhism
67	6	form	from
80	35	suppersession	supersession
85	9	views	view
85	40	attended	attend
92	11	be	(delete)
96	22	then	than
101	13	The Khalsa . . . God's!	The Khalsa belongs to God, victory is God's!
102	9	at	it
107	26	as a individual	individuals

107	31	service	services
113	3	challenge	challenges
119	20	indiguetion	indignation
128	4	1977	1577
131	33	who	He
134	22	worldy	worldly
144	7	epilog	epilogue
145	21	and	you
145	23	there	their
148	30	Nams	Name
148	36	leads	lead
153	16	(AG,)	(AG, 1412)
155	30	intellect	intuition
161	10	numbus	nimbus
162	31	in	is
163	17	fom	form
169	26	amy	may
170	4	of	on
173	9	joining	join
177	4	social	social functions
179	35	cantle	candle
180	17	celilate	celibate
180	19	Charity	Chastity
181	9	letter	later
185	5	recipents	recepients
187	31	yours	your
187	32	Tongue the mant	Charm, the gem
190	3	Ramkal	Ramkali
191	22	excepted	expected
192	26	celebration	celebrations
197	28	Emperor	Emperor's
200	28	Sikh	Khalsa
201	12	mytic	mystic
204	19	Selections from	(delete)
205	3	complication	compilation
206	4	Chardy	Chaudry
208	9	Mohan	Mahan
208	28	Mehta	Mehtab
210	25	Turu	Taru